MANAGERIAL ECONOMICS

MANAGERIAL ECONOMICS

Shashi Kumar

genNEXT publication

Managerial Economics

Rs. 890

ISBN: 978-93-80222-20-2

Published in 2010 in India by
Gennext Publication
23 Main Ansari Road, Darya Ganj,
New Delhi-110002
E-Mail:GenNextpublication@hotmail.com
Phone: 23282060

Printed at: Young Art Press, Delhi

Contents

Preface

Managerial economics pertains to the economics of management essential for managers. It includes Demand, Supply, Production, Cost, Profit, Revenue and Pricing Practices. This volume presents complete treatment of the subject with numerous examples. It emphasizes on day to day examples and clearly enlightens all topics.

This textbook presents practical simple tools and concepts of managerial economics for students as well as managers practicing in business environment. It presents the essentials of managerial economics in a lucid style. This volume exclusively incorporates this discipline to other managerial functions.

Detailed chapters are included on topics such as Mathematical Economics, Demand and Supply, Production, Cost, Profit, Revenue, Competition, Monopoly, Monopolistic Competition, Duopoly and Oligopoly and Pricing Practices.

This volume teaches students how to make better business decisions using economics and succeed in their field. Each chapter gives real world examples and relevant managerial economics principles in a straightforward manner.

This volume is an essential addition to any student and business manager library; especially anyone needed to make important, informed decisions in the presence of scarce resources. A valuable source of knowledge for all students, teachers, consultants and lay person who are interested in gaining knowledge of managerial economics.

The well-written materials ensure that students are able to understand all topics clearly. Author is confident that this book will be a handy tool for the students learning business communication. Sincere feedback, suggestions and comments are always welcome.

Shashi Kumar

1

Introduction

Economics is the study of how individuals and societies make choices subject to constraints. The need to make choices arises from scarcity. From the perspective of society as a whole, scarcity refers to the limitations placed on the production of goods and services because factors of production are finite. From the perspective of the individual, scarcity refers to the limitations on the consumption of goods and services because of limited of personal income and wealth.

Definition: Economics is the study of how individuals and societies choose to utilize scarce resources to satisfy virtually unlimited wants.

Definition: Scarcity describes the condition in which the availability of resources is insufficient to satisfy the wants and needs of individuals and society.

The concepts of scarcity and choice are central to the discipline of economics. Because of scarcity, whenever the decision is made to follow one course of action, a simultaneous decision is made to forgo some other course of action. Thus, any action requires a sacrifice. There is another common admonition that also underscores the all pervasive concept of scarcity: if an offer seems too good to be true, then it probably is.

Individuals and societies cannot have everything that is desired because most goods and services must be produced with scarce productive resources. Because productive resources are scarce, the amounts of goods and services produced from these ingredients must also be finite in supply. The concept of scarcity is summarized in the economic admonition that there is no "free lunch." Goods, services, and productive resources that are scarce have a positive price. Positive prices reflect the competitive interplay between the supply of and demand for scarce resources and commodities. A commodity with a positive price is referred to as an economic good. Commodities that have a zero price because they are relatively unlimited in supply are called free goods.

What are these scarce productive resources? Productive resources, sometimes called factors of production or productive inputs, are classified into one of four broad categories: land, labour, capital, and entrepreneurial ability. Land generally refers to all natural resources. Included in this category are wildlife, minerals, timber, water, air, oil and gas deposits, arable land, and mountain scenery.

Labour refers to the physical and intellectual abilities of people to produce goods and services. Of course, not all workers are the same; that is, labour is not homogeneous. Different individuals have different physical and intellectual attributes. These differences may be inherent, or they may be acquired through education and training. Although the Declaration of Independence proclaims that everyone has certain unalienable rights, in an economic sense all people are not created equal. Thus some people will become fashion models, professional athletes, or college professors; others will work as clergymen, cooks, police officers, bus drivers, and so forth. Differences in human talents and abilities in large measure explain why some individuals' labour services are richly rewarded in the market and others, despite their noble calling, such as many public school teachers, are less well compensated.

Capital refers to manufactured commodities that are used to produce goods and services for final consumption. Machinery, office buildings, equipment, warehouse space, tools, roads, bridges, research and development, factories, and so forth are all a part of a nation's capital stock. Economic capital is different from financial capital, which refers to such things as stocks, bonds, certificates of deposits, savings accounts, and cash. It should be noted, however, that financial capital is typically used to finance a firm's acquisition of economic capital. Thus, there is an obvious linkage between an investor's return on economic capital and the financial asset used to underwrite it.

In market economies, almost all income generated from productive activity is returned to the owners of factors of production. In politically and economically free societies, the owners of the factors of production are collectively referred to as the household sector. Businesses or firms, on the other hand, are fundamentally activities, and as such have no independent source of income. That activity is to transform inputs into outputs. Even firm owners are members of the household sector. Financial capital is the vehicle by which business acquire economic capital from the household sector. Businesses accomplish this by issuing equity shares and bonds and by borrowing from financial intermediaries, such as commercial banks, savings banks, and insurance companies.

Entrepreneurial ability refers to the ability to recognize profitable opportunities, and the willingness and ability to assume the risk associated with marshaling and organizing land, labour, and capital to produce the goods and services that are most in demand by consumers. People who exhibit this ability are called entrepreneurs. In market economies, the value of land, labour, and capital is directly determined through the interaction of supply and demand. This is not the case for entrepreneurial ability. The return to the entrepreneur is called profit. Profit is defined as the difference between total revenue earned from the production and sale of a good or service and the total cost associated with producing that good or service. Although profit is indirectly determined by the interplay of supply and demand, it is convenient to view the return to the entrepreneur as a residual.

OPPORTUNITY COST

The concepts of scarcity and choice are central to the discipline of economics. These concepts are used to explain the behavior of both producers and consumers. It is important to understand, however, that in the face of scarcity whenever the decision is made to follow one course of action, a simultaneous decision is made to forgo some other course of action. When a high school graduate decides to attend college or university, a simultaneous decision is made to forgo entering the work force and earning an income. Scarcity necessitates trade-offs. That which is forgone whenever a choice is made is referred to by economists as opportunity cost. That which is sacrificed when a choice is made is the next best alternative. It is the path that we would have taken had our actual choice not been open to us. Definition: Opportunity cost is the highest valued alternative forgone whenever a choice is made.

MACROECONOMICS VERSUS MICROECONOMICS

Scarcity, and the manner in which individuals and society make choices, are fundamental to the study of economics. To examine these important issues, the field of economics is divided into two broad subfields: macroeconomics and microeconomics.

As the name implies, macroeconomics looks at the big picture. Macroeconomics is the study of entire economies and economic systems and specifically considers such broad economic aggregates as gross domestic product, economic growth, national income, employment, unemployment, inflation, and international trade. In general, the topics covered in macroeconomics are concerned with the economic environment within which firm managers operate. For the most part, macroeconomics focuses on the variables over which the managerial decision maker has little or no control but may be of considerable importance in the making of economic decisions at the micro level of the individual, firm, or industry.

Definition: Macroeconomics is the study of aggregate economic behavior. Macroeconomists are concerned with such issues as national income, employment, inflation, national output, economic growth, interest rates, and international trade.

By contrast, microeconomics is the study of the behavior and interaction of individual economic agents. These economic agents represent individual firms, consumers, and governments. Microeconomics deals with such topics as profit maximization, utility maximization, revenue or sales maximization, production efficiency, market structure, capital budgeting, environmental protection, and governmental regulation.

Definition: Microeconomics is the study of individual economic behavior. Macroeconomists are concerned with output and input markets, product pricing, input utilization, production costs, market structure, capital budgeting, profit maximization, production technology, and so on.

MANAGERIAL ECONOMICS

Managerial economics is the application of economic theory and quantitative methods (mathematics and statistics) to the managerial decision-making process. Simply stated, managerial economics is applied microeconomics with special emphasis on those topics of greatest interest and importance to managers. The role of managerial economics in the decision-making process is illustrated in figure below.

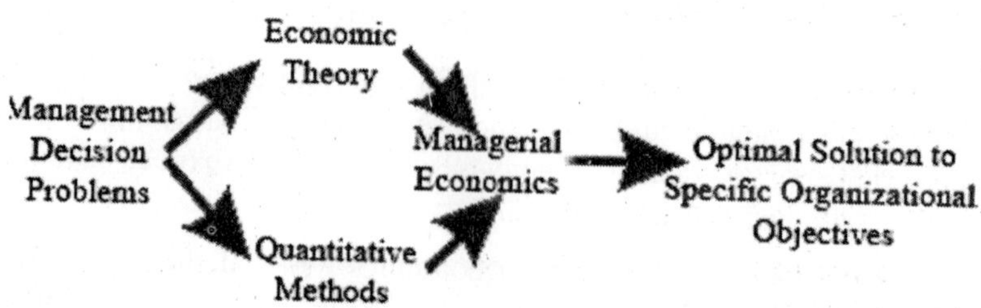

Definition: Managerial economics is the synthesis of microeconomic theory and quantitative methods to find optimal solutions to managerial decision-making problems.

To illustrate the scope of managerial economics, consider the case the owner of a company that produces a product. The manner in which the firm owner goes about his or her business will depend on the company's organizational objectives. Is the firm owner a profit maximizer, or is management more concerned something else, such as maximizing the company's market share? What specific conditions must be satisfied to optimally achieve these objectives? Economic theory attempts to identify the conditions that need to be satisfied to achieve optimal solutions to these and other management decision problems.

As we will see, if the company's organizational objective is profit maximization then, according to economic theory, the firm should continue to produce widgets up to the point at which the additional cost of producing an additional widget (marginal cost) is just equal to the additional revenue earned from its sale (marginal revenue).To apply the "marginal cost equals marginal revenue" rule, however, the firm's management must first be able to estimate the empirical relationships of total cost of widget production and total revenues from widget sales. In other words, the firm's operations must be quantified so that the optimization principles of economic theory may be applied.

THEORIES AND MODELS

The world is a very complicated place. In attempting to understand how markets operate, for example, the economist makes a number of simplifying assumptions. Without these assumptions, the ability to make predictions about cause-and-effect relationships becomes unmanageable. The "law" of demand asserts that the price of a good or service and its quantity demanded are inversely related, ceteris paribus.

This theory asserts that, other factors remaining unchanged (i.e., ceteris paribus), individuals will tend to purchase increasing amounts of a good or service as prices fall and decreasing amounts as the prices rise. Of course, other things do not remain unchanged. Along with changes in the price of the good or service, disposable income, the prices of related commodities, tastes, and so on, may also change. It is difficult, if not impossible, to generalize consumer behavior when multiple demand determinants are simultaneously changing.

Definition: Ceteris paribus is an assertion in economic theory that in the analysis of the relationship between two variables, all other variables are assumed to remain unchanged.

It is good to remember that economics is a social, not a physical, science. Economists cannot conduct controlled, laboratory experiments, which makes economic theorizing all the more difficult. It also makes economists vulnerable to ridicule. One economic quip, for example, asserts that if all the economists in the world were laid end to end, they would never reach a conclusion. This is, of course, an unfair criticism. In business, the objective is to reduce uncertainty. The study of economics is an attempt to bring order out of seeming chaos. Are economists sometimes wrong?

Certainly. But the alternative for managers would be to make decisions in the dark.

What then are theories? Theories are abstractions that attempt to strip away unnecessary detail to expose only the essential elements of observable behavior. Theories are often expressed in the form of models. A model is the formal expression of a theory. In economics, models may take the form of diagrams, graphs, or mathematical statements that summarize the relationship between and among two or more variables. More often than not, there will be more than one theory to explain any given economic phenomenon. When this is the case, which theory should we use?

"GOOD" THEORIES VERSUS "BAD" THEORIES

The ultimate test of a theory is its ability to make predictions. In general, "good" theories predict with greater accuracy than "bad" theories. If one theory is known to predict a particular phenomenon with 95% accuracy, and another theory of the same phenomena is known to predict with 96% accuracy, the former theory is replaced by the latter theory. It is in the nature of scientific progress that "good" theories replace "bad" theories. Of course, "good" and "bad" are relative concepts. If one theory predicts an event with greater accuracy, then it will replace alternative theories, no matter how well those theories may have predicted the same event in the past.

Another important observation in the process of theorizing is that all other factors being equal, simpler models, or theories, tend to predict better than more complicated ones. This principle of parsimony is referred to as Ockham's razor, which was named after the fourteenth-century English philosopher William of Ockham.

Definition: Ockham's razor is the principle that, other things being equal, the simplest explanation tends to be the correct explanation.

The category of "bad" theories includes two common errors in economics. The most common error, perhaps, relates to statements or theories regarding cause and effect. It is tempting in economics to look at two sequential events and conclude that the first event caused the second event.

Clearly, this is not always the case, some financial news reports not with standing. For example, a report that the Dow Jones Industrial Average fell 200 points might be attributed to news of increased tensions in the Middle East. Empirical research has demonstrated, however, while specific events may indirectly affect individual stock prices, daily fluctuations in stock market averages tend, on average, to be random. This common error is called the fallacy of post hoc, ergo propter hoc (literally, "after this, therefore because of this").

Related to the pitfall of post hoc, ergo propter hoc is the confusion that often arises between correlation and causation. Case and Fair (1999) offer the following illustration. Large cities have many automobiles and also have high crime rates. Thus, there is a high correlation between automobile ownership and crime. But, does this mean that automobiles cause crime? Obviously not, although many other factors that are highly correlated with a high concentration of automobiles (e.g., population density, poverty, drug abuse) may provide a better explanation of the incidence of crime. Certainly, the presence of automobiles is not one of these factors.

The second common error in economic theorizing is the fallacy of composition. The fallacy of composition is the belief that what is true for a part is necessarily true for the whole. An example of this may be found in the paradox of thrift. The paradox of thrift asserts that while an increase in saving by an individual may be virtuous ("a penny saved is a penny earned"), if all individuals in an economy increase their saving, the result may be no change, or even a decline, in aggregate saving. The reason is that an increase in aggregate saving means a decrease in aggregate spending, resulting in lower national output and income. Since saving depends upon income, increased savings may be less advantageous under certain circumstances for the economy as a whole. At a more fundamental level, while it may be rational for an individual to run for the exit when he is the only person in a burning theater, for all individuals in a crowded burning theater to decide to run for the exit would not be.

THEORIES VERSUS LAWS

It is important to distinguish between theories and laws. The distinction relates to the ability to make predictions. Laws are statements of fact about the real world. They are statements of relationships that are, as far as is commonly known, invariant with respect to specified underlying assumptions or preconditions. As such, laws predict with absolute certainty. "The sun rises in the east" is an example of a law. A law in economics is the law of diminishing marginal returns. This law asserts that for an efficient production process, as increasing amounts of a variable input are combined with one or more fixed inputs, at some point the additions to total output will get progressively smaller.

By contrast, a theory is an attempt to explain or predict the behavior of objects or events in the real world. Unlike laws, theories cannot predict events with complete accuracy. There are very few laws in economics, although some economic theories are inappropriately referred to as "laws." This is because economics deals with people, whose behavior is not absolutely predictable.

DESCRIPTIVE VERSUS PRESCRIPTIVE MANAGERIAL ECONOMICS

Managerial economics has both descriptive and prescriptive elements. Managerial economics is descriptive in that it attempts to interpret observed phenomena and to formulate theories about possible cause-andeffect relationships. Managerial economics is prescriptive in that it attempts to predict the outcomes of specific management decisions. Thus, the principles developed in a course in managerial economics may be used to prescribe the most efficient way to achieve an organization's objectives, such as profit maximization, sales (revenue) maximization, and maximizing market share.

Managerial economics can be utilized by goal-oriented managers in two ways. First, given the existing economic environment, the principles of managerial economics may provide a framework for evaluating whether managers are efficiently allocating resources (land, labour, and capital) to produce the firm's output at least cost. If not, the principles of economics may be used as a guide for reallocating the firm's operating budget away from, say, marketing and toward retail sales to achieve the organization's objectives.

Second, the principles of managerial economics can help managers respond to various economic signals. For example, given an increase in the price of output or the development of a new lower cost production technology, the appropriate response generally would be for a firm to increase output.

QUANTITATIVE METHODS

Quantitative methods refer to the tools and techniques of analysis, including optimization analysis, statistical methods, game theory, and capital budgeting. Managerial economics makes special use of mathematical economics and econometrics to derive optimal solutions to managerial decision-making problems. Managerial economics attempts to bring economic theory into the real world. Consider, for example, the formal (mathematical) demand model represented by Equation (1.1).

$$Q_D = f\left(\mathrm{P}, \mathrm{I}, \mathrm{P_s}, \mathrm{A}\right) \tag{1.1}$$

Equation (1.1) says that the quantity demand of a good or service commodity QD is functionally related to its selling price P, per-capita income I, the price of a competitor's product Ps, and advertising expenditures A.2 By collecting data on Q, P, I, and Ps it should be possible to quantify this relationship. If we assume that this relationship is linear, Equation (1.1) may be specified as

$$Q_D = b_0 + b_1 P + b_2 I + b_3 P_r + b_4 A \tag{1.2}$$

It is possible to estimate the parameters of Equation (1.2) by using the methodology of regression analysis discussed in Green (1997), Gujarati (1995), and Ramanathan (1998).The resulting estimated demand equation, as well as other estimated relationships, may then be used by management to find optimal solutions to managerial decision-making problems. Such decision-making problems may entail optimal product pricing or optimal advertising expenditures to achieve such organizational objectives as revenue maximization or profit maximization.

Economic theory is concerned with how society answers the basic economic questions of what goods and services should be produced, and in what amounts, how these goods and services should be produced (i.e., the choice of the appropriate production technology), and for whom these goods and services should be produced.

In market economies, what goods and services are produced by society is a matter determined not by the producer, but rather by the consumer. Profit-maximizing firms produce only the goods and services that their customers demand. Firms that produce commodities that are not in demand by consumers—manual typewriters to day, for example—will flounder or go out of business entirely. Consumers express their preferences through their purchases of goods and services in the market. The authority of consumers to determine what goods and services are produced is often referred to as consumer sovereignty. Woe to the arrogant manager who forgets this fundamental economic fact of life.

Definition: Consumer sovereignty is the authority of consumers to determine what goods and services are produced through their purchases in the market.

PRODUCTION METHODS

How goods and services are produced refers to the technology of production, and this is determined by the firm's management. Production technology refers to the types of input used in the production process, the organization of those factors of production, and the proportions in which those inputs are combined to produce goods and services that are most in demand by the consumer.

Throughout this text, we will generally assume that firm owners and managers are profit maximizers. It is the inexorable search for profit that determines the methodology of production. As will be demonstrated in subsequent chapters, a necessary condition for profit maximization is cost minimization. In competitive markets, firms that do not combine productive inputs in the most efficient (least costly) manner possible will quickly be driven out of business.

FOR WHOM ARE GOODS AND SERVICES PRODUCED?

Those who are willing, and able, to pay for the goods and services produced are the direct beneficiaries of the fruits of the production process. While the what and the how questions lend themselves to objective economic analysis, answers to the for whom question are fraught with numerous philosophical and analytical pitfalls. Debates about fairness are inevitable and often revolve around such issues as income distribution and ability to pay.

Income determines an individual's ability to pay, and income is derived from the sale of the services of factors of production. When you sell your labour services, you receive payment. The rental price of labour is referred to as a wage or a salary. When you rent the services of capital, you receive payment. Economists refer to the rental price of capital as interest. When you sell the services of land, you receive rents. The return to entrepreneurial ability is called profit. Wages, interest, rents, and profits define an individual's income.

In market economies, the returns to the owners of these factors of production are largely determined through the interaction of supply and demand. Thus, an individual's income is a function of the quality and quantity of the factors of production owned. Questions about the distribution of income are ultimately questions about the distribution of the ownership of factors of production and the supply and demand of those factors. The solutions to the for whom questions typically are the domain of politicians, sociologists, theologians, and special-interest economists, indeed, anyone concerned with the highly subjective issues of "fairness." This book eschews such thorny moral debates. What follows will focus on finding objectives answers to the what and how economic questions.

CHARACTERISTICS OF PURE CAPITALISM

Although there are as many economic systems as there are countries, we will discuss the basic elements of pure capitalism. Purely capitalist economies are characterized by exclusive private ownership of productive resources and the use of markets to allocate goods and services. Pure capitalism stands in stark contrast to socialism, which is characterized by partial or total public ownership of productive resources and centralized decision making to allocate resources.

Capitalism in its pure form has probably never existed. In all countries characterized as capitalist, government plays an active role in the promotion of overall economic growth and the allocation of goods and services through its considerable control over resources. The reason we examine capitalism in its pure form is essentially twofold. To begin with, most western, developed, economies fundamentally are capitalist, or market, economies. Moreover, and perhaps more important, understanding capitalism in its pure form will better position the analyst to understand deviations and gradations from this "ideal" state. Economies that are characterized by a blend of public and private ownership is known as mixed economies.

Most of the discussion in this text will assume that our prototypical firm operates within a purely capitalist market system. Although the complete set of conditions necessary for pure capitalism is not likely to be found in reality, an understanding of the essential elements of pure capitalism is fundamental to an analysis of subtle and not-so-subtle variations from this extreme case.

PRIVATE PROPERTY

In pure capitalism, all productive resources are owned by private individuals who have the right to dispose of that property as manner they see fit. This institution is maintained over time by the right of an individual to bequeath property to his or her heirs.

FREEDOM OF ENTERPRISE AND CHOICE

Freedom of enterprise is the freedom to obtain and organize productive resources for the purpose of producing goods and services for sale in markets. Freedom of choice is the freedom of resource owners to dispose of their property as they see fit, and the freedom of consumers to purchase whatever goods and services they desire, constrained only by the income derived from the sale or rental of privately owned productive resources.

RATIONAL SELF-INTEREST

Rational self-interest refers to the behavior of individuals in a consistent manner to optimize some objective function. Rational self-interest is also referred to by economists as bounded rationality. In the case of the consumer, the postulate of rationality asserts that an individual attempts to maximize the total satisfaction derived from the consumption of goods and services, subject to his or her wealth, income, product prices, insights, and knowledge of market conditions.

The postulate of rationality also has its counterpart in the theory of the firm. Rational firm owners attempt to maximize some organizational objective, subject resource constraints, input prices, market structure, and so on. Entrepreneurs organize productive resources to produce goods and services for sale in markets to maximize profit or some other, equally rational, objective. While it is may be true that not all consumers seek to maximize their utility from their purchases of goods and services and not all firms attempt to maximize profit from the production and sale of output, these are probably the dominant forms of human behavior.

COMPETITION

There are a number of conditions necessary for pure (perfect) competition to exist. For example, there must be buyers and sellers for any particular good or service. This condition ensures that no single individual economic unit has market power to control prices. Large numbers of buyers and sellers ensure the widespread diffusion of economic power, thereby limiting the potential for abuse of such power. Another necessary condition for perfect competition to exist is relatively easy entry into and exit from the market. This condition implies that there are no or low economic, legal, or regulatory restrictions on the production, sale, or consumption of goods and services. In other words, individuals may easily enter into the production and sale of economic goods, while individuals may also enter into any market to transact goods and services as they see fit.

MARKETS AND PRICES

Markets are the basic coordinating mechanisms of capitalism. Price is the essential underlying information transmission mechanism. Unless there is deception or misunderstanding of the facts, a voluntary exchange between two parties must benefit both parties to the transaction; otherwise they would not have entered into the transaction in the first place. It is in markets, both for outputs and inputs, that buyers and sellers meet to further their own self-interest, unfettered by artificial impediments.

The price system is an elaborate mechanism through which the free choices of individuals are recorded and communicated. The price system, if allowed to operate freely, informs market participants which goods are in greatest demand, and, consequently, where productive resources are most needed. The price system enables society to collectively register its decisions about how resources ought to be allocated and how the resulting output should be distributed. In general, institutional impediments tend to impair the functioning of the price mechanism. Although government intervention in the marketplace often results in socially efficient outcomes, governments that impose the fewest restrictions on the functioning of the price mechanism tend to be the most efficient. Extensive and intrusive government intervention, characteristic of centrally planned economies, is the least efficient mode: such economies have the slowest growth and generally do the poorest job at raising living standards. It should be noted, however, that while economies with minimal government interference tend to grow rapidly, individuals with the greatest amounts of the most productive resources will receive the greatest proportion of an economy's output. Therefore, there appears to be a significant efficiency–equity trade-off in the case of pure capitalism.

The concept of laissez-faire describes limited government participation in the operation of free markets and free choices. Each of the foregoing characteristics of pure capitalism assumes that there are no outside impediments to the market system. For the most part, the government's role is strictly limited to the provision of "public goods," such as public roads or national defense, and the administration of a judicial system to interpret and enforce contracts and private property rights.

THE ROLE OF GOVERNMENT IN MARKET ECONOMIES

MACROECONOMIC POLICY

Government participates in economic activity at the microeconomic and macroeconomic levels. Macroeconomic policy may be divided in monetary policy and fiscal policy. Monetary policy is concerned with the regulation of the money supply and credit. Monetary policy in the United States is conducted by the Federal Reserve. The other part of macroeconomic policy is fiscal policy. Fiscal policy deals with government spending and taxation. Fiscal policy in the United States may be initiated by the president or Congress but only Congress has the power to levy taxes. In formulating economic policy proposals, the president relies on advice from members of the cabinet, the Office of Management and Budget, and the Council of Economic Advisers.

In general, the objective of macroeconomic policy, sometimes referred to as stabilization policy, is to moderate the negative effects of the business cycle, the recurring expansions and contractions in overall economic activity. Periods of economic expansion, or economic "booms," are often accompanied by a general and sustained increase in the prices of goods and services, or inflation. Periods of economic contraction are associated with rising unemployment. Macroeconomic policy is directed toward maintaining full employment and price level stability.

MICROECONOMIC POLICY

Economics is the study of how consumers use their limited incomes to purchase goods and services to maximize their utility (satisfaction or happiness). Consumers are also owners of factors of production (land, labour, and capital), the services of which are offered to the highest bidder to generate the income necessary to purchase goods and services from firms. Finally, firms purchase the services of the factors of production to produce goods and services for sale in the market. The revenues generated from the sale of these goods and services are then returned to the owners of the factors of production in the form of wages, interest, and rents. What remains of total revenue after the services of the factors of production have been paid for is called profits. While the prices of land, labour, and capital are directly determined in the resource market, profits are residual payments to the entrepreneur, which is another source of consumer income.

In 1776 Adam Smith argued in Wealth of Nations that the actions of self-interested individuals are driven, as if by an invisible hand, to promote the general public welfare. This, Smith wrote, is because the interaction of self-interested buyers and sellers in perfectly competitive markets would tend to promote economic efficiency. When economic efficiency is realized, consumers' utility, firms' profits, and the public welfare are maximized. Since, however, the conditions necessary to achieve economic efficiency are not always present, competitive markets are not always perfect. There are generally two justifications for the government's role in economy. One justification for government intervention is that the market does not always result in economically efficient outcomes. The other is that some people do not like the market outcome and use the government to alter the outcome, often for the benefit of some narrowly defined special interest group. The following discussion will focus on the role of the government to promote efficient economic outcomes.

The concept of economic efficiency is often associated with the term Pareto efficiency. An outcome is said to be Pareto efficient if it is not possible to make one person in society better off, say through some resource allocation, without making some other person in society worse off. Two related concepts are production efficiency and consumption efficiency.

Production efficiency occurs when firms produce given quantities of goods and services at least cost. From society's perspective, production efficiency takes place when society's resources are fully employed and are used in the best, most productive way.

Consumption efficiency occurs when consumers derive the greatest level of happiness, satisfaction, or utility from the purchase of goods and services with their limited income. Consumers, in other words, receive the greatest "bang for the buck."

Efficiency in production and consumption depend on a number of conditions, including perfect information and the absence of externalities. When information is not perfect, or when externalities exist, market imperfections arise and economic efficiency is not achieved.

The main information transmission mechanism in market economies is the system of prices. A change in the market price is a signal to producers and consumers that more or less of a good or service is desired.

When market prices are "right," producers and consumers will make the best possible decisions. When prices are "wrong," producers and consumers will not make the best possible decisions. Producers will not utilize the least-cost combination of factors of production, with resulting resource misallocation and waste, while consumers, by failing to allocate their limited incomes in the most efficient manner possible, will not maximize their satisfaction.

It is often argued that when information is not perfect and market solutions are not optimal, the government should step in and require that a certain amount of information be made available. Government policies pursuant to this viewpoint have resulted in companies printing ingredients on product labels, providing health warnings on cigarettes packages, and so on.

In most developed countries, government mandates that new pharmaceuticals be tested and certified before being made available to the public, while members of certain professions, such as lawyers, doctors, nurses, and teachers, must be licensed or certified.

Another justification of government participation in economic activity is the existence of externalities. Economic efficiency requires that the participants in any market transaction fully absorb all the benefits and costs associated with that transaction. If this is the case, the market price of that good or service will fully reflect those benefits and costs. However, if a third party not directly involved in the transactions receives some of the costs or benefits of that transaction, externalities are said to exist. When the third party receives some of the benefits of the transaction, the externalities are said to be positive. If, on the other hand, the third party absorbs some of the costs of the transaction, the externalities are said to be negative.

Education is an example of a service that generates positive externalities. Increased literacy and higher levels of education, for example, make workers more productive, and democracies operate more efficiently with a better informed electorate. Unfortunately, if producers of education do not receive all the benefits of their efforts, educational services tend to be underprovided. But if it is agreed that positive externalities exist, then one role of government is to step in and subsidize the production of education to bring the output of these goods and services to more socially optimal levels.

Pollution, which is a by-product of the production process, is an example of negative externalities: too much of a good or service is being produced because firms are not absorbing all the costs associated with producing that good or service. When the public is forced to pay higher medical bills because of illnesses associated with air and water pollution, resources are diverted away from more socially desirable ends. When negative externalities exist, government will often step in and tax production, or, in the case of pollution, force firms to undertake measures to eliminate undesirable by-products. In either case, production costs are raised, and output (and pollution) is reduced to more socially desirable levels.

THEORY OF THE FIRM

The concept of the "firm" or the "company" is commonly misunderstood. Too often, the corporate entities are confused with the people who own or operate the organizations. In fact, a firm is an activity that combines scarce productive resources to produce goods and services that are demanded by society.

Firms are more appropriately viewed as an activity that transforms productive inputs into outputs of goods and services. The manner in which productive resources are combined and organized will depend of the organizational objective of the owner–operator or, as in the case of publicly owned companies, the decisions of the designated agents of the company's shareholders.

Scarce productive resources are many and varied. Consider, for example, the productive resources that go into the production of something as simple as a chair. First, there are various types of labour employed, such as designers, machine tool operators, carpenters, and sales personnel. If the chair is made of wood, decisions must be made regarding the type or types of wood that will be used. Will the chair have upholstery of some kind? If so, then decisions must be made on material, quality, and patterns. Will the chair have any attachments, such as small wheels on the bottom of the legs for easy moving? Will the wheels be made of metal, plastic, or some composite material?

The point is that even something as relatively simple as a chair may require quite a large number of resources in the production process. It should be clear, therefore, that when one is discussing economic and business relationships in the abstract, making too many allowances for reality has its limitations. To overcome this problem, we will assume that production is functionally related to two broad categories of inputs, labour and capital.

THE OBJECTIVE OF THE FIRM

Economists have traditionally assumed that the goal of the firm is to maximize profit p. This behavioral assumption is central to the neoclassical theory of the firm, which posits the firm as a profit-maximizing "black box" that transforms inputs into outputs for sale in the market. While the precise contents of the "black box" are unknown, it is generally assumed to contain the "secret formula" that gives the firm its competitive advantage. In general, neoclassical theory makes no attempt to explain what actually goes on inside the "black box," although the underlying production function is assumed to exhibit certain desirable mathematical properties, such as a favourable position with respect to the law of diminishing returns, returns to scale, and substitutability between and among productive inputs. The appeal of the neoclassical model is its application to a wide range of profit maximizing firms and market situations.

Neoclassical theory attempts to explain the behavior of profit maximizing firms subject to known resource constraints and perfect market information. It is important, however, to distinguish between current period profits and the stream of profits over some period of time. Often, managers are observed making decisions that reduce this year's profit in an effort to boost net income in future. Since both present and future profits are important, one approach is to maximize the present, or discounted, value of the firm's stream of future profits.

This more complete model of firm behavior also has the advantage of incorporating the important elements of time and uncertainty. Here, the primary goal of the firm is assumed to be expected wealth maximization, and is generally considered to be the primary objective of the firm.

REALISTIC ASSUMPTION OF PROFIT MAXIMIZATION

The assumption of profit maximization has come under repeated criticism. Many economists have argued that this behavioral assertion is too simplistic to describe the complex nature and managerial thought processes of the modern large corporation. Two distinguishing characteristics of the modern corporation weaken the neoclassical assumption of profit maximization. To begin with, the modern large corporation is generally not owner operated. Responsibility for the day-to-day operations of the firm is delegated to managers who serve as agents for shareholders.

One alternative to neoclassical theory based on the assumption of profit maximization is transaction cost theory, which asserts that the goal of the firm is to minimize the sum of external and internal transaction costs subject to a given level of output, which is a first-order condition for profit maximization. According to Ronald Coase (1937), who is regarded as the founder of the transaction cost theory, firms exist because they are excellent resource allocators. Thus, consumers satisfy their demand for goods and services more efficiently by ceding production to firms, rather than producing everything for their own use.

Still another theory of firm behavior, which is attributed to Herbert Simon (1959), asserts that corporate executives exhibit satisfying behavior. According to this theory, managers will attempt to maximize some objective, such as executive salaries and perquisites, subject to some minimally acceptable requirement by shareholders, such as an "adequate" rate of return on investment or a minimum rate of return on sales, profit, market share, asset growth, and so on. The assumption of satisfying behavior is predicated on the belief that it is not possible for management to know with certainty when profits are maximized because of the complexity and uncertainties associated with running a large corporation. There are also non-economic organizational objectives, such as good citizenship, product quality, and employee goodwill.

The closely related theory of manager-utility maximization was put forth by Oliver Williamson (1964). Williamson argued that managers seek to maximize their own utility, which is a function of salaries, perquisites, stock options, and so on. It has been argued, however, that managers who place their own self-interests before the interests of shareholders by failing to exploit profit opportunities may quickly find themselves looking for work. This will come about either because shareholders will rid themselves of managers who fail to maximize earnings and share prices or because the company finds itself the victim of a corporate takeover. William Baumol (1967), on the other hand, has argued that sales or market share maximization after shareholders' earnings expectations have been satisfied more accurately reflects the organizational objectives of the typical large modern corporation.

Marris and Wood (1971) have argued that the objective of management is to maximize the firm's valuation ratio, which is related to the growth rate of the firm. The firm's valuation ratio is defined as the ratio of the stock market value of the firm to its highest possible value. The highest possible value of this ratio is 1. According to this view, since managers are primarily motivated by job security, they will attempt to achieve a corporate growth rate that maximizes profits, dividends, and shareholder value. The importance of the valuation ratio is that it may be used as a proxy for a shareholder satisfaction with the performance of management. The higher the firm's valuation ratio, the less likely that managers will be ousted.

Still another important contribution to an understanding of firm behavior is principal–agent. According to this theory, the firm may be seen as a nexus of contracts between principals and "stakeholders" (agents). The principal–agent relationship may be that between owner and manager or between manager and worker. The principal–agent problem may be summarized as follows: What are the least-cost incentives that principals can offer to induce agents to act in the best interest of the firm? Principal–agent theory views the principal as a kind of "incentive engineer" who relies on "smart" contracts to minimize the opportunistic behavior of agents. Owner–manager and manager–worker principal–agent problems will be examined in greater detail in the next two sections.

Definition: This principal–agent problem arises when there are inadequate incentives for agents (managers or workers) to put forth their best efforts for principals (owners or managers). This incentive problem arises because principals, who have a vested interest in the operations of the firm, benefit from the hard work of their agents, while agents who do not have a vested interest, prefer leisure.

Although these alternative theories of firm behavior stress some relevant aspects of the operation of a modern corporation, they do not provide a satisfactory alternative to the broader assumption of profit maximization. Competitive forces in product and resource markets make it imperative for managers to keep a close watch on profits. Otherwise, the firm may lose market share, or worse yet, go out of business entirely. Moreover, alternative organizational objectives of managers of the modern corporation cannot stray very far from the dividend-maximizing self-interests of the company's shareholders. If they do, such managers will be looking for a new venue within which to ply their trade.

Regardless of the specific firm objective, however, managerial economics is less interested in how decision makers actually behave than in understanding the economic environment within which managers operate and in formulating theories from which hypotheses about cause and effect may be inferred. In general, economists are concerned with developing a framework for predicting managerial responses to changes in the firm's operating environment. Even if the assumption of profit maximization is not literally true, it provides insights into more complex behavior. Departures from these assumptions may thus be analyzed and recommendations made. In fact, many practicing economists earn a living by advising business firms and government agencies on how best to achieve "efficiency" by bringing the "real world" closer to the ideal hypothesized in economic theory. Indeed, the assumption of profit maximization is so useful precisely because this objective is rarely achieved in reality.

OWNER–MANAGER PROBLEM

A distinguishing characteristic of the large corporation is that it is not owner operated. The responsibility for day-to-day operations is delegated to managers who serve as agents for shareholders. Since the owners cannot closely monitor the manager's performance, how then shall the manager be compelled to put forth his or her "best" effort on behalf of the owners? If a manager is paid a fixed salary, a fundamental incentive problem emerges. If the firm performs poorly, there will be uncertainty over whether this was due to circumstances outside the manager's control was the result of poor management. Suppose that company profits are directly related to the manager's efforts. Even if the fault lay with a goldbricking manager, this person can always claim that things would have been worse had it not been for his or her herculean efforts on behalf of the shareholders. With absentee ownership, there is no way to verify this claim. It is simply not possible to know for certain why the company performed poorly. When owners are disconnected from the day-to-day operations of the firm, the result is the owner–manager/principal–agent problem.

To understand the essence of the owner–manager/principal–agent problem, suppose that a manager's contract calls for a fixed salary of Rs. 200,000 annually. While the manager values income, he or she also values leisure. The more time devoted to working means less time available for leisure activities. A fundamental conflict arises because owners want managers to work, while managers prefer leisure. The problem, of course, is that the manager will receive the same Rs. 200,000 income regardless of whether he or she puts in a full day's work or spends the entire day enjoying leisure activity. A fixed salary provides no incentive to work hard, which will adversely affect the firm's profits. Without the appropriate incentive, such as continual monitoring, the manager has an incentive to "goof off."

Definition: The owner–manager/principal–agent problem arises when managers do not share in the success of the day-to-day operations of the firm. When managers do not have a stake in company's performance, some managers will have an incentive to substitute leisure for a diligent work effort.

INCENTIVE CONTRACTS

Will the offer of a higher salary compel the manager to work harder? The answer is no for the same reason that the manager did not work hard in the first place. Since the owners are not present to monitor the manager's performance, there will be no incentive to substitute work for leisure. A fixed-salary contract provides no penalty for goofing off. One solution to the principal–agent problem would be to make the manager a stakeholder by offering the manager an incentive contract. An incentive contract links manager compensation to performance. Incentive contracts may include such features as profit sharing, stock options, and performance bonuses, which provide the manager with incentives to perform in the best interest of the owners.

Definition: An incentive contract between owner and manager is one in which the manager is provided with incentives to perform in the best interest of the owner.

Suppose, for example, that in addition to a salary of Rs. 200,000 the manager is offered 10% of the firm's profits. The sum of the manager's salary and a percentage of profits is the manager's gross compensation. This profit-sharing contract transforms the manager into a stakeholder. The manager's compensation is directly related to the company's performance. It is in the manager's best interest to work in the best interest of the owners.

Exactly how the manager responds to the offer of a share of the firm's profits depends critically on the manager's preferences for income and leisure. But one thing is certain. Unless the marginal utility of an additional Rupee of income is zero, it will be in the manager's best interest not to goof off during the entire work day. Making the manager a stakeholder in the company's performance will increase the profits of the owner.

OTHER MANAGEMENT INCENTIVES

The principal–agent problem helps to explain why a manager might not put forth his or her effort on behalf of the owner. There are, however, other reasons why a manager would work in the best interest of the owner that are quite apart from the direct incentives associated with being a stakeholder in the success of the firm. These indirect incentives relate directly to the self-interest of the manager. One of these incentives is the manager's own reputation.

Managers are well aware that their current position may not be their last. The ability of managers to move to other more responsible and lucrative positions depends crucially on demonstrated managerial skills in previous employments. An effective manager invests considerable time, effort, and energy in the supervision of workers and organization of production. The value of this investment will be captured in the manager's reputation, which may ultimately be sold in the market at a premium. Thus, even if the manager is not made a stakeholder in the firm's success through profit sharing, stock options, or performance bonuses, the manager may nonetheless choose to do a good job as a way of laying the groundwork for future rewarding opportunities.

Another incentive, which was discussed earlier, relates to the manager's job security. Shareholders who believe that the firm is not performing up to its potential, or is not earning profits comparable to those of similar firms in the same industry, may then move to oust the incumbent management. Closely related to a shareholder revolt is the threat of a takeover. Sensing that a firm's poor performance may be the result of underachieving or incompetent managers another company might move to wrest control of the business from present shareholders. Once in control, the new owners will install a more effective management team to increase net earnings and raise shareholder value.

MANAGER–WORKER/PRINCIPAL–AGENT PROBLEM

The principal–agent problem also arises in the relationship between management and labour. Suppose that the manager is a stakeholder in the firm's operations. While manager's well-being is now synonymous with that of the owners, there is potentially a principal–agent problem between manager and worker. Without a stake in the company's performance, there will be an incentive for some workers to substitute leisure for hard work. Since it may not be possible to closely and constantly monitor worker performance, the manager is confronted with the principal–agent problem of providing incentives for diligent work. As before, the solution is to transform the worker into a stakeholder.

Definition: The manager–worker/principal–agent problem arises when workers do not have a vested interest in a firm's success. Without a stake in the company's performance, there will be an incentive for some workers not to put forth their best efforts.

PROFIT AND REVENUE SHARING

As in the case of the owner–manager/principle–agent problem, workers can be encouraged to put forth their best efforts by linking their compensation to the firm's profitability. Another way to enhance worker performance is to tie compensation to the firm's revenues. This method of compensation is particularly important when worker performance directly impact revenues rather than operating costs. The most common form of revenue sharing is the sales commission. When we think of sales commissions, we tend to think of insurance agents, real estate brokers, automobile salespersons, and so on. But sales commissions take a variety of forms. The familiar system in which bartenders and waiters earn tips also constitutes a revenue-based incentive scheme.

There are, however, problems associated with revenue-based incentive schemes. One problem is that such compensation mechanisms may lead to unethical behavior toward customers. This is especially true when customer contact is on a one-time or impersonal basis. The negative stereotypes associated with some professions, such as telephone marketers or used-car salespeople, attest to the potential dangers of linking compensation to revenues. Another problem with linking compensation to revenues is that there is generally no incentive for workers to minimize cost. Corporate executives who inflate expense accounts in attempts to curry favour with potential clients and bartenders who give free drinks attest to some of the problems associated with revenue-based incentive schemes.

OTHER WORKER INCENTIVES

Other methods of encouraging workers to put forth their best efforts are piecework, time clocks, and spot checks. Piecework involves payment based on the number of units produced. Sweatshop operations, once common in the textile industry, are examples of this type of revenue-based incentive scheme. Of course, when worker compensation is based on piecework high quantity often comes at the expense of low product quality. Low-quality products may lead to customer dissatisfaction, which in turn results in lower sales, revenues, and profits.

Time clocks indicate whether workers show up for work on time and stay till the ends of their shifts. However, time clocks do not monitor worker performance while at the workplace. Thus, the use of time clocks is an inferior solution to the manager–worker/principal–agent problem. A more effective solution, which verifies that not only the worker is on the job but that the worker is performing up to expectations, is the spot check. To be effective, spot checks must be unpredictable. Otherwise, workers will know when to work hard and when goofing off will not be noticed.

There are two distinct problems with spot checks. To be effective, random spot checks must be frequent enough to raise the expected penalty to the worker who is caught goldbricking. Frequent spot checks, however, are costly and reduce the firm's profitability. In addition, frequent spot checks can have a negative effect on worker morale. Low worker morale will negatively affect productivity and profitability. In general, incentive-based schemes based on threats are inferior to compensation-based solutions, such as revenue or profit sharing, to the principal–agent problem.

CONSTRAINTS ON THE OPERATIONS OF THE FIRM

Suppose that the objective of the firm is to maximize short-run profits (or wealth, or value). In attempting to achieve this objective, the firm faces a number of constraints. These constraints might include a scarcity of essential productive resources, such as a certain type of skilled labour, specific raw materials, as might occur because of labour discontent in the country of a foreign supplier, limitations on factory or warehouse space, and unavailability of credit. Constraints might also take the form of legal restrictions on the operations of the firm, such as minimum wage laws, pollution emission standards, and legal restrictions on certain types of business activity. Such constraints are often imposed by government to achieve perceived social (welfare) goals.

For many business and economic applications, it is necessary to think in terms of the optimizing managerial objectives subject to one or more side constraints. This process is referred to as constrained optimization. For example, it might be the goal of a firm to maximize profits subject to limitations on operating budgets or the level of output. The existence of these constraints usually means that the range of possibilities available to the firm is limited.

Thus, profit maximization in the strict sense may not be possible. Put differently, the maximum attainable profits in the presence of such constraints are likely to be less than they would have been in the absence of the restrictions. Although most of this text deals with developing principles of firm behavior based on theories of unconstrained profit maximization, we will also introduce the powerful mathematical techniques of Lagrange multipliers and linear programming for dealing with constrained optimization problems.

ACCOUNTING PROFIT VERSUS ECONOMIC PROFIT

To say that products that can be produced profitably will be, and those that cannot be produced profitably will not begs the question of what we mean by "profit." What is commonly thought of as profit by the accountant may not match the meaning assigned to the term by an economist. An economist's notion of profit goes back to the basic fact that resources are scarce and have alternative uses. To use a certain set of resources to produce a good or service means that certain alternative production possibilities were forgone. Costs in economics have to do with forgoing the opportunity to produce alternative goods and services. The economic, or opportunity, cost of any resource in producing some good or service is its value or worth in its next best alternative use.

Given the notion of opportunity costs, economic costs are the payments a firm must make, or incomes it must provide, to resource suppliers to attract these resources away from alternative lines of production. Economic costs (TC) include all relevant opportunity costs. These payments or incomes may be either explicit, "out-of-pocket" or cash expenditures, or implicit. Implicit costs represent the value of resources used in the production process for which no direct payment is made. This value is generally taken to be the money earnings of resources in their next best alternative employment. When a computer software programmer quits his or her job to open a consulting firm, the forgone salary is an example of an implicit cost. When the owner of an office building decides to open a hobby shop, the forgone rental income from that store is an example of an implicit cost. When a housewife decides to redeem a certificate of deposit to establish a day-care center for children, the forgone interest earnings represent an implicit cost. In short, any sacrifice incurred when the decision is made to produce a good or service must be taken into account if the full impact of that decision is to be correctly assessed.

Economic profits are equal to total revenue less total economic costs, which is the sum of explicit and implicit costs. Accounting profits, on the other hand, are equal to total revenue less total explicit costs.

It is, of course, a simple matter to make accounting profit equivalent to economic profit by making explicit all relevant implicit costs. Suppose, for example, that an individual quits a Rs. 40,000 per year job as the manager a family restaurant to open a new restaurant. Since this is a sacrifice incurred by the budding restauranteur, the forgone salary is an implicit cost. On the other hand, this implicit cost can easily be made explicit by putting the restaurant owner "on the books" for a salary of Rs. 40,000.The somewhat arbitrary distinction between explicit and implicit costs is illustrated in the following problem.

NORMAL PROFIT

Another important concept in economics is that of normal profit. Normal profit, sometimes referred to as normal rate of return, is the level of profit required to keep a firm engaged in a particular activity. Alternatively, normal profit represents the rate of return on the next best alternative investment of equivalent risk. It is the level of profit necessary to keep people from pulling their investments in search of higher rates of return. If a firm is well established and has a good earnings record, and if there is little to no possibility of financial loss during a specified period of time, then the normal rate of return is approximately equal to the interest rate on a risk-free government bond. If the firm's earnings are erratic and its future prospects questionable, then the risk-free rate of return must be augmented by a risk premium. Either way, normal profit is a form of opportunity cost. Viewed in this way, it is easy to see that normal profit represents a component of total economic cost.

VARIATIONS IN PROFITS ACROSS INDUSTRIES AND FIRMS

It was pointed out earlier that profit is the mechanism whereby society signals resource owners and entrepreneurs where goods and services are in greatest demand. If market economies are dynamic and efficient, this would imply that profits tend to be equal across industries and among firms. Yet, this is hardly the case. Established industries, such as textiles and basic metals, tend to generate a lower rate of return than such high-technology industries as computer hardware and software, telecommunications, health care, and biotechnology. There are several theories that help to explain these profit differences.

Although free-market economies tend to be relatively efficient and dynamic, it is this very dynamism that often gives rise to above-normal and below-normal profits. In general, we would expect risk-adjusted rates of return to be the same across all industries and firms. The frictional theory of profit, however, helps explain why this is rarely the case. To see this, we make a distinction between short-run and long-run competitive equilibrium. If we assume that firms are profit maximizers, then a firm is in shortrun equilibrium if it is earning an above-normal rate of return. The existence of above-normal rates of return tends to attract investment capital, thereby resulting in an increase in industry output, falling product prices, and lower profits. If a firm is earning below-normal rates of return, then investment capital will tend to exit the industry, resulting in lower output, rising product prices, higher prices, and increased profits.

Firms that are just earning a normal rate of return are said to be in longrun equilibrium. When firms are in long-run equilibrium, investment capital will neither enter nor exit the industry. In this case, output neither expands nor contracts, and product prices and profits remain unchanged. In reality, industries are rarely in long-run competitive equilibrium because of recurring supply-side and demand-side "shocks" to the economic system. Examples of supply-side shocks may result from changes in production technology or changes in resource prices, such as fluctuations in energy prices brought about by recurrent changes in OPEC production policies. On the demand side of the market, these shocks may result from the introduction of new products and changing consumer preferences, such as was the case with the introduction of personal computers in 1980s.

The risk-bearing theory of profit suggests that above-normal profits are required to attract productive resources into industries with above-average risk, such as petroleum exploration. This line of reasoning is quite analogous to the idea that the rate of return on corporate equities should be higher than that for corporate bonds to compensate the investor for the increased uncertainty associated with the returns on these financial assets.

Sometimes a firm will earn above-normal profits because it is in a position to exercise market power. Market power relates to the ability of a firm or an industry to raise the selling price of its product by restricting output. The degree of a firm's market power is usually related to the level of competition. If a firm has many competitors, each selling essentially the same good or service, then that firm's ability to raise price will be severely limited. To raise prices in the face of stiff competition would result in a dramatic decline in sales. As we will discuss later, this is characteristic of firms operating in perfectly competitive industries. At the other extreme, a firm that produces output for the entire industry has a great deal of discretion over its selling price through adjustments in output. This is the extreme case of a monopoly. Such a dominant position in the market may be achieved through patent protection, government restrictions that limit competition, or through cost advantages associated with large scale production.

An extension to the competitive theory of firm behavior is the marginal efficiency theory of profit. According to this theory, the firm's ability to extract above-normal profits in the long-run stems from being a more efficient (least-cost) producer. In this case, a firm is able to generate high profits by staying ahead of the competition by adopting the most efficient methods of production and management techniques. Above-normal profits might also be generated through the introduction of a new product or production technique. The innovation theory of profit postulates that above-average profits are the rewards associated with being the first to introduce a new product or technology. Steve Jobs, cofounder of Apple Computer, became a multimillionaire after pioneering the desktop personal computer. Such above-normal profits, however, invite a host of imitators and thus are usually short-lived. Usually within a relative short period of time, above normal profits will be competed away, and some individual producers may be forced to drop out of the industry.

Managerial economics is the application of economic theory and quantitative methods (mathematics and statistics) to the managerial decision making process. In general, economic theory is the study of how individuals and societies choose to utilize scarce productive resources (land, labour, capital, and entrepreneurial ability) to satisfy virtually unlimited wants. Quantitative methods refer to the tools and techniques of analysis, which include optimization analysis, statistical methods, forecasting, game theory, linear programming, and capital budgeting.

Economic theory is concerned with how society answers the basic economic questions of what goods and services should be produced, and in what amounts, how these goods and services should be produced (i.e., the choice of the appropriate production technology), and for whom these goods and services should be produced. In market economies, what goods and services are produced by society is determined not by the producer, but rather by the consumer.

Profit-maximizing firms produce only the goods and services their customers demand. How goods and services are produced refers to the technology of production, and this is determined by the firm's management. Profit maximization implies cost minimization. In competitive markets, firms that do not combine productive inputs in the most efficient (least costly) manner possible will quickly be driven out of business. The for whom part of the question designates the individuals who are willing, and able, to pay for the goods and services produced.

The study of economics is divided into two broad subcategories: macroeconomics and microeconomics. Macroeconomics is the study of entire economies and economic systems and specifically considers such broad economic aggregates as gross domestic product, economic growth, national income, employment, unemployment, inflation, and international trade. In general, the topics covered in macroeconomics are concerned with the economic environment within which firm managers operate. For the most part, macroeconomics focuses on variables over which the managerial decision maker has little or no control, although they may be of considerable importance when economic decisions are mode at the micro level of the individual, firm, or industry. Macroeconomics also examines the role of government in influencing these economic aggregates to achieve socially desirable objectives through the use of monetary and fiscal policies.

Microeconomics, on the other hand, is the study of the behavior and interaction of individual economic agents. These economic agents represent individual firms, consumers, and governments. Microeconomics deals with such topics as profit maximization, utility maximization, revenue or sales maximization, product pricing, input utilization, production efficiency, market structure, capital budgeting, environmental protection, and governmental regulation. Microeconomics is the study of the behavior of individual economic agents, such as individual consumers and firms, and the interactions between them.

Unlike macroeconomics, microeconomics is concerned with factors that are directly or indirectly under the control of management, such as product quantity, quality, pricing, input utilization, and advertising expenditures. Managerial economics also explicitly recognizes that a firm's organizational objective, usually profit maximization, is subject to one or more operating constraints (size of firm's operating budget, shareholders' expected rate of return on investment, etc.).

The dominant organizational objective of firms in free-market economies is profit maximization. Other important organizational objectives, which may be inconsistent with the goal of profit maximization, include a variety of noneconomic objectives, satisficing behavior, and wealth maximization.

The assumption of profit maximization has come under repeated criticism. Many economists have argued that this behavioral assertion is too simplistic to describe the complexity of the modern large corporation and the managerial thought processes required. Other theories emphasize different aspects of the operations of the modern, large corporation. Despite these attempts, no other theory of firm behavior has been able to provide a satisfactory alternative to the broader assumption of profit maximization. Profit maximization (loss minimization) involves maximizing the positive difference (minimizing the negative difference) between total revenue and total economic cost, that is, total economic profit. Total revenue is defined as the price of a product times the number of units sold. Total economic cost includes all relevant costs associated with producing a given amount of output. These costs include both explicit, "out-of-pocket" expenses and implicit costs.

Economic profit is distinguished from accounting profit, which is the difference between total revenue and total explicit costs. Total economic profit considers all relevant economic costs associated with the production of a good or a service. Another important concept is normal profit, which refers to the minimum payment necessary to keep the firm's factors of production from being transferred to some other activity. In other words, normal profit refers to the profit that could be earned by a firm in its next best alternative activity. Economic profit refers to profit in excess of these normal returns.

Noneconomic organizational objectives tend to emphasize such intangibles as good citizenship, product quality, and employee goodwill. The achievement of other organizational objectives, such as earning an "adequate" rate of return on investment, or attaining some minimum acceptable rate of sales, profit, market share, or asset growth, is the result of satisficing behavior on the part of senior management. Satisficing behavior is predicated on the belief that it is not possible for senior management to know when profits are maximized because of the complexities and uncertainties associated with running a large corporation. Finally, maximization of shareholder wealth involves maximizing the value of a company's stock by maximizing the present value of the firm's net cash inflows at the appropriate discount rate.

In summary, managerial economics might best be described as applied microeconomics. As an applied discipline, managerial economics integrates economic theory with the techniques of quantitative analysis, including mathematical economics, optimization analysis, regression analysis, forecasting, linear programming, and risk analysis. Managerial economics attempts to demonstrate how the optimality conditions postulated in economic theory can be applied to real-world business situations to optimize firms' organizational objectives.

Note: Conn's, Inc. (Conn's) is a US based specialty retailer. The company offers home appliances and consumer electronics products through its retail outlets. In addition, Conn's also provides in-house credit finance options for its customers' product purchases. The company is headquartered in Beaumont, Texas and employed 3,235 people as on January 2009. For detailed information related to this chapter reader can visit www.conns.com

2

The Essentials of Demand and Supply

Managerial economics is the synthesis of microeconomic theory and quantitative methods to find optimal solutions to managerial decision-making problems. In previous chapters we reviewed the basic elements of two of the quantitative methods most frequently used in managerial economics: mathematical economics and econometrics. In this chapter, we will demonstrate how presumably quantifiable economic functional relationships involving one dependent variable and one or more explanatory variables may be used to predict market-clearing prices in idealized, perfectly competitive markets.

Students who have made it this far in their economic studies have already been exposed to the market paradigm of demand and supply. While the principles of demand and supply presented in this chapter may be familiar, the manner in which this material is presented may not be. The discussion that follows establishes the procedural framework for much of what is to come.

The basic market paradigm presented in this chapter is a stylized version of what occurs in the real world. The model is predicated on a number of assumptions that are rarely, if ever, satisfied in practice, including perfect and symmetric information, market transactions that are restricted to private goods and services, and that no market participants having market power.

When there is "perfect and symmetric information," all that is knowable about the goods and services being transacted is known in equal measure by all market participants. For markets to operate efficiently, both the buyer and the seller must have complete and accurate information about the essentials of demand and supply quantity, quality, and price of the good or service being exchanged. Asymmetric information exists when some market participants have more and better information about the goods and services being exchanged. Fraud can arise in the presence of asymmetric information.

In extreme cases, the knowledge that some market participants have access to privileged information may result in a complete breakdown of the market, such as might occur if it became widely believed that stock market transactions were dominated by insider trading.

Goods and services are said to be "private" when all the production costs and consumption benefits are borne exclusively by the market participants. That is, there are no indirect, third-party effects. Such third-party effects, called externalities, may affect either consumers or producers.

The most common example of a negative externality in production is pollution. Finally, "market power" refers to the ability to influence the market price of a good or service by shifting the demand or supply curve.

A violation of any of the three assumptions just given could lead to failure of the market to provide socially optimal levels of particular goods or services. When this occurs, direct or indirect government intervention in the market may be deemed to be in the public's best interest.

THE LAW OF DEMAND

The assumption of profit-maximizing behavior assumes that owners and managers know the demand for the firm's good or service. The demand function asserts that there is a measurable relationship between the price that a company charges for its product and the number of units that buyers are willing and able to purchase during a specified time period. Economists refer to this behavioral relationship as the law of demand, which is sometimes called the first fundamental law of economics.

Definition: The law of demand states that the quantity demanded of a good or service is inversely related to the selling price, ceteris paribus (all other determinants remaining unchanged).

The term "law of demand" is actually a misnomer. As discussed in first chapter, laws are facts. Laws are assertions of fact. Laws predict events with certainty. By contrast, theories are probabilistic statements of cause the law of demand and effect. The law of demand is a theory, as is invariably the case when human nature is involved.

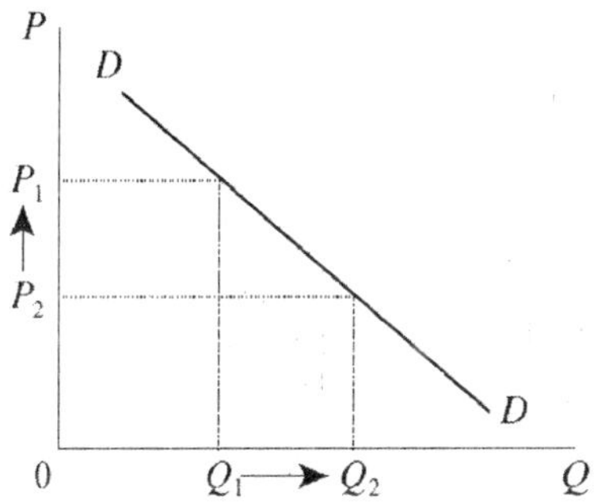

Figure: The demand curve.

Symbolically, the law of demand may be summarized as

$$Q_D = f(P) \qquad (2.1a)$$

and

$$\frac{dQ_D}{dP} < 0 \qquad (2.1b)$$

Equation (2.1a) states that Q_D, the quantity demanded of a good or service, is functionally related to the selling price P. Inequality (2.1b) asserts that quantity demanded and price are inversely related. This relationship is illustrated in Figure above. The downward-sloping demand curve illustrates the inverse relationship between the quantity demanded of a good or service and its selling price.

The validity of the law of demand may be argued on the basis of common sense and simple observation. At a more sophisticated level, the validity of the law of demand may be argued on the basis of diminishing marginal utility and income and substitution effects.

INCOME EFFECT

For most goods, the income effect asserts that as a product's price declines (increases), an individual's real income (purchasing power) increases (decreases). The increase in real purchasing power resulting from a fall in prices enables the individual to consume greater quantities of a commodity, while the opposite is true for an increase in prices. In other words, an increase in real purchasing power generally (although not always) leads to increase in quantity demanded. The goods of the types for which this phenomenon holds are referred to as normal goods. Unfortunately, the income effect does not always have the expected positive effect on the quantity demanded of a good. In some cases, as an individual's purchasing power increases, the quantity demand for that good falls. Goods of these types are called inferior goods. Examples of such goods may be potatoes, bus tickets, soup bones, and bologna. We will return to this issue shortly when considering separately the effect of changes in money income on the demand for goods and services.

SUBSTITUTION EFFECT

The more powerful substitution effect entails no such ambiguities. The substitution effect reflects changes in consumers' opportunity costs. The substitution effect states that as a product's price declines, consumers will substitute the now less expensive product for similar goods that are more expensive. In the majority of cases, the income effect and the substitution effect complement and reinforce each other. That is, a decline in the price of a good will not only have a positive substitution effect, but will have a positive income effect as well. As a result, the ordinary demand curve will be downward sloping. Even in the case of inferior goods, where the income effect is negative, the ordinary demand curve will exhibit a downward slope because the substitution effect, which is always positive with a drop in price, outweighs the negative income effect.

THE MARKET DEMAND CURVE

The law of demand is a theoretical explanation of the expected behavior of individual economic units when confronted with a change in the price of a commodity. Yet our concern, at the present, is less with the behavior of individual economic agents than with the market demand for the product of an industry.

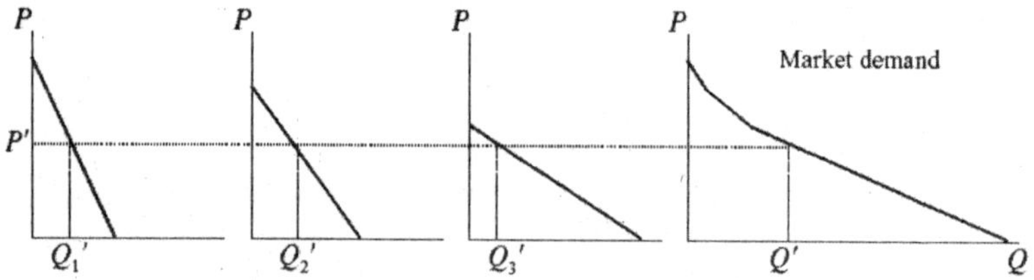

Figure: The market demand curve is the horizontal summation of the individual demand curves.

We must, therefore, extend our analysis to justify what we would hope to be a downward-sloping market demand curve. To derive the hypothetical market demand function for a particular industry's product, let us first consider three hypothetical individual demand functions for the product in question

$$Q_{D,1} = a_1 + b_1 P \tag{2.2a}$$

$$Q_{D,2} = a_2 + b_2 P \tag{2.2b}$$

$$Q_{D,3} = a_3 + b_3 P \tag{2.2c}$$

where the $Q_{D,i}$ terms represent the individual's demand for the commodity, the a_i terms are positive constants, and the bi terms the unit change in quantity demanded given a change in the selling price.

Definition: The market demand curve is the horizontal summation of the individual demand curves.

For any given price, the market demand curve is the sum of the horizontal distances from the vertical axis to each individual demand curve. Summing together Equations (2.2) we get

$$Q_{D,i} + Q_{D,2} + Q_{D,3} = (a_1 + a_2 + a_3) + (b_1 + b_2 + b_3)P \tag{2.3}$$

Or

$$Q_D = a + bP \tag{2.4}$$

where a $= a_1 + a_2 + a_3$ and b $= b_1 + b_2 + b_3$. In general, for the n-consumer case

$$Q_{D,M} = \sum_{i=1\to n} Q_{D,i} = \sum_{i=1\to n} a_i = \sum_{i=1\to n} b_i P \tag{2.5}$$

where $Q_{D,M}$ is market demand.

The market demand curve establishes a relationship between the product's price and the quantity demanded; all other determinants of market demand are held constant. The relationship between changes in price and changes in quantity demanded are illustrated as movements along the demand curve. When economists refer to a change in the quantity demanded (in response to a change in price), they are referring to a movement along the demand curve. As we will see, this is to be distinguished from a change in demand (illustrated as a shift in the entire demand curve), which results when a determinant of demand, other than its selling price, is changed. This semantic distinction is made necessary because two dimensional representations of a demand function can accommodate a relationship between two variables only—in this case price and quantity, the independent and dependent variables, respectively.

OTHER DETERMINANTS OF MARKET DEMAND

We know, of course, that price is not the only factor that influences an economic agent's decision to purchase quantities of a given good or service. Other demand determinants include income, consumer preferences, the prices of related goods, price expectations, and population.

INCOME

Typically, an increase in a consumer's money income will result in increased purchases of goods and services, other things remaining equal (including the selling price). More precisely, a ceteris paribus increase in an individual's money income will usually lead to an increase in the demand for a good or service. Conceptually, this is not the same thing as an increase in quantity demanded of a good or service due to an increase in an individual's real income that has resulted from a fall in price. Similarly, a ceteris paribus decline in an individual's money income will result in a decrease in demand. As before, such goods are called normal goods. Most goods and services fall into this category. An increase in demand for a normal good resulting from an increase in income may be illustrated in Figure below.

In the case of so-called interior goods, however, the demand for a good or a service actually declines with an increase in money income. The result would be a leftward shift in the demand curve. Inferior goods are largely a matter of individual preferences. As their income rises, some individuals prefer to substitute train or plane travel for slower, and presumably less expensive, long-distance bus rides. On the other hand, other people really like riding buses. For this group, long-distance bus travel is a normal good.

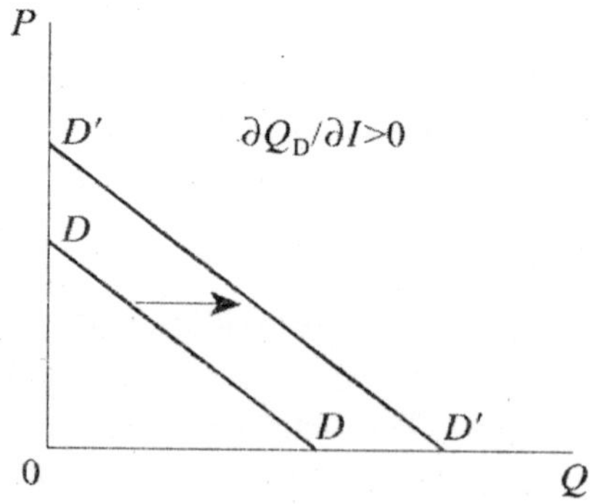

Figure: An increase in demand resulting from an increase in money income.

TASTES OR PREFERENCES (T)

Another determinant of market demand is individuals' tastes, or preferences, for a particular product. After seeing a McDonald's television commercial, for example, one person might be compelled to purchase an increased quantity of hamburgers, even though the price of hamburgers had not fallen or his income had remained the same. This increased demand for hamburgers would be represented as a rightward shift in the demand curve. Similarly, if after reading an article in the New York Times about the health dangers associated with diets high in animal fat and salt, the same person might decide to cut down on his intake of hamburgers, which would be shown as a left-shift in his demand curve for hamburgers. The effect of an increase in taste is similar to that depicted for an increase in income in Figure above.

PRICES OF RELATED GOODS: SUBSTITUTES (PS) AND COMPLEMENTS (PC)

The prices of related goods can also affect the demand for a particular good or service. Related goods are generally classified as either substitute goods or complementary goods.

Substitutes are goods that consumers consider to be closely related. As the price of good X rises, the quantity demanded of that good will fall according to the law of demand. If good Y is a substitute for good X, the demand for good Y will rise as the consumer substitutes into it. The willingness of the consumer to substitute one good for another varies from good to good and is rarely an either/or proposition. For example, although not perfect substitutes for most consumers, Coca-Cola and Pepsi-Cola might be classified as "close" substitutes. Other examples of goods that may be classified as substitutes are oleomargarine and butter, coffee and tea, and beer and ale.

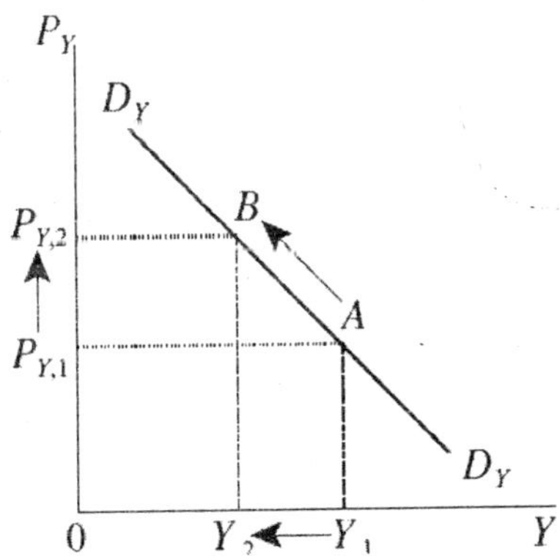

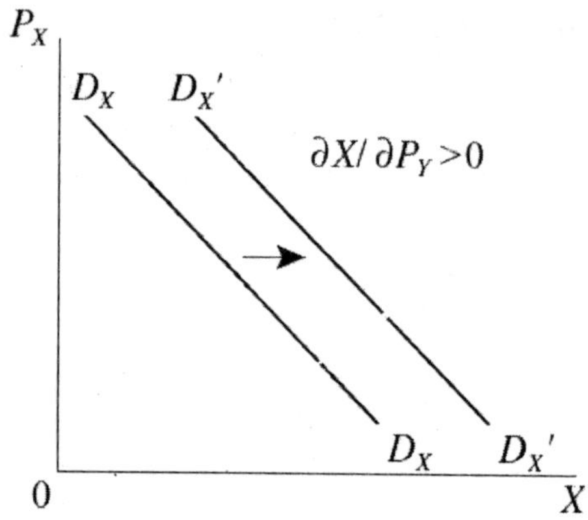

Figure: An increase in demand resulting froma decrease in the price of a substitute good.

If goods X and Y are substitutes, then we would expect that as the price of Y rises the quantity demanded of Y falls, and the demand for X, other things remaining constant (including the price of X, income, etc.) increase. This interrelationship is illustrated in Figure above.

Note that in above figure as the price of good Y rises from $P_{Y,1}$ to $P_{Y,2}$ the quantity demanded of good Y falls from Y_1 to Y_2 (a movement along the D_YD_Y curve from point A to point B), resulting in an increase in the demand for good X. This is illustrated by a right-shift in the demand function for X from D_XD_X to $D_{X'}D_{X'}$. Analogously, a fall in the price of product Y, say from $P_{Y,2}$ to $P_{Y,1}$, would result in an increase in the quantity demanded of good Y, or a movement along the demand curve from point B to point A, would result in a left-shift of the demand curve for good X.

Complements are products that are normally consumed together. Examples of such product pairs include corned beef and cabbage, tea and lemon, coffee and cream, peanut butter and jelly, tennis rackets and tennis balls, ski boots and skis, and kites and kite string.

If goods X and Y are complements, we would expect that as the price of good Y falls and the quantity demanded of good Y increases, we will also witness an increase in the demand for good X. In figure below as the price of Y falls from $P_{Y,1}$ to $P_{Y,2}$ the quantity demanded of good Y increases from Y_1 to Y_2 (a movement along the D_YD_Y curve from point A to point B). The lower price of good Y, say for kites, not only results in an increase in the quantity demanded of kites, but also results in an increase in the demand for good X, kite string. This increase in the demand for good X is shown as a right-shift in the entire demand function for good X. Similarly, an increase in the price of good Y not only would result in a decline in the quantity demanded of good Y, but also would result in a fall in the demand for good X, which is illustrated as left-shift in the demand function for good X.

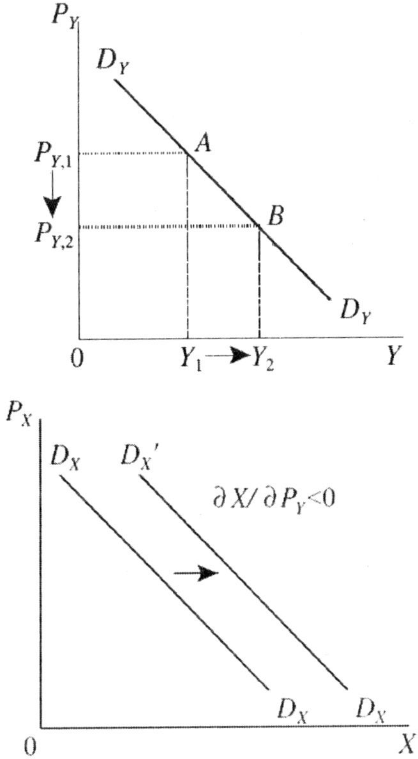

Figure: An increase in demand resulting from a decrease in the price of a complementary good.

PRICE EXPECTATIONS (P_E)

If we expect that the price of a good or service will be lower in the future, the demand for that product will be lower today, resulting in a left-shift of today's demand function. Converscly, if we expect the price to be higher tomorrow, the demand will be greater today, resulting in a right-shift in the demand function.

POPULATION (N)

As we discussed earlier, the market demand curve for a good or a service is the horizontal summation of demand curves of individuals that make up the market. Changes in the number of consumers in the market, perhaps because of an increase in the general population, will result in changes in demand.

An increase in population, perhaps because of immigration, increased birthrates, or demographic changes, likely will cause an increase in the demand for a product, which will be illustrated diagrammatically as a right-shift in the demand curve. Similarly, a decrease in population will likely cause a decrease in the demand for a product, which will be illustrated diagrammatically as a left-shift in the demand curve.

The relationship between the demand for a good and service and the set of determinants just discussed may be expressed as

$$Q_D = f(P, I, T, P_s, P_c, P_e, N) \tag{2.6}$$

OTHER DEMAND DETERMINANTS

We have mentioned only a very few of the possible factors that will influence the demand for a product. Other demand determinants might include income expectations, changes in interest rates, changes in foreign exchange rates, and the impact of wealth effects.

In actual demand analysis, an indepth familiarity with specific market conditions will usually help one to identify the relevant demand determinants that need to be considered in analyzing market behavior.

THE MARKET DEMAND EQUATION

The functional relationship summarized in Equation (2.6) suggests only that a relationship exists between QD and a collection of hypothesized explanatory variables. While such an expression of causality is useful, it says nothing about the specific functional relationship, nor does it say anything about the magnitude of the interrelationships.

To quantify the hypothesized relationship in Equation (2.6), it is necessary to specify a functional form. Using the techniques discussed in Green (1997), Gujarati (1995), and Ramanathan (1998), we may proceed to estimate the values of the coefficients.

As indicated earlier, the most commonly used functional form is the linear equation. We might, therefore, express Equation (2.6) as

$$Q_D = b_0 + b_1 P + b_2 I + b_3 P_s + b_4 P_c + b_5 P_e + b_6 N \tag{2.7}$$

where

$b_1 < 0,\ b_2 > 0,\ b_3 > 0,\ b_4 < 0,\ b_5 > 0,\ b_6 > 0$

The coefficients bi are the first partial derivatives of the demand function. They indicate how Q_D will change from a one unit change in the value of the independent variables. For many purposes, it is useful to concentrate only on the relationship between quantity demanded and the price of the commodity under consideration while holding the other variables constant. Equation (2.7) may be rewritten as

$$Q_D = \zeta + b_1 P \tag{2.8}$$

where $\zeta = b_0 + b_1 I_0 + b_3 P_{s,0} + b_4 P_{c,0} + b_5 P_{e,0} + b_6 N_0$

It should be clear from Equation (2.8) and the discussion thus far that a change in Pwill result in a change in the quantity demanded and, thus, a movement along the curve labeled DD. On the other hand, a change in any of the demand determinants will result in a change in the value of the horizontal intercept (ζ) resulting in a change in demand and a shift in the entire demand curve. For example, a decline in consumers income will result in a decline in the value of ζ to ζ', resulting in a left-shift of the demand function from DDto D'D'

MARKET DEMAND VERSUS FIRM DEMAND

While the discussion thus far has focused on the market demand curve, it is, in fact, the demand curve facing the individual firm that is of most interest to the manager who is formulating price and output decisions. In the case of a monopolist, when firm output constitutes the output of the industry, the market demand curve is identical to the demand curve faced by the firm. Consequently, the firm will bear the entire impact of changes in such demand determinants as incomes, tastes, and the prices of related goods. Similarly, the pricing policies of the monopolist will directly affect the consumer's decisions to purchase the firm's output.

In most cases, however, the firm supplies only a small portion of the total output of the industry. Thus, the firm's demand curve is not identical to that of the market as a whole. One major difference between firm and market demand may be the existence of additional demand determinants, such as pricing decisions made by the firm's competitors. Another important difference is that the quantitative impact of changes in such determinants as taste, income, and prices of related goods will be smaller because of the firm's smaller share of the total market supply. It is the demand function faced by the individual firm that is of primary concern in managerial economics.

THE LAW OF SUPPLY

While we have discussed some of the conditions under which consumers are willing, and able, to purchase quantities of a particular good or service, we have yet to say anything about the willingness of producers to produce those very same goods and services. Once we have addressed this matter, we will be in a position to give form and substance to the elusive concept of "the market."

Definition: The law of supply asserts that quantity supplied of a good or service is directly (positively) related to the selling price, ceteris paribus. As we will see in later chapters on production and cost, under certain conditions, including short-run production, the hypothesis of a profit maximization, and perfect competition in resource markets, the law of supply is based on the law of diminishing marginal returns (sometimes called the law of diminishing marginal product). In fact, as we will see later, the supply curve of an individual firm is simply a portion of the firm's marginal cost curve, which at some point rises in response to the law of diminishing returns.

The law of diminishing returns is not an economic relationship but a technological relationship that is empirically consistent. In fact, the law of diminishing marginal returns may be the only true law in economics. The law of diminishing marginal returns in fact makes the law of supply a stronger relationship than the "law" of demand. With that, consider the following hypothetical market supply function.

Symbolically, the law of supply may be summarized as follows:

$$Q_S = g(P) \tag{2.9a}$$

and

$$\frac{sQ_s}{dP} > 0 \tag{2.9b}$$

Equation (2.9a) states that the quantity supplied QS of a good or service is functionally related to the selling price P. Inequality (2.9b) asserts that quantity supplied of a product and its price are directly related. The upward-sloping supply curve illustrates the positive relationship between the quantity demanded of a good or service and its selling price. The market supply curve shows the various amounts of a good or service that profit-maximizing firms are willing to supply at each price. As with the market demand curve, the market supply curve is also the horizontal summation of the individual firms' supply curves. Unlike the earlier discussion of the market demand schedule as the horizontal summation of the individual consumer demand schedules, an investigation of the supply schedule for an individual firm will be deferred.

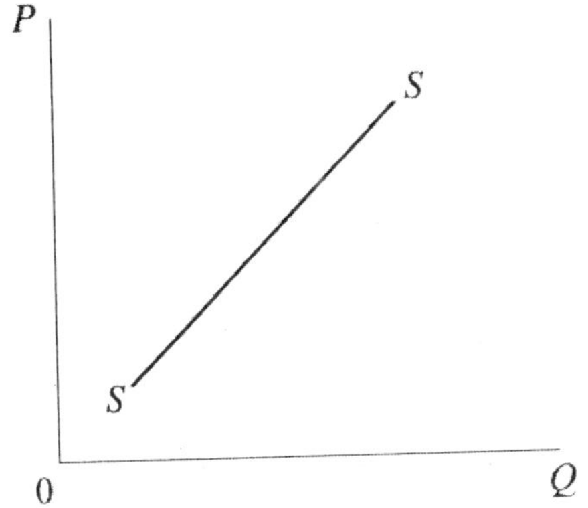

Figure: The supply curve.

The market supply curve establishes a relationship between price and quantity supplied. Changes in the price and the quantity supplied of a good or service are represented diagrammatically as a movement along the supply curve. Changes in supply determinants are illustrated as a shift in the entire supply curve.

DETERMINANTS OF MARKET SUPPLY

Of course, the market price of a good or service is not the only factor that influences a firm's decision to alter the quantity supplied of a particular good or service. To get a "feel" for whether a firm will increase or decrease the quantity supplied of a particular good or service (assuming the product's price is given) in response to a particular supply-side stimulus, let us assume that the firms that make up the supply side of the market are "profit maximizers." Total profit is defined as

$$\pi(Q) = TR(Q) - TC(Q) \tag{2.10}$$

where π is total profit, TR is total revenue, and TC is the total cost, which are defined as functions of total output Q. Moreover, total revenue may be expressed as the product of the selling price of the product times the quantity sold.

$$TR = PQ \tag{2.11}$$

Total cost, on the other hand, is assumed to be an increasing function of a firm's output level, which is a function of the productive resources used in its production. Equation (2.12) expresses total cost as a function of labour and capital inputs.

$$TC = h(Q) = h[k(L, K)] = l(L, K) \tag{2.12}$$

If the firm purchases productive resources in a perfectly competitive factors market, the total cost function might be expressed as

$$TC = TFC + TVC$$

$$= TFC + P_L L + P_K K \tag{2.13}$$

where TFC represents total fixed cost (a constant), P_L is the price of labour, which is determined exogenously, L the units of labour employed, P_K is the rental price of capital, also determined exogenously, and K the units of capital employed. Fixed costs represent the cost of factors of production that cannot be easily varied in the short run. Rental payments for office space as specified for the term of a lease represent a fixed cost.

Equation (2.13) indicates that as a firm's output level expands, the costs associated with higher output levels increase. In general, let us say that the change in any factor that causes a firm's profit to increase will result in a decision to increase the quantity the firm supplies to the market, other things remaining the same.

Conversely, any change that causes a decline in profits will result in a decline in quantity supplied, other things remaining the same. We have already seen that an increase in product price, which increases total revenue, will result in an increase in the quantity supplied, or a movement to the right and along the supply function. Now let's consider other supply side determinants.

PRICES OF PRODUCTIVE INPUTS (P_L)

By the logic just set forth, a drop in the price of a resource used to produce a product will reduce the total cost of production. If the selling price of the product is parametric, the decrease in the price of resources will result in an increase in the firm's profits, resulting in a right-shift of the supply function.

Conversely, a rise in input prices, which increases total cost and reduces profit, at a given price, will result in a left-shift in the supply function. The relationship between supply and a decline in the price of a resource is illustrated in figure below.

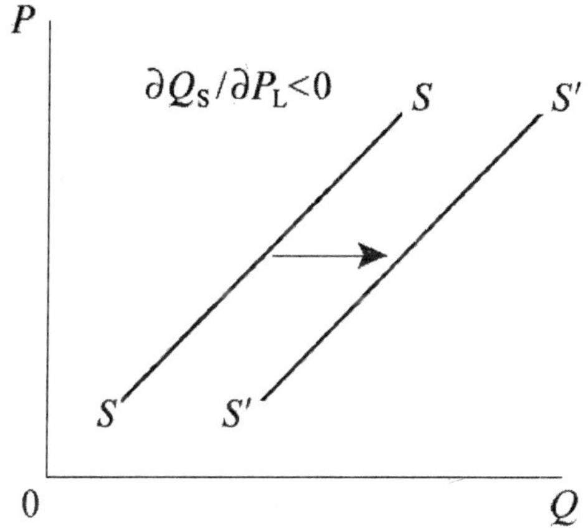

Figure: An increase in supply resulting from a decrease in factor prices.

TECHNOLOGY (E)

Advances in methods of management or production imply increases in productive efficiency. Increased efficiency means that either more output can be obtained from some given level of inputs, or some given level of output can be obtained using fewer inputs. In either case, improvements in the managerial or technological arts imply lower total costs of production, other things remaining the same, which implies increased profits, and, therefore, a right-shift in the entire supply schedule.

TAXES AND SUBSIDIES (R)

An increase in taxes levied on a firm's operations translates to an increase in the total cost of production, which implies a reduction in profits, other things remaining the same. The result would be a reduction in supply, or a left-shift in the supply curve. Conversely, a reduction in taxes, which is analytically equivalent to, say, a government subsidy, improves the firm's profits, thereby resulting in a right-shift in the supply schedule (an increase in supply).

PRICES OF RELATED GOODS: SUBSTITUTES (P_S) AND COMPLEMENTS (P_C)

The prices of related goods can also affect the supply of a particular good or service. As in the case of demand, these related goods are generally classified as either substitute goods or complementary goods.

Substitutes are goods that may be produced using the same (fixed) production facilities. Suppose, for example, that land can be used to grow wheat or corn. An increase in the price of corn would cause farmers to devote more land to the production of corn and less to the production of wheat. Thus, even though the price of wheat may have initially remained unchanged, the increase in the price of corn causes a reduction in the supply of wheat.

Complements are goods that are produced together. Beef and cowhide leather, for example, are complements in production. An increase in the price of beef will cause an increase in the quantity supplied of beef, which may also result in an increase in the supply of cowhide leather, even though the price of cowhide leather initially remained unchanged.

PRICE EXPECTATIONS (P_E)

If firm owners expect an increase in the product's selling price, they can be expected to withhold some output from the market, thereby building up inventories, for later sale at the anticipated higher price. Notice that this would probably result in a reduction in total revenues, and profits, today in favour of expected higher profits tomorrow. This would result in a reduction in supply, or a left-shift in the supply curve. Conversely, firm owners who anticipate a decline in selling prices can be expected to draw down inventories below what are considered optimal levels for sale today, thereby causing the supply curve to shift to the right.

NUMBER OF FIRMS IN THE INDUSTRY (F)

Other things being equal, including the selling price of a given product, an influx of firms into an industry will result in an increase in total supply. The result would be a right-shift in the supply function. Conversely, if firms exit the industry, the supply curve would be expected to shift to the left. The relationship between the supply of a good and service and the set of supply determinants discussed thus far may be expressed as

$$QS = f(P, P_L, E, R, P_s, P_c, P_e, F) \tag{2.14}$$

where

$$\partial Q_S/\partial P > 0, \partial Q_S/\partial P_L < 0, \partial Q_s/\partial E > 0, \partial Q_s/\partial R < 0, \partial Q_s/\partial P_s < 0, \partial Q_s/\partial P_c > 0,$$

$$\partial Q_s/\partial P_e < 0 \quad and\ \partial Q_S/\partial E > 0 .$$

Remember that a change in the quantity supplied of a good or service refers to the relationship between changes in the price of the good or service in question and changes in the quantity supplied. This is illustrated diagrammatically as a movement along the supply curve. A change in supply, on the other hand, refers to the relationship between changes in any other supply determinant, such as factor prices and production technology, which is shown diagrammatically shift in the entire supply curve.

THE MARKET MECHANISM: THE INTERACTION OF DEMAND AND SUPPLY

We can now use the concepts of demand and supply to explain the functioning of the market mechanism. Consider above figure, which brings together the market demand and supply curves. In our hypothetical market, the market equilibrium price is P. At that price, the quantity of a good or service that buyers are able and willing to buy is precisely equal to Q, the amount that firms are willing to supply. At a price below P, the quantity demanded exceeds the quantity supplied. In this situation, consumers will bid among themselves for the available supply of Q, which will drive up the selling price. Buyers who are unable or unwilling to pay the higher price will drop out of the bidding process. At the higher price, profit-maximizing producers will increase the quantity supplied. As long as the selling price is below P, excess demand for the product will persist and the bidding process will continue. The bidding process will come to an end when, at the equilibrium price, excess demand is eliminated. In other words, at the equilibrium price, the quantity demanded by buyers is equal to the quantity supplied.

It is important to note that in the presence of excess demand, the adjustment toward equilibrium in the market emanates from the demand side. That is, prices are bid up by consumers eager to obtain a product that is in relatively short supply. Suppliers, on the other hand, are, in a sense, passive participants, taking their cue to increase production as prices rise.

On the other side of the market equilibrium price is the situation of excess supply. At a price above P, producers are supplying amounts of Q in excess of what consumers are willing to purchase. In this case, producers' inventories will rise above optimal levels as unwanted products go unsold. Since holding inventories is costly, producers will lower price in an effort to move their product. At the lower price, the number of consumers who are willing and able to purchase, say, hamburgers increases. Producers, on the other hand, will adjust their production schedules downward to reflect the reduced consumer demand.

In this case, where the quantity supplied exceeds the quantity demanded, producers become active players in the market adjustment process. That is, in the presence of excess supply, producers provide the impetus for lower product prices in an effort to avoid unwanted inventory accumulation. Consumers, on the other hand, are passive participants, taking their cue to increase consumption in response to lower prices initiated by the actions of producers but having no direct responsibility for the lower prices.

CHANGES IN SUPPLY AND DEMAND: THE ANALYSIS OF PRICE DETERMINATION

Now let us use the analytical tools of supply and demand to analyze the effects of a change in demand and/or a change in supply on the equilibrium price and quantity. Consider first the case of a change in demand.

DEMAND SHIFTS

Suppose, for example, that medical research finds that hamburgers have highly desirable health characteristics, triggering an increase in the public's preference for hamburgers. Other things remaining constant, this would result in a right-shift in the demand curve for hamburgers. This results in an increase in the equilibrium price and quantity demanded for hamburgers. Consider Figure below.

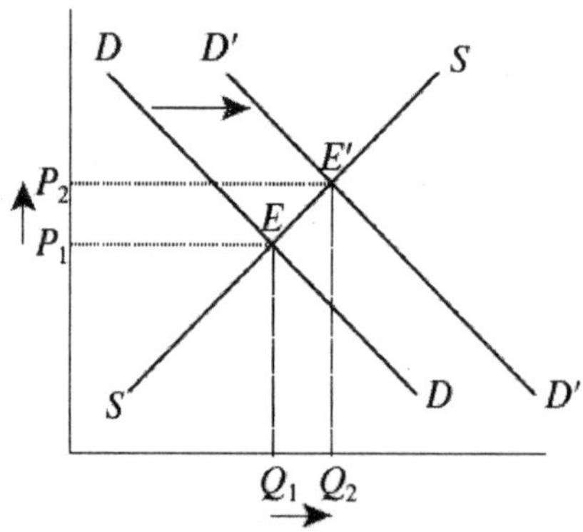

Figure: A rise in the equilibrium price and quantity resulting from an increase in demand.

If medical research, on the other hand had discovered that hamburgers exhibited highly undesirable health properties, one could have predicted a reduction in the demand for hamburgers, or a left-shift in the demand curve, resulting, in turn, in a decline in both equilibrium price and quantity demanded.

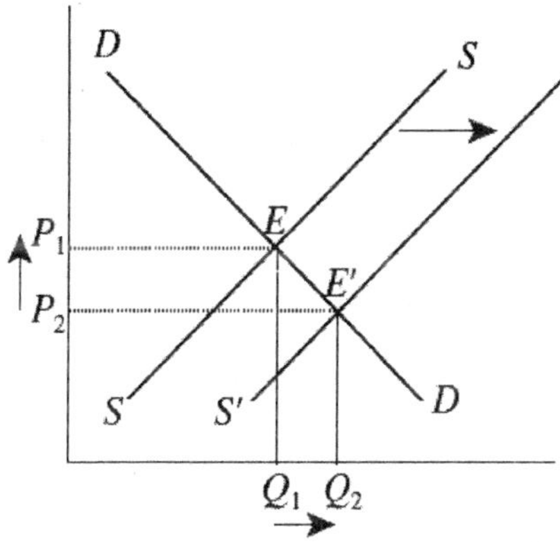

Figure: A fall in the equilibrium price and a rise in the equilibrium quantity resulting from an increase in supply.

SUPPLY SHIFTS

Suppose there is a sharp decline in the price of cattle feed. The result will be an increase in the supply of hamburgers at every price, other things remaining the same. This, of course, would result in a right-shift of the supply function. The result, which is illustrated in Figure above, is a decline in the equilibrium price and an increase in quantity supplied. Conversely, a left-shift in the supply curve would have raised the equilibrium price and lowered the equilibrium quantity. In either the case of a demand shift or a supply shift, the effect on the equilibrium price and quantity is unambiguous. Can as much be said if both the demand curve and the supply curve shift simultaneously?

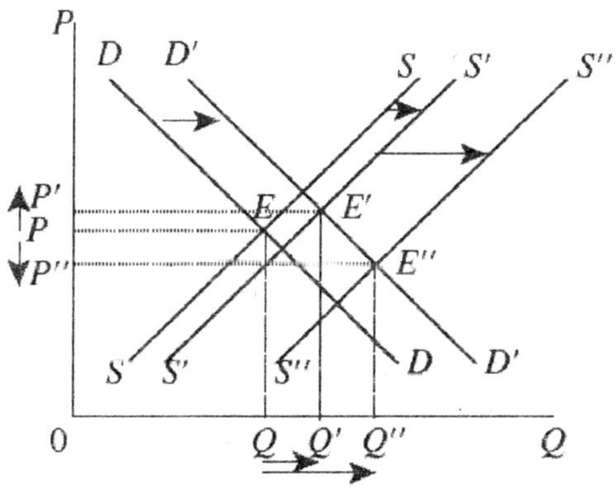

Figure: An increase in demand and supply may result in an unambiguous rise in the equilibrium quantity and an ambiguous change in the equilibrium price.

DEMAND AND SUPPLY SHIFTS

As illustrated in Figure above, a shift in the demand curve or a shift in the supply curve resulted in unambiguous changes in equilibrium price and quantity demanded. When changes in both demand and supply occur simultaneously, however, it is more difficult to predict the effect on price and quantity demanded. This can be illustrated by considering four possible cases.

Case 1: An Increase in Demand and an Increase in Supply

As illustrated in Figure above, a right-shift in both the demand and supply curves yields an unambiguous increase in quantity demanded. The effect on the equilibrium price, however, is indeterminate.

As shown earlier, if the increase in supply is relatively less than the increase in demand, the result will be a net increase in price. This is seen in Figure above by comparing the market clearing price at E with E'.On the other hand, if there occurs a large increase in supply, relative to the increase in demand, the result will be a net decrease in the equilibrium price. This is seen by comparing the market clearing price at E with E" in Figure above.

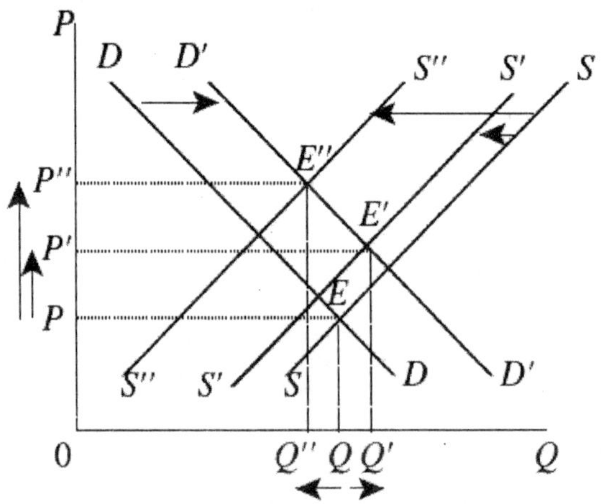

Figure: An increase in demand and a decrease in supply may result in an unambiguous rise in the equilibrium price and an ambiguous change in the equilibrium quantity.

Case 2: An Increase in Demand and a Decrease in Supply

As illustrated in figure above, a right-shift in the demand curve and a left-shift in the supply curve result in an unambiguous increase in the equilibrium price, although the effect on the equilibrium quantity is indeterminate.

If the decrease in supply is relatively less than the increase in demand, the result will be an increase in equilibrium price and quantity. This is seen in Figure above by comparing the equilibrium price and quantity at E with E'. If, however, the decrease in supply is relatively more than the increase in demand, the result will be an increase in the equilibrium price but a decrease in the equilibrium quantity. This can be seen by comparing the equilibrium price and quantity at E with E'' = in Figure above.

Case 3: A Decrease in Demand and a Decrease in Supply

As can be seen in figure below, a left-shift in both the demand and supply curves will result in an unambiguous decline in the equilibrium quantity and an indeterminate change in the equilibrium price.

If the decrease in supply is relatively less than the decrease in demand, the result will be a decrease in the equilibrium price and quantity. This is seen by comparing equilibrium price and quantity at E with E' in Figure below. If, however, the decrease in supply is relatively greater than the decrease in demand, the result will be a decrease in the equilibrium quantity, but an increase in the equilibrium price. This can be seen by comparing the equilibrium price and quantity at E with E'' in Figure below.

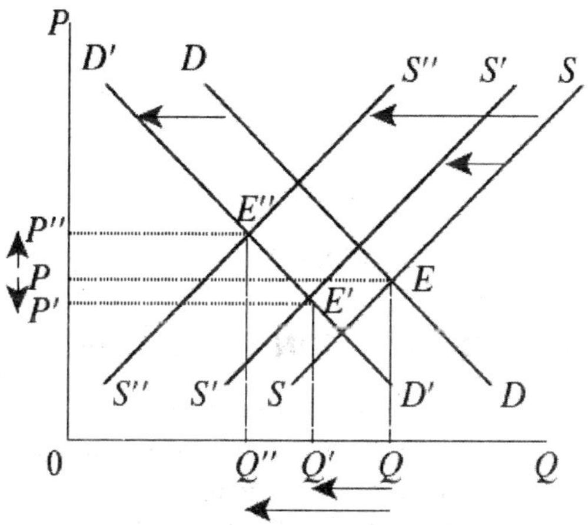

Figure: A decrease in both demand and supply may result in an unambiguous fall in the equilibrium quantity but an ambiguous change in the equilibrium price.

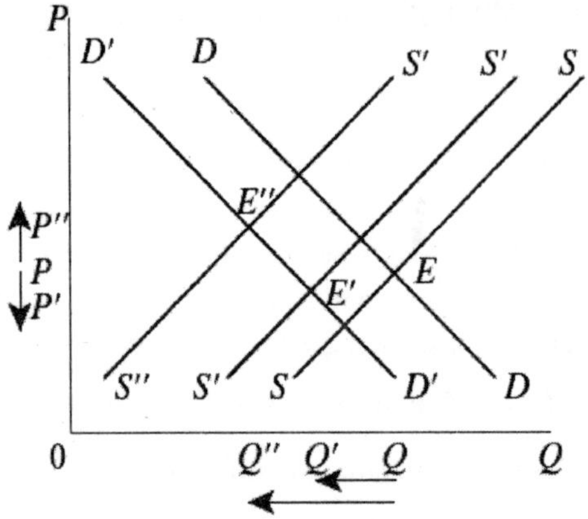

Figure: A decrease in demand and an increase in supply may result in an unambiguous fall in the equilibrium quantity and an ambiguous change in the equilibrium price.

Case 4: A Decrease in Demand and an Increase in Supply

In our final case, a left-shift in the demand curve and a right-shift in the supply curve will result in an unambiguous decline in the equilibrium price, but an indeterminate change in the equilibrium quantity. This situation is depicted in Figure above.

If the increase in supply is relatively less than the decrease in demand, the result will be a decrease in the equilibrium price and quantity. This is seen by comparing the equilibrium price and quantity at E with E' in Figure above. If, however, the increase in supply is relatively greater than the decrease in demand, the result will be an increase in the equilibrium quantity and a decrease in the equilibrium price. This can be seen by comparing the equilibrium price and quantity at E with E '' in Figure above.

$$300-50P=140+30P \quad P^{*}=2 \quad Q^{*}=300-50(2)=140+30(2)=200$$

THE RATIONING FUNCTION OF PRICES

How realistic is the assumption of market equilibrium? In a dynamic economy it is unrealistic to presume that markets adjust instantaneously to demand and supply disturbances. Although temporary shortages and surpluses are inevitable, it is important to realize that unfettered markets are stable in the sense that the prices tend to converge toward equilibrium following an exogenous shock. The converse would be to assume that markets are inherently unstable and that prices diverge or spiral away from equilibrium, which would be a recipe for market disintegration on a regular basis. The fact that we do not observe this kind of chaos should reinforce our faith in the underlying logic and stability of the free market process.

The system of markets and prices performs two closely related, and very important, functions. In Figure above we observed that when the market price of a good or service is above or below the equilibrium price, surpluses or shortages arise. The question confronting any economy when the quantity demanded exceeds the quantity supplied is how to allocate available supplies among competing consumers. In free-market economies, this task is typically accomplished by an increase in prices. The process by which shortages are eliminated by allocating available goods and services to consumers willing and able to pay higher prices calls on control the rationing function of prices. Price rationing means that whenever there is a need to distribution of a good or service that is in limited supply, the price will rise until the quantity demanded equals the quantity supplied and equilibrium in the market is restored.

Definition: The rationing function of prices refers to the increase or a decrease in the market price to eliminate a surplus or a shortage of a good or service. The rationing function is considered to be a short-run phenomenon because other demand determinants are assumed to be constant.

As we observed earlier, shortages set into motion a process whereby consumers effectively bid among themselves for available goods and services. As the price is bid up, suppliers make more goods and services available for sale, while some consumers drop out of the bidding process. Fundamental to this bidding process is the notion of willingness and ability to pay. The ideal of "willingness and ability to pay" is fundamental to the allocation of available goods and services. The willingness and ability of a consumer to pay for a good or service is fundamentally a function of consumers' tastes and preferences, and income and wealth. What all this implies, of course, is that in market economies the more well-to-do participants have greater command over goods and services than consumers of more modest means.

While price rationing is a fundamental characteristic of market economies, it is not the only way to allocate goods and services that are in short supply. Alternative rationing mechanisms are necessary when the market is constrained from performing this function. Under what circumstances might the market price fail to increase to eliminate a shortage?

PRICE CEILINGS

At various times, and under a variety of circumstances, state and federal governments have found it necessary to "interfere" in the market. This interference has sometimes involved measures that short-circuit the price-rationing function of markets. Government officials accomplish this by prohibiting price increases to eliminate shortages when they arise. A ban on price increases above a certain level is called a price ceiling. The rationale underlying the imposition of a price ceiling typically revolves around the issue of "fairness." Sometimes such interference is justified, but more often than not price ceilings result in unintended negative consequences. To understand what is involved, consider Figure above.

Definition: A price ceiling is a maximum price for a good or service that has been legally imposed on firms in an industry.

Figure above depicts the situation of excess demand $Q_{1'} - Q_{1''}$ = at price P1 arising from a decrease in the supply. Of course, the excess demand might also have arisen from an increase in the demand for a good or service. Figure above might be used to illustrate the market for consumer goods and services in the United States during World War II. As resources were shifted into the production of military goods and services to prosecute the war effort, fewer commodities were available for domestic consumption. If the

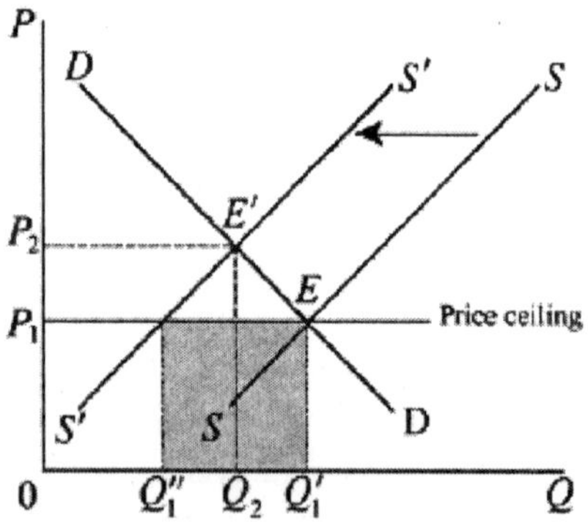

Figure: Market intervention: the effects of price ceilings in times of shortage.

government had done nothing, prices on a wide range of consumer goods (gasoline, meat, sugar, butter, automobile tires, etc.) would have risen sharply from P_1 to P_2. Without price controls, the equilibrium quantity would have fallen from $Q_{1'}$ to Q_2. Thus, the rationing function of prices would have guaranteed that only the well-to-do had access to available, nonmilitary commodities. In the interest of "fairness," and to maintain morale on the home front, the government imposed price ceilings, such as 1 in Figure above, on a wide range of consumer goods.

The imposition of a price ceiling means shortages will not be automatically eliminated by increases in price. With price ceilings, the price-rationing mechanism is not permitted to operate. Some other mechanism for allocating available supplies of consumer goods is required. When shortages were created by the imposition of price ceilings during World War II, the federal government instituted a program of ration coupons to distribute available supplies of consumer goods. Ration coupons are coupons or tickets that entitle the holder to purchase a given amount of a particular good or service during a given time period. During World War II, families were issued ration coupons monthly to purchase a limited quantities of gasoline, meat, butter, and so on.

Definition: Ration coupons are coupons or tickets that entitle the holder to purchase a given amount of a particular good or service during a given time period.

It should be noted that the use of ration coupons to bypass the price rationing mechanism of the market will be effective as long as no trading in ration coupons is all owed. If transactions in trading coupons are not effectively prohibited, the results will be almost identical to a market-driven outcome. Illegal transactions are referred to as "black markets." Individuals who are willing and able to pay will simply bid up the price of coupons and eliminate the price differential between the market and ceiling prices.

In addition to ration coupons, there are a variety of other non–price rationing mechanisms. Perhaps the most common of all such non– price rationing mechanisms is queuing, or waiting in line. This was the non–price rationing mechanism that arose in response to the decision by Congress to impose a price ceiling of 57¢ per gallon of unleaded gasoline following the 1973–74 OPEC embargo on shipments of crude oil to the United States.

Definition: Queuing is a non–price rationing mechanism that involves waiting in line.

Analytically, higher crude oil prices resulted in a left-shift in the supply of curve of gasoline (why?). Without the price ceiling, the result would have been a sharp increase of gasoline prices at the pump, which the Congress deemed to be "unfair." As a result, shortages of gasoline developed. Since the price rationing mechanism was not permitted to operate, there were very long lines at gas stations. Under the circumstances, gasoline still went to drivers willing and able to pay the price, which in this case, in addition to the pump price, included the opportunity cost of waiting in line for hours on end.

Another version of queuing is the waiting list. Waiting lists are prevalent in metropolitan areas with rent control laws. Rent control is a price ceiling on residential apartments. When controlled rents are below market clearing rents, a shortage of rent-controlled apartments is created. Prospective tenants are placed on a waiting list to obtain apartments as housing units become available. Rent controls were initially imposed during World War II. With the end of the war and the return of the GIs, and the subsequent baby boom, the demand curve for rental housing units soared. Elected politicians, sensing the pulse of their constituency, decided to continue with rent controls in some form, no doubt intoning the "fairness" mantra."

The initial result was a serious housing shortage in urban centers. Applicants were placed on waiting lists, but the next available rental units were slow to materialize. Other non–price rationing mechanisms included so called key money (bribes paid by applicants to landlords to move up on the waiting list), the requirement that prospective tenants purchase worthless furniture at inflated prices, exorbitant, non refundable security deposits, and, of course, so-called favoured customers or individuals who receive special treatment. One of the more despicable incarnations of the favoured customer relates to racial, religious, and other forms of group discrimination.

Definition: A favoured customer is an individual who receives special treatment.

Rent controls tend to create housing shortages that become more severe over time. Population growth shifts the demand for rental units to the right, which tends to exacerbate shortages in the rental housing market. What is more, if permitted rent increases do not keep pace with rising maintenance costs, fuel bills, and taxes, the supply of rental units may actually decline as landlords abandoned unprofitable buildings. This was particularly notable in New York City in the 1960s and 1970s, when apartment buildings abandoned by landlords in the face of rising operating costs transformed the South Bronx into an area reminiscent of war-ravaged Berlin in 1945. Rent stabilization in the cities encouraged the development of suburban communities, which ultimately led to "urban sprawl."

Another tactic for dealing with the economic problems associated with rent controls was the genesis, at least in New York City, of the cooperative. "Co-ops," which are not subject to rent controls, are former rental units in apartment buildings. Ownership of shares in the corporation convey the right to occupy an apartment. The prices of these shares are market determined.

Unfortunately, the transformation of rental units into co-ops and office space further exacerbated New York City's housing shortage. Just why rent controls in New York City have persisted for so long is understandable. To begin with, landlords are a particularly unlikable lot. Second, there are many more tenants than landlords, and each tenant has a vote. Pleasing this population is a lure not easily overlooked by politicians, whose planning horizon tends to extend only as far as the next election.

But there is some good news. Having recognized the fundamental flaws associated with interfering in the housing market, newer generations of politicians, obliged to deal with the problems of inner-city blight in part created by rent controls have undertaken to revitalize urban centers. Among these measures has been the elimination or dramatic reduction in the number of rental units subject to price ceilings. The result has been a resurgence in new rental housing construction, which has put downward pressure on rents.

Price Floors

The counterpart to price ceilings is the price floor. Whereas price ceilings are designed to keep prices from rising above some legal maximum, price floors are designed to keep prices from falling below some legal minimum. Perhaps the most notable examples of prices floors are agricultural price supports and minimum wages. This situation is depicted in Figure above.

The situation depicted in Figure above is that of an excess supply (surplus) for a commodity, say tobacco, resulting from an increase in supply. Of course, the excess supply might also have arisen from a decrease in the demand. Here, the government is committed to maintaining a minimum tobacco price at P_1, perhaps for the purpose of assuring tobacco farmers a minimum level of income. The result of a price floor is to create an excess supply of tobacco of $Q_1'' = Q_1'$. In the absence of a price floor, the equilibrium price of tobacco would have fallen from P_1 to P_2 and the equilibrium quantity would have increased from Q_1' to Q_2. In the labour market, price floors in the form of minimum wage legislation are ostensibly designed to provide unskilled workers with a "living wage," although the result is usually an increase in the unemployment rate of unskilled labour.

Definition: A price floor is a legally imposed minimum price that may be charged for a good or service.

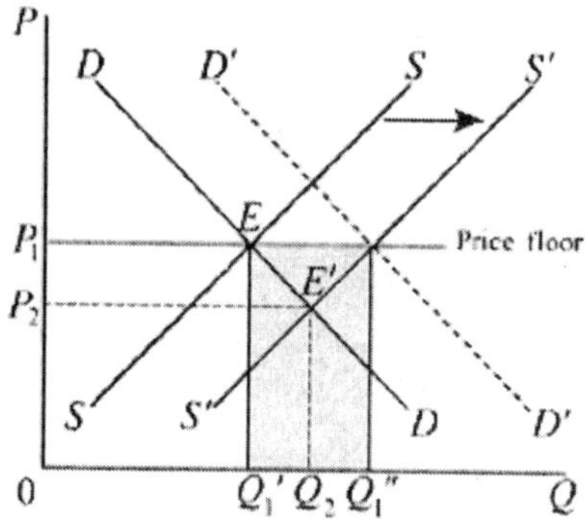

Figure: Market intervention: the effects of price floors in times of surplus.

The problem with price floors is that they create surpluses, which ultimately have to be dealt with. In the case of agricultural price supports, to maintain the price of the product at P_1 in Figure above the government has two policy options: either pay certain farmers not to plant, thereby keeping the supply curve from shifting from SS to S'S', or enter the market and effectively buy up the surplus produce, which is analytically equivalent to shifting the demand curve from DD to D'D'. In either case, the taxpayer picks up the bill for subsidizing the income of the farmers for whose benefit the price floor has been imposed.

Actually, the tobacco farmer case illustrates the often schizophrenic nature of government policies. On the one hand, the federal government goes to great lengths to extol the evils of smoking, while at the same time subsidizing tobacco production.

Minimum wage legislation also impacts the taxpayer. Suppose, for example, that there is an increase in unskilled labour in a particular industry because of immigration. This results in a shift to the right of the labour supply curve, which could drive the wage rate below the mandated minimum. A surplus of unskilled labour leads to unemployment. This is a serious result, since not only would many unskilled workers be willing to accept a wage below the minimum (as opposed to no wage at all), but these workers now are hard put to obtain on-the-job experience needed to enable them to earn higher wages and income in the future. The taxpayer picks up the bill for many of these unemployed workers, who show up on state welfare rolls.

THE ALLOCATING FUNCTION OF PRICES

While the price rationing mechanism of the market may be viewed as a short-run phenomenon, the allocating function of price tends to be a long-run phenomenon. In the long run, all price and non-price demand and supply determinants are assumed to be variable. In the long run, price changes signal consumers and producers to devote more or less of their resources to the consumption and production of goods and services. In other words, free markets determine not only final distribution of final goods and services, but also what goods and services are produced and how productive resources will be allocated for their production.

Definition: The allocating function of prices refers to the process by which productive resources arc reallocated between and among production processes in response to changes in the prices of goods and services.

To see this, consider the increase in the demand for restaurant meals in the United States that developed during the 1970s. This increase in demand for restaurant meals resulted in an increase in the price of eating out, which increased the profits of restauranteurs. The increase in profits attracted investment capital into the industry. As the output of restaurant meals increased, the increased demand for restaurant workers resulted in higher wages and benefits. This attracted workers into the restaurant industry and away from other industries,. where the diminished demand for labour resulted in lower wages and benefits.

Note: Sobeys is a private grocery retailer which operates 1,300 stores under retail banners that include Sobeys, IGA, IGA extra, Foodland, Price Chopper and Thrifty foods. The company primarily operates in Canada. The company is owned by Empire Company Limited. Sobeys is headquartered in Nova Scotia, Canada and employs about 75,000 people. Reader can visit their site corporate.sobeys.com. For a detailed study of connected to this chapter.

3

Production

The discussion thus far has focused primarily on the demand side of the market. We have seen, for example, that a firm's total revenue will depend, in part, on the selling price of the product, which is determined by the interaction of consumer and producer behavior in the market. We have also investigated the conditions under which a firm might increase its revenues by changing the selling price of its product. In spite of all that has thus far been accomplished, we have yet to examine the conditions under which firms produce the goods and services that are demanded by consumers, and perhaps more importantly from the perspective of senior management, the associated costs of production. If we are to investigate more closely the first-order and second-order conditions for a firm to maximize its profits, we must understand not only the revenue component of the profit equation, but the cost component as well. In this chapter we will examine the general problem of transforming productive resources in goods and services for sale in the market.

THE ROLE OF THE FIRM

The firm is an organizational activity that transforms factors of production, or productive inputs, into outputs of goods and services. Economics itself is the study of how society chooses to satisfy virtually unlimited human wants subject to scarce productive resources. In fact, this economic problem can be viewed as a constrained optimization problem in which the objective is to maximize some index of human happiness, which is assumed to be a function of the consumption of limited, or scarce, amounts of goods and services.

Let us examine this fundamental economic paradigm a bit more closely. For theoretical purposes, it is useful to assume that human material wants and desires are insatiable. While this might not be so for any individual commodity, by and large the vast majority of individuals are never completely satisfied with what they have. Consumers will, in general, always want more of something. Unfortunately, consumers cannot have everything they want for the simple reason that the productive inputs necessary to produce these goods and services are finite. In other words, outputs of goods and services (Q) are limited because the productive resources necessary to produce them are limited.

Productive resources, or inputs, or factors of production are used by firms to produce goods and services. These productive resources may conceptually be divided into two broad categories—human and nonhuman resources. Nonhuman resources may be further classified as land, raw materials, and capital. While these classifications are arbitrary, they are conceptually convenient.

Land (e.g., arable land for farming, or the land under buildings and roads) may be described as a "gift of nature." Raw materials include such natural resources as coal, oil, copper, sand, and trees. Finally, capital represents manufactured inputs that are used in the production of final goods and services. Capital goods include tools, machinery, equipment, office buildings, and storage facilities.

In an economic sense, "capital" does not refer to such financial assets as money, corporate equities, savings accounts, and U.S. Treasury securities. There is a loose conceptual connection between the economic and financial definitions of the term in that firms that wish to acquire capital equipment will do so only if the additional return from an investment in capital goods is sufficient to cover the opportunity cost of the interest that might have been earned by investing in a financial asset.

Human resources, on the other hand, might be classified as labour and entrepreneurial ability. labour consists of the physical and mental talents of individuals engaged in the production process. labour services are similar to services derived from nonhuman resources in that the rental value of labour services (wages, salaries, health benefits, etc.) is determined by the interaction of supply and demand conditions in the market for factors of production. labour is unique among the other factors of production, however, in that in a free society, labour decides for itself how intensively its services will be made available in the production process.

Entrepreneurial ability is a special subset of human resources because without the entrepreneur, all other factors of production cannot be combined. In other words, the services of land, labour, and capital are "rented" to the highest bidder through the interaction of supply and demand.

The bidders are entrepreneurs. An individual may, of course, be both a labourer and entrepreneur in the same production process. Nevertheless, the entrepreneur is unique in that it is through his or her initiative and enterprise that the other factors of production are organized in the first place.

The entrepreneur is distinguished from the "hired hand" in a number of other ways. The entrepreneur, for example, makes the non routine decisions for the firm. The entrepreneur determines the firm's organizational objectives. The entrepreneur is an innovator, constantly on the alert for the best (least expensive) production techniques. The entrepreneur also endeavors to ascertain the wants and needs of the public to be able to introduce new and better products, and to discontinue production of goods and services that are no longer in demand. The entrepreneur is a risk taker in the expectation of earning a profit.

It should be pointed out once again that it is assumed that the expectation of earning profit is the motivating incentive for all commercial activities in a free economy. Without the profit motive, it is assumed that entrepreneurs would not incur risk the financial risks associated with combining productive resources to produce final goods and services for sale in the market. In the absence of the profit motive, the production of goods and services in quantities that are most in demand by society would not occur. Moreover, whenever the profit incentive is diluted—say, through a tax on profits—fewer goods and services will be produced by the private sector in exchange for an increase in goods and services produced by the public sector. Whether society is better off or worse off will ultimately depend on which sector is most responsive to society's needs and preferences and which sector is most efficient in the utilization of productive resources in the delivery of those goods and services. The disappointing economic experiences of centrally planned economies in the communist countries of eastern Europe and Asia in the latter half of the twentieth century, compared with that of the essentially free market economies of western Europe, North America, and Japan often convincing testimony to the power of the profit motive in promoting the general economic well-being of society at large. To quote from Adam Smith: "By pursuing his own interest he (the entrepreneur) frequently promotes that of society more effectively than when he really intends to promote it."

THE PRODUCTION FUNCTION

The technological relationship that describes the process whereby factors of production are efficiently transformed into goods and services is called the production function. Mathematically, a production function utilizing capital, labour, and land inputs may be written as

$$Q = f(K, L, M) \tag{3.1}$$

where K is capital, L is labour, and M is land.

The production function defines the maximum rate of output per unit of time obtainable from a given set of productive inputs. Obviously, some firms organize inputs inefficiently, thereby producing less than the maximum possible level of goods and services. In a competitive market environment, however, firms that do not adopt the most efficient (cost-effective) production technology will not prosper and may, if fact, be forced to curtail operations as their market position is undermined by more aggressive competitors.

In free-market economies there is a tendency for more efficient operations to drive less efficient firms out of an industry. For the sake of pedagogical, theoretical, and graphical convenience, let us assume that all productive inputs may be classified as either labour (L) or capital goods (K). Equation (3.1) may therefore be rewritten as

$$Q = f(K, L) \tag{3.2}$$

In most cases, labour and capital may be substituted, albeit in varying degrees. As we will see, the precise manner in which these inputs are combined will depend on the relative rental price and marginal productivity of the factor of production. A firm that operates efficiently will choose that combination of productive inputs that minimizes the total cost of producing a given level of output. Equivalently, a firm that operates efficiently will choose that combination of productive inputs that will maximize production subject to a given operating budget.

It should be noted that the production function signifies the technological relationship between inputs and outputs. It is an engineering concept, devoid of any economic content. The production function defines the maximum output obtainable from a particular combination of inputs. Input prices must be combined with the production function to determine which of the many possible combinations of inputs is the most desirable given the firm's objectives, such as profit maximization.

THE COBB–DOUGLAS PRODUCTION FUNCTION

Production functions take many forms. In fact, there is a unique production function associated with each and every production process. In practice, it may not be possible to precisely define the mathematical relationship between the output of a good or service and a set of productive inputs. In spite of this, it is possible to approximate a firm's production function. Perhaps the most widely used functional form of the production process for empirical and instructional purposes is the Cobb–Douglas production function. The appeal of the Cobb–Douglas production function stems from certain desirable mathematical properties. The general form of the Cobb–Douglas production function for the two-input case may be written

$$Q = AK^{\alpha} L^{\beta} \tag{3.3}$$

where A, α and β are known parameters and K and L represent the explanatory variables capital and labour, respecitvely. It is further assumed that $0 \leq (\alpha, \beta) \leq 1$.

Consider, for example, the following empirical Cobb–Douglas production function:

$$Q = 25K^{0.5} L^{0.5} \tag{3.4}$$

SUBSTITUTABILITY

When a given level of output is generated, factors of production may or may not be substitutable for each other. The Cobb–Douglas production function also illustrates the fundamental economic problem of constrained optimization. Although there are theoretically an infinite number of output levels possible, the firm is typically subject to a predetermined operating budget that limits the amount of productive resources that can be acquired by the firm.

Because of this restriction, an increase in the use of one factor of production requires that less of some other factor be employed. The degree of substitutability of inputs is important because it suggests that managers are able to alter the input mix required to produce a given level of output in response to changes in input prices.

RETURNS TO SCALE

Suppose that output is described as a function of capital and labour. Suppose that capital and labour are multiplied by some scalar. If output increases by that same scalar, the term constant returns to scale (CRTS) opplies. In table above we observe that when labour and capital inputs are raised by a factor of 2, as when labour and capital are doubled from 2 units to 4 units, then output is raised by the same scalar (i.e., output increases from 50 to 100 units). If capital and labour are multiplied by a scalar and output increases by a multiple greater than the scalar, the condition is referred to as increasing returns to scale (IRTS). Finally, if capital and labour are multiplied by a scalar and output increases by a multiple less than the scalar, the condition is referred to as decreasing returns to scale (DRTS).

LAW OF DIMINISHING MARGINAL PRODUCT

Finally, the Cobb–Douglas production function exhibits a very important technological relationship—the law of diminishing marginal product (also referred to as the law of diminishing returns). This law, sometimes referred to as the second fundamental law of economics, states that when at least one productive input is held fixed while at least one other productive resource is increased, output will also increase but by successively smaller increments. The law of diminishing marginal product is a short-run production concept.

As will be discussed in the next section, the "short run" in production refers to that period of time during which at least one factor of production is held fixed in amount. Mathematically, the law of diminishing marginal product requires that the first partial derivative of the production function with respect to a variable input be positive and the second partial derivative negative. In table above, for example, when capital is held constant at K = 1, and labour is successively increased from L = 1 to L = 6, output increases from 25 to 61 units, but successive marginal increments are 10, 8, 7, 6, and 5.

It was noted earlier that the production function is characterized as efficient (i.e., the most output obtainable from a given level of input usage). Efficient utilization of productive inputs is characterized by production possibilities defined on the production surface in figure below. Any point above the production surface is unobtainable given the level of inputs available to the firm and the prevailing state of production technology. Any point below the production surface characterizes inefficiency.

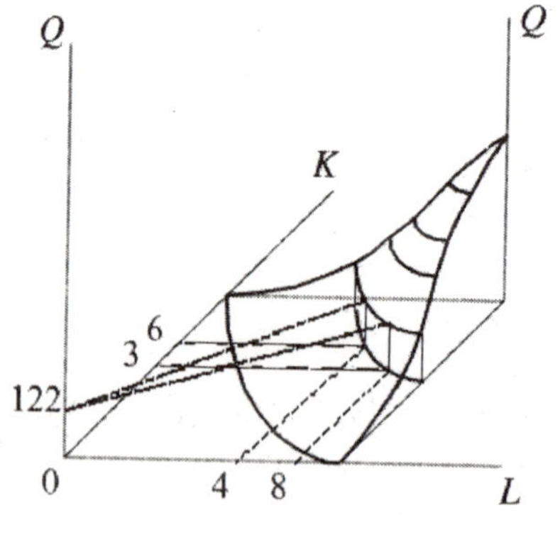

Figure: The production surface.

SHORT-RUN PRODUCTION FUNCTION

In the production process, economists distinguish between the short run and the long run. The short run in production refers to that period of time during which at least one factor of production is held constant. The law of diminishing marginal product is a short-run phenomenon. The long run in production occurs when all factors of production are variable. Denoting K_0 as a fixed amount of capital, the short-run production function may be written

$$Q_L = f\left(K_0, L\right) = TP_L \tag{3.5}$$

Equation (5.5) is sometimes referred to as to total product of labour, or more simply as TP_L.

The decision maker must determine the optimal amount of the variable input (L) given its price (P_L) and the price of the resulting output (P). It is assumed that the state of technology is captured in the specification of the production function and that production is efficient. Note that the subscript L in Equation (3.5) denotes the level of output dependent on the level of labour usage. Equivalently, if labour is assumed to be the fixed input, the shortrun production function would be written

$$Q_K = f\left(K, L_0\right) = TP_K \tag{3.6}$$

KEY RELATIONSHIPS: TOTAL, AVERAGE, AND MARGINAL PRODUCTS

There is a crucial relationship between any total concept and its related average and marginal concepts. Since the present discussion deals with production, we will explore the relationship between the total product of labour and the related average product of labour (AP_L) and marginal product of labour (MP_L). The reader is advised, however, that the fundamental relationships established here are perfectly general and may be applied to any functional relationship.

TOTAL PRODUCT OF LABOUR

If we assume that the level of capital usage is fixed, the total product of labour is described by Equation (3.5). This short-run production function defines the maximum amount of output attainable from any given level of labour usage given some fixed level of capital usage.

AVERAGE PRODUCT OF LABOUR

The average product of labour AP_L is simply the total product per unit of labour usage and is determined by dividing the total product of labour by the total amount of labour usage. This relationship is defined in Equation (3.7).

$$AP_L = \frac{TP_L}{L} = \frac{Q_L}{L} = \frac{f(K_{0,}L)}{L} \tag{3.7}$$

MARGINAL PRODUCT OF LABOUR

The marginal product of labour MP_L is defined as the incremental change in output associated with an incremental change in the amount of labour usage. Mathematically, since the amount of capital is constant, this is equivalent to the first partial derivative of the production function with respect to labour:

$$MP_L = \frac{\partial TP_L}{\partial L} = \frac{\partial Q_L}{\partial L} = \frac{\partial f(K_{0,}L)}{\partial L} \tag{3.8}$$

Similarly, the marginal product of capital is defined as

$$MP_K = \frac{\partial TP_K}{\partial K} = \frac{\partial Q_K}{\partial K} = \frac{\partial f(K,L_0)}{\partial K} \tag{3.9}$$

Consider, for example, the Cobb–Douglas production function

$$Q = AK^{\alpha} L^{\beta}$$

The respective marginal products are

$$MP_L = \frac{\partial Q_L}{\partial L} = \beta AK^{\alpha} L^{\beta-1} \tag{3.10}$$

$$MP_K = \frac{\partial Q_K}{\partial K} = \alpha AK^{\alpha-1} L^{\beta} \tag{3.11}$$

MATHEMATICAL RELATIONSHIP BETWEEN APL AND MPL

The mathematical relationship between the average product of labour (or any average concept) and the marginal product of labour (or any related marginal concept) may be illustrated by the use of optimization analysis. Consider again the definition of the average product of labour

$$AP_L = \frac{TP_L}{L} = \frac{Q_L}{L} = \frac{f(K_{0,}L)}{L}$$

Taking the first derivative of Equation (3.7) with respect to labour and setting the results equal to zero yields

$$\frac{\partial TP_L}{\partial L} = \frac{L(\partial Q_L/\partial L) - Q_L(\partial L/\partial L)}{L^2} = 0$$

which implies

$$MP_L - \frac{Q_L}{L} = 0 \quad MP_L = AP_L$$

since $1/L^2$ is positive. That is, when the average product of labour is maximized, the marginal product of labour is equal to the average product of labour.

Equation may also be used to highlight another important relationship between the average product of labour and the marginal product of labour. When $MP_L > AP_L$, then $\partial AP_L/\partial L > 0$, which implies that the average product of labour is rising. When $MP_L < AP_L$, then $\partial AP_L/\partial L < 0$, which says that the average product of labour is falling. Only when $MP_L < AP_L$ and $\partial AP_L/\partial L = 0$ will the average product of labour be stationary (either a maximum or a minimum). The second-order condition for minimum average product of labour is $\partial AP_L/\partial L < 0$.

In general, for any total function it can be easily demonstrated that when the marginal value is greater than the average value (i.e., M > A), then A will be rising. When M < A, A will be falling. Finally, when M = A, A will neither be falling nor rising but at a local optimum (maximum or minimum). To illustrate this relationship, consider the simple example of a student who takes a course in which the final grade is based on the average of 10 quizzes. A maximum of 100 points may be earned on each quiz. Thus, a maximum of 1,000 points may be earned during the semester, or a maximum average for the course of 1,000/10 = 100.

Suppose that the student has taken six quizzes and has earned a total of 480 points, for an average grade of 480/6 = 80. If the student receives a grade of 90 on the seventh quiz, then the student's average will rise from 80 to 570/7 = 81.4. That is, since the marginal grade is greater than the average grade to that point, the student's average will rise. On the other hand, if the student received a grade of 70 on the seventh quiz, the student's average will fall to 550/7 = 78.6. Finally, if the student receives a grade of 80 on the seventh quiz then, clearly, there will be no change in the student's average (i.e., 560/7 = 80).

THE LAW OF DIMINISHING MARGINAL PRODUCT

It was noted earlier that the Cobb–Douglas production function exhibits a number of useful mathematical properties. One of these properties is the important technological relationship known as the law of diminishing marginal product (law of diminishing returns). This concept can be described with the use of a simple illustration.

Consider a tomato farmer who has a 10-acre farm and as much fertilizer, capital equipment, water, labour, and other productive resources as is necessary to grow tomatoes. The only input that is fixed in supply is farm acreage. The farmer decides that to maximize output, additional workers will have to be hired. With the exception of farm acreage, each worker has as many productive resources to work with as necessary.

Initially, as one might expect, output expands rapidly. At least in the early stages of production, as more workers are assigned to the cultivation of tomatoes, the additional output per worker might be expected to increase. This is because in the beginning land is relatively abundant and labour is relatively scarce. While each worker has as much land and other resources to work with as is necessary for efficient production, at least some land initially stands fallow. labour can be said to be fully utilized while land can be said to be underutilized. As more labourers are added to the production process, total output rises; beyond some level of labour usage, however, incremental additions to output from the addition of more workers, while positive, will begin to decline. That is, while each additional worker contributes positively to total output, beyond some point the amount of land allocated to each worker will decline. No matter how much water, fertilizer, and other inputs are made available to each worker, the amount of output per worker will begin to fall. At this point, land has become over utilized while labour has become fully utilized.

The law of diminishing marginal product sets in at the point at which the contribution to total output from an additional worker begins to fall. In fact, if successively more workers are added to the production process, the amount of land allocated to each worker becomes so small that we might even expect zero marginal product; that is, total output has been maximized. It is even conceivable that beyond the point of maximum production, as more workers are added to the production process, output will actually decline. This is because workers may interfere with each other or will perhaps trample on some of the tomatoes. In the extreme, we cannot rule out the possibility of negative marginal product of a variable input.

Definition: The law of diminishing marginal product states that as increasing amounts of a variable input are combined with one or more fixed inputs, at some point the marginal product of the variable input will begin to decline.

Numerous empirical studies have attested to the veracity of the law of diminishing marginal product. As noted earlier, this phenomenon is exhibited mathematically in the Cobb–Douglas production function. A necessary condition for the law of diminishing returns is that the first partial derivative of the production function be positive, indicating that as more of the variable input is added to the production process, output will increase. A sufficient condition, however, is that the second partial derivative be negative, indicating that the additions to total output from additions of the variable input will become smaller. Consider again Equation (3.10).

$$MP_L = \frac{\partial Q_L}{\partial L} = \beta A K^{\alpha} L^{\beta-1} > 0 \qquad (3.10)$$

Since A, α, and β are assumed to be positive constant, and $|\alpha|$, $|\beta| < 1$, then Equation (5.10) is clearly positive, since $L\beta^{-1} > 0$. A positive marginal product of labour is expected, since we would expect output to increase as incremental units of a variable input are added to the production process. Our concern is with the change in marginal product, given incremental increases in the amount of labour used. To determine this we must take the second partial derivative of the total product of labour function or, which is the same thing, the first partial derivative of Equation (3.10).

$$\frac{\partial MP_L}{\partial L} = \frac{\partial^2 Q_L}{\partial L^2} = \beta(\beta-1) A K^{\alpha} L^{\beta-2} < 0$$

since $\beta - 1 < 0$ and $L^{\beta-2} > 0$

Problem: Consider the following Cobb–Douglas production function:

$Q = 25K^{0.5}L^{0.5}$

Verify that this expression exhibits the law of diminishing marginal product with respect to capital.

Solution: The marginal product of capital is given as

$$MP_K = \frac{\partial Q_K}{\partial K} = 0.5(25)K^{0.5-1}L^{0.5} = 12.5K^{-0.5}L^{0.5} > 0$$

since L and K are positive. The second partial derivative of the production function is

$$\frac{\partial MP_K}{\partial K} = \frac{\partial^2 Q_K}{\partial K^2} = -0.5(12.5)K^{-1.5}L^{0.5} < 0$$

which is clearly negative, since $K^{-1.5} = 1/K^{-1.5} > 0$.

THE OUTPUT ELASTICITY OF A VARIABLE INPUT

Another useful relationship in production theory is the coefficient of output elasticity of a variable input, which illustrates an interesting relationship between the marginal product and the average product of a productive input. By definition, the output elasticity of labour is

$$\varepsilon_L = \frac{\%\Delta Q}{\%\Delta L} = \left(\frac{\partial Q_L}{\partial L}\right)\left(\frac{L}{Q_L}\right)$$

$$= MP_L\left(\frac{1}{AP_L}\right) = \frac{MP_L}{AP_L}$$

The output elasticity of labour is simply the ratio of the marginal product of labour and the average product of labour. As we will see later, this relationship has some interesting implications for production theory.

Problem: The Cobb–Douglas production function is widely used in economic and empirical analysis because it possesses several useful mathematical properties. The general form of the Cobb–Douglas production function is given as $Q = AK^{\alpha}L^{\beta}$

where A is a positive constant and $0 < \alpha < 1$, $0 < \alpha < 1$.

a. The law of diminishing marginal product states that as units of a variable input are added to a fixed input, output will increase at a decreasing rate. Suppose that capital (K) is the fixed input and that labour (L) is the variable input. Demonstrate the law of diminishing marginal product using the Cobb–Douglas production function.

b. Assuming that capital is the constant factor of production, what is the proportional change in output resulting from a proportional change in labour input?

Solution:

a. With capital the constant factor of production, the mathematical conditions for the law of diminishing returns are

$$MP_L = \frac{\partial Q}{\partial L} > 0$$

$$\frac{\partial MP_L}{\partial L} = \frac{\partial^2 Q}{\partial L^2} < 0$$

Taking the partial derivative of the Cobb–Douglas production function with respect to labour yields

$$\frac{\partial Q}{\partial L} = \beta A K^{\alpha} L^{\beta-1} = \beta\left(AK^{\alpha}L^{\beta}\right)L^{-1} = \frac{\beta Q}{L} > 0$$

for K, L > 0

This result demonstrates that as more labour is added to fixed capital, output will rise. Taking the second partial derivative of Q with respect to L, we obtain

$$\frac{\partial^2 Q}{\partial L^2} = (\beta - 1)\beta A K^{\alpha} L^{\beta-2} = (\beta-1)\beta\left(AK^{\alpha}L^{\beta}\right)L^{-2}$$

$$= \frac{(\beta-1)\beta Q}{L} < 0$$

for K, L > 0

This result demonstrates that output increases at a decreasing rate.

b. The output elasticity with respect to L is given as

$$\varepsilon_L = \left(\frac{\partial Q}{\partial L}\right)\left(\frac{L}{Q}\right) = \frac{MP_L}{AP_L} = \left(\frac{\beta Q}{L}\right)\left(\frac{L}{Q}\right) = \beta$$

That is, the proportional change in output resulting from proportional changes in labour input (the output elasticity of labour) is equal to β, a constant. It can be easily demonstrated that the output elasticity of capital (ε_K) is equal to α.

RELATIONSHIPS AMONG THE PRODUCT FUNCTIONS

MARGINAL PRODUCT

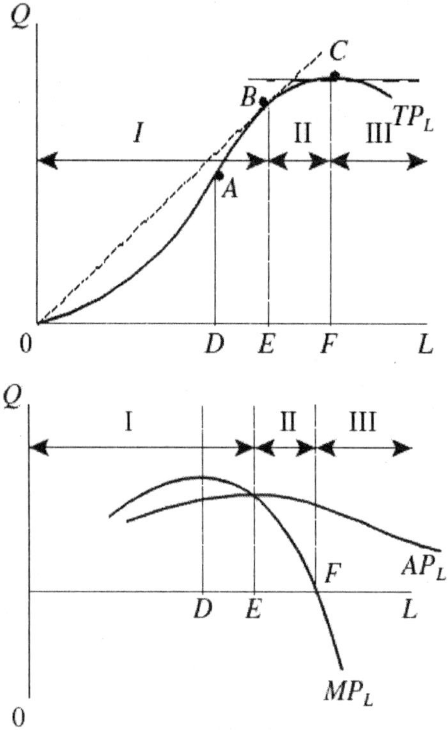

Figure: (a) & (b) Stages of production.

In Figure above, illustrates the short-run relationships among the total, average, and marginal product functions, which the marginal product of labour, which is the first partial derivative of the total product of labour function, is the value of the slope of a tangent at a particular point on the TP_L curve. We can see from Figure (a) that as we move from point 0 on the TP_L curve, the slope of the tangent steadily increases in value until we reach inflection point A. From point A to point C the marginal product of labour is still positive, but its value steadily decreases to zero, which is at the top of the TP_L "hill." Beyond point C the slope of the value of the tangent (TP_L) becomes negative. These relationships are illustrated in Figure (b), where the TP_L function reaches its maximum at the labour usage level 0D, which is at the inflection point, thereafter declining steadily until TP_L L = 0 at 0F. For labour usage beyond point 0F, then TP_L becomes negative, resulting in the decline in TP_L.

In figure (a) the distance 0A along TP_L represents increasing marginal product of labour. This range of labour usage is represented by the distance 0D and is characterized by increasing incremental contributions to total output arising from incremental applications of labour input. This phenomenon, if it occurs at all, is likely to take place at lower output levels. This is because at low output levels the fixed input is likely to be underutilized, making it likely that additional applications of the variable input will result in increased efficiency arising from specialization, management, communications, and so on.

Once efficiency gains from specialization have been exhausted, however, the production process will be characterized by the law of diminishing marginal product. This phenomenon sets in at the labour usage DF, which corresponds to the distance AC along the TP_L curve. The law of diminishing marginal product sets in at the inflection point A and continues until $TP_L = 0$ at point C. To reiterate, the law of diminishing marginal product says that as more and more of the variable input is added to the production process with the amount utilized of at least one factor of production remaining constant, beyond some point, incremental additions to output will become smaller and smaller.

Finally, movement along the TP_L curve beyond point C is characterized by negative marginal product of labour. Beyond the level of labour usage 0F in Figure (a), incremental increases in labour usage will actually result in a fall in total output. In Figure (b) this phenomenon is illustrated by $MP_L < 0$; that is, the MP_L curve falls below the horizontal axis for output levels in excess of 0F.

AVERAGE PRODUCT

The average product of labour may be illustrated diagrammatically as the value of the slope of a ray through the origin to a given point on the total product curve. To see this, consider the definition of the marginal product of labour for discrete changes in output.

$$MP_L = \frac{\Delta Q}{\Delta L} = \frac{Q_2 - Q_1}{L_2 - L_1} \tag{3.14}$$

Suppose that we arbitrarily select as our initial price quantity combination the origin (i.e., $Q_1 = L_1 = 0$). Substituting these values into Equation (3.14) we get

$$MP_L = \frac{Q_2 - 0}{L_2 - 0} = \frac{Q_2}{L_2} = AP_L \qquad (3.15)$$

This is the same result as in Equation (3.12).

Referring to figure (a), we see that as we move up along the TP_L curve from the origin, AP_L reaches a maximum at point B, steadily declining thereafter. Note also that at point B the average product of labour is precisely the value of the marginal product of labour because at that point the ray from the origin and the tangent at that point are identical. This is seen in Figure (b) at the labour usage 0E, where the AP_L curve intersects the MP_L curve. Finally, unlike the marginal product of labour (or any other productive input), the average product of labour cannot be negative because labour and output can never be negative.

THE THREE STAGES OF PRODUCTION

Stage I of production is defined as the range of output from L = 0 to, but not including, the level of labour usage at which $AP_L = MP_L$. Alternatively, stage I of production is defined up to the level of labour usage at which the average product of labour is maximized. In this range, labour is over utilized, whereas capital is underutilized. This can be seen by the fact that $MP_L > AP_L$ thus "pulling up" output per unit of labour. If we assume that the wage rate per worker and the price per unit of output are constant, then increasing output per worker suggests that average revenue generated per worker is rising, which suggests that average profit per worker is also rising. It stands to reason, therefore, that no firm would ever actually operate within this region of labour usage (0 to $MP_L = AP_L$), since additions to the labour force will increase average worker productivity and, under the appropriate assumptions, average profit generated per worker as well.

Stage II of production is defined in Figure above as the labour usage levels 0E to 0F. In this region, the marginal product of labour is positive but is less than the average product of labour, thus "pulling down" output per worker, which implies that average revenue generated per worker is also falling. In this region, labour becomes increasingly less productive on average.

Finally, stage III of production is defined along the TPL function for labour input usage in excess of 0F, where $MP_L < 0$. As it is apparent that production will not take place in stage I of production because an incremental increase in labour usage will result in an increase in output per worker and, under the appropriate assumptions, an increase in profit per worker, so it is also obvious that production will not take place in stage III.

This is because an increase in labour usage will result in a decline in total output accompanied by an increase in total cost of production, implying a decline in profit.

Stage III is also the counterpart to stage I of production. Whereas in stage I labour is overutilized and capital is underutilized, in stage III the reverse is true; that is, labour is underutilized and capital is overutilized. In other words, because of the symmetry of production, labour that is overutilized implies that capital is underutilized, and vice versa. Since stages I and III of production for labour have been ruled out as illogical from a profit maximization perspective, it also follows that stages III and I of production for capital have been ruled out for the same reasons.

We may infer that stage II of production for labour, and also for capital, is the only region in which production will take place. The precise level of labour and capital usage in stage II in which production will occur cannot be ascertained at this time.

For a profit-maximizing firm, the efficient capital–labour combination will depend on the prevailing rental prices of labour (P_L) and capital (P_K), and the selling price of a unit of the resulting output (P). More precisely, as we will see, the optimal level of labour and capital usage subject to the firm's operating budget will depend on resource and output prices, and the marginal productivity of productive resources. A discussion of the optimal input combinations will be discussed in the next chapter.

ISOQUANTS

Figure below illustrates once again the production surface for Equation (3.4). From our earlier discussion we noted that because of the substitutability of productive inputs, for many productive processes it may be possible to utilize labour and capital in an infinite number of combinations. Figure below illustrates four such input combinations to produce 122 units of output. It should be noted once again that efficient production is defined as any input combination on the production surface. The locus of points II in Figure below is called an isoquant.

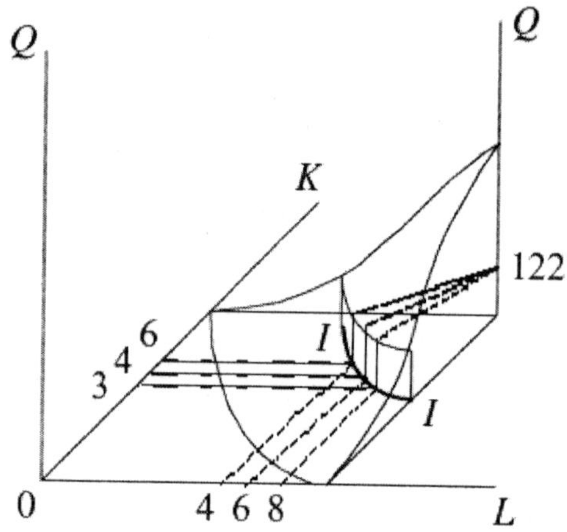

Figure: The production surface and an isoquant at Q = 122.

Definition: An isoquant defines the combinations of capital and labour (or any other input combination in n-dimensional space) necessary to produce a given level of output.

If fractional amounts of labour and capital are assumed, then an infinite number of such combinations is possible. While Figure above explicitly shows only one such isoquant at Q = 122 for Equation (3.4), it is easy to imagine that as we move along the production surface, an infinite number of such isoquants are possible corresponding to an infinite number of theoretical output levels. Figure below is referred to as an isoquant map. For any given production function there are an infinite number of isoquants in an isoquant map. In general, the function for an isoquant map may be written

$$Q_0 = f(K, L) \tag{3.16}$$

where Q0 denotes a fixed level of output. Solving Equation (3.16) for K yields

$$Q_0 = f(K, L) \tag{3.17}$$

The slope of an isoquant is given by the expression

$$\frac{dK}{dL} = gk(L, Q_0) = MRTS_{KL} < 0 \tag{3.18}$$

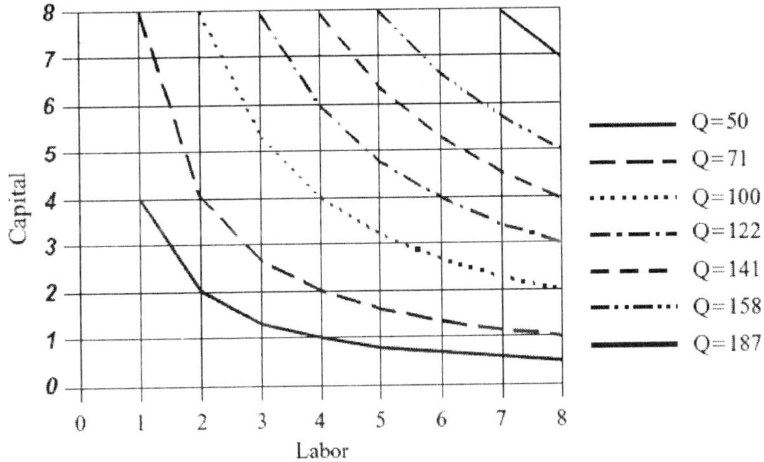

Figure: Selected isoquants for the production function

$Q - 25K^{0.5}L^{0.5}$.

It measures the rate at which capital and labour can be substituted for each other to yield a constant rate of output. Equation (3.18) is also referred to as the marginal rate of technical substitution of capital for labour ($MRTS_{KL}$). The marginal rate of technical substitution summarizes the concept of substitutability discussed earlier. $MRTS_{KL}$ says that to maintain a fixed output level, an increase (decrease) in the use of capital must be accompanied by a decrease (increase) in the use of labour. It may also be demonstrated that

$$MRTS_{KL} = -\frac{MP_L}{MP_K} \tag{3.19}$$

Equation (3.19) says that the marginal rate of technical substitution of capital for labour is the ratio of the marginal product of labour (MP_L) to the marginal product of capital (MP_K).

Definition: If we assume two factors of production, capital and labour, the marginal rate of technical substitution ($MRTS_{KL}$) is the amount of a factor of production that must be added (subtracted) to compensate for a reduction (increase) in the amount of a factor of production to maintain a given level of output. The marginal rate of technical substitution, which is the slope of the isoquant, is the ratio of the marginal product of labour to the marginal product of capital (MP_L/MP_K).

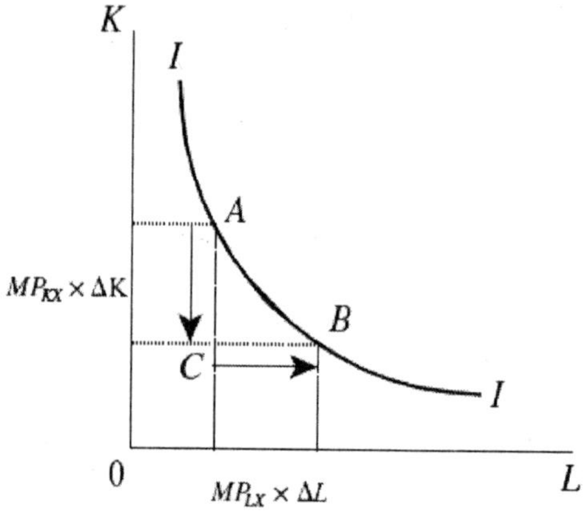

Figure: Slope of an isoquant: marginal rate of technical substitution.

To see this, consider figure above, which illustrates a hypothetical isoquant. By definition, when we move from point A to point B on the isoquant, output remains unchanged. We can conceptually break this movement down into two steps. In going from point A to point C, the reduction in output is equal to the loss in capital times the contribution of that incremental change in capital to total output (i.e., $MP_K \Delta K < 0$). In moving from point C to point B, them contribution to total output is equal to the incremental increase in labour time marginal product of that incremental increase (i.e., $MP_L \Delta L > 0$). Since to remain on the isoquant there must be no change in total output, it must be the case that $-MP_K \times \Delta K = MP_L \times \Delta L$

Rearranging Equation (5.20) yields

$$\frac{\Delta K}{\Delta L} = -\frac{MP_L}{MP_K}$$

For instantaneous rates of change, Equation (3.20) becomes

$$\frac{dK}{dL} = -\frac{MP_L}{MP_K} = MRTS_{KL} < 0 \qquad (3.21)$$

Equation (3.21) may also be derived by applying the implicit function theorem to Equation (3.2). Taking the total derivative of Equation (3.2) and setting the results equal to zero yields

$$dQ = \left(\frac{\partial Q}{\partial L}\right) dL + \left(\frac{\partial Q}{\partial K}\right) dK = 0 \qquad (3.22)$$

Equation (3.22) is set equal to zero because output remains unchanged in moving from point A to point B in figure below. Rearranging Equation (3.22) yields

$$\frac{\partial Q/\partial L}{\partial Q/\partial K} = \frac{dK}{dL}$$

or

$$\frac{dK}{dL} = -\frac{MP_L}{MP_K}$$

Another characteristic of isoquants is that for most production processes they are convex with respect to the origin. That is, as we move from point A to point B in figure below, increasing amounts of labour are required to substitute for decreased equal increments of capital. Mathematically, convex isoquants are characterized by the conditions $dK/dL < 0$ and $d^2K/dL^2 > 0$. That is, as MP_L declines as more labour is added by the law of diminishing marginal product, MP_K increases as less capital is used. This relationship illustrates that inputs are not perfectly substitutable and that the rate of substitution declines as one input is substituted for another. Thus, with MP_L declining and MP_K increasing, the isoquant becomes convex to the origin.

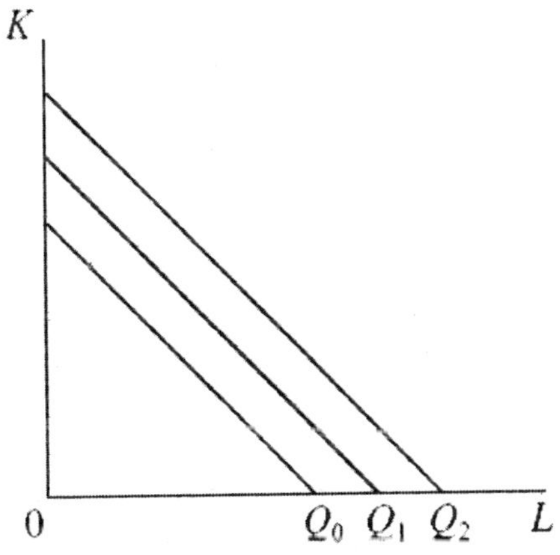

Figure: Perfect input substitutability.

The degree of convexity of the isoquant depends on the degree of substitutability of the productive inputs. If capital and labour are perfect substitutes, for example, then labour and capital may be substituted for each other at a fixed rate. The result is a linear isoquant, which is illustrated in figure above. Mathematically, linear isoquants are characterized by the conditions $dK/dL < 0$ and $d^2K/dL^2 = 0$. Examples of production processes in which the factors of production are perfect substitutes might include oil versus natural gas for some heating furnaces, energy versus time for some drying processes, and fish meal versus soybeans for protein in feed mix.

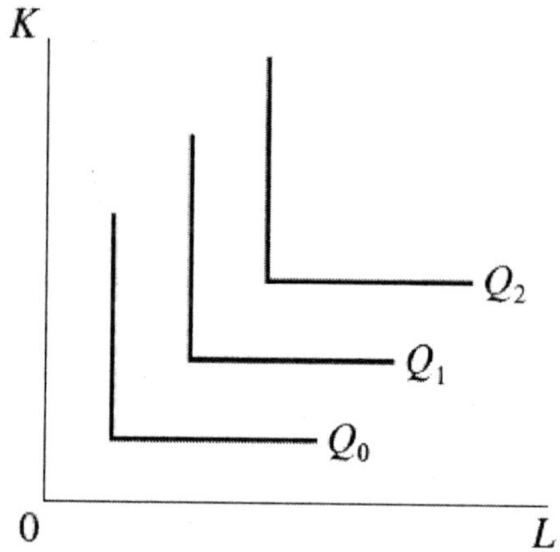

Figure: Fixed input combinations.

Some production processes, on the other hand, are characterized by fixed input combinations, that is, $MRTS_{K/L} = KL$. This situation is illustrated in figure below. Note that the isoquants in this case are "L shaped." These isoquants are discontinuous functions in which efficient input combinations take place at the corners, where the smallest quantity of resources is used to produce a given level of output. Mathematically, discontinuous functions do not have first and second derivatives. Examples of such fixed-input production processes include certain chemical processes that require that basic elements be used in fixed proportions, engines and body parts for automobiles, and two wheels and a frame for a bicycle.

LONG-RUN PRODUCTION FUNCTION RETURNS TO SCALE

It was noted earlier that the long run in production describes the situation in which all factors of production are variable. A firm that increases its employment of all factors of production may be said to have increased its scale of operations. Returns to scale refer to the proportional increase in output given some equal proportional increase in all productive inputs. As discussed earlier, constant returns to scale (CRTS) refers to the condition where output increases in the same proportion as the equal proportional increase in all inputs. Increasing returns to scale (IRTS) occur when the increase in output is more than proportional to the equal proportional increase in all inputs. Decreasing returns to scale (DRTS) occur when the proportional increase in output is less than proportional increase in all inputs. To illustrate these relationships mathematically, consider the production function

r	Returns to scale
= 1	Constant
> 1	Increasing
< 1	Decreasing

$$Q = f(x_1, x_2, ..., x_n) \tag{3.23}$$

where output is assumed to be a function of n productive inputs. A function is said to be homogeneous of degree r if, and only if,

$$f(tx_1, tx_2, ..., tx_n) \equiv t^r f(x_1, x_2, ..., x_n)$$

or

$$t^r Q \equiv f(tx_1, tx_2, ..., tx_n) \tag{3.24}$$

where t > 0 is some factor of proportionality. Note the identity sign in expression (3.24). This is not an equation that holds for only a few points but for all $t, x_1, x_2, ..., x_n$. This relationship expresses the notion that if all productive inputs are increased by some factor t, then output will increase by some factor t^r, where r > 0. Expression (3.24) is said to be a function that is homogeneous of degree r.

Returns to scale are described as constant, increasing, or decreasing depending on whether the value of r is greater than, less than, or equal to unity. Constant returns to scale is the special case of a production function that is homogeneous of degree one, which is often referred to as linear homogeneity.

ESTIMATING PRODUCTION FUNCTIONS

The Cobb–Douglas production function is also the most commonly used production function in empirical estimation. Consider again Equation (3.3).

$$Q = AK^{\alpha}L^{\beta} \tag{3.3}$$

Cobb–Douglas production functions may be estimated using ordinary-least-squares regression methodology. Ordinary least squares regression analysis is the most frequently used statistical technique for estimating business and economic relationships. In the case of Equation (3.3), ordinary least squares may be used to derive estimates of the parameters A, α and β on the basis observed values of the dependent variable Q and the independent variables K and L. To apply the ordinary-least-squares methodology, however, the equation to be estimated must be linear in parameters, which Equation (3.3) clearly is not. This minor obstacle is easily overcome. Taking logarithms of Equation (3.3) we obtain

$$\log Q = \log A + \alpha \log K + \beta \log L \tag{3.25}$$

The estimated parameter values α and β are no longer slope coefficients but elasticity values. To begin, recall that y = log x, then

$$\frac{dy}{dx} = \frac{1}{x}$$

or

$$dy = \frac{dx}{x}$$

Now, taking the first partial derivatives of Equation (3.25) with respect to K and L, we obtain

$$\frac{\partial \log Q}{\partial \log K} = \alpha$$

and

$$\frac{\partial \log Q}{\partial \log L} = \beta$$

But $\partial \log Q - \partial Q/Q$, $\partial \log K - \partial K/K$, and $\partial \log L - \partial L/L$. Therefore

$$\frac{\partial \log Q}{\partial \log K} = \frac{\partial Q/Q}{\partial K/K} = \left(\frac{\partial Q}{\partial K}\right)\left(\frac{K}{Q}\right) = \alpha = \varepsilon_K \tag{3.26}$$

Similarly,

$$\frac{\partial \log Q}{\partial \log L} = \frac{\partial Q/Q}{\partial K/L} = \left(\frac{\partial Q}{\partial K}\right)\left(\frac{L}{Q}\right) = \beta = \varepsilon_L \tag{3.27}$$

These parameter values represent output elasticities of capital and labour, while the sum of these parameters is the coefficient of output elasticity (returns to scale), that is,

$$\varepsilon_Q = \varepsilon_K + \varepsilon_L \tag{3.28}$$

Note: Broadcom Corporation (Broadcom) is a provider of semiconductors for wired and wireless communications. It provides a portfolio of system-on-a-chip (SoC) and software solutions to manufacturers of computing and networking equipment, digital entertainment and broadband access products, and mobile devices. The company operates in the North America, Asia Pacific, and Europe. It is headquartered in Irvine, California and employs 7,402 people, including full-time, contract and temporary employees. For further knowledge regarding this chapter reader can visit www.broadcom.com

4

Cost

In last chapter we reviewed the theoretical implications of the technological process whereby factors of production are efficiently transformed into goods and services for sale in the market. The production function defines the maximum rate of output per unit of time obtainable from a given set of productive inputs. The production function, however, was presented as a purely technological relationship devoid of any behavioral assertions underlying motives of management. The optimal combination of inputs used in the production process will differ depending on the firm's organizational objectives. The objective of profit maximization, for example, may require that the firm use one set of productive resources, while maximization of revenue or market share may require a completely different set.

The substitutability of inputs in the production process indicates that any given level of output may be produced with multiple factor combinations. Deciding which of these combinations is optimal not only depends on a well-defined organizational objective but also requires that management attempt to achieve this objective while constrained by a limited operating budget and constellation of factor prices. Changes in the budget constraints or factor prices will alter the optimal combination of inputs. The purpose of this chapter is to bridge the gap between production as a purely technological relationship and the cost of producing a level of output to achieve a well-defined organizational objective.

THE RELATIONSHIP BETWEEN PRODUCTION AND COST

The cost function of a profit-maximizing firm shows the minimum cost of producing various output levels given market-determined factor prices and the firm's budget constraint. Although largely the domain of accountants, the concept of cost to an economist carries a somewhat different connotation. As already discussed in the first chapter, economists generally are concerned with any and all costs that are relevant to the production process. These costs are referred to as total economic costs. Relevant costs are all costs that pertain to the decision by management to produce a particular good or service.

Total economic costs include the explicit costs associated with the day-to-day operations of a firm, but also implicit (indirect) costs. All costs, both explicit and implicit, are opportunity costs. They are the value of the next best alternative use of a resource. What distinguishes explicit costs from implicit costs is their "visibility" to the manager. Explicit costs are sometimes referred to as "out-of-pocket" costs. Explicit costs are visible expenditures associated with the procurement of the services of a factor of production. Wages paid to workers are an example of an explicit cost.

By contrast, implicit costs are, in a sense, invisible: the manager will not receive an invoice for resources supplied or for services rendered. To understand the distinction, consider the situation of a programmer who is weighing the potential monetary gains from leaving a job at a computer software company to start a consulting business. The programmer must consider not only the potential revenues and out-of-pocket expenses (explicit costs) but also the salary forgone by leaving the computer company.

The programmer will receive no bill for the services he or she brings to the consulting company, but the forgone salary is just as real a cost of running a consulting business as the rent paid for office space. As with any opportunity cost, implicit costs represent the value of the factor's next best alternative use and must therefore be taken into account. As a practical matter, implicit costs are easily made explicit. In the scenario just outlines, the programmer can make the forgone salary explicit by putting himself or herself "on the books" as a salaried employee of the consulting firm.

SHORT-RUN COST

The theory of cost is closely related to the underlying production technology. We will begin by assuming that the firm's short-run total cost (TC) of production is given by the expression

$$TC = f(Q) \tag{4.1}$$

As we discussed in last chapter, the short run in production is defined as that period of time during which at least one factor of production is held at some fixed level. Assuming only two factors of production, capital (K) and labour (L), and assuming that capital is the fixed factor (K_0), then Equation (4.1) may be written

$$TC = f\left[g\left(K_0, L\right)\right] \tag{4.2}$$

Equation (4.2) simply says that the short-run total cost of production is a function of output, which is itself a function of the level of capital and labour usage. In other words, total cost is a function of output, which is a function of the production technology and factors of production, and factors of production cost money. Equation (4.2) is a general statement that relates the total cost of production to the usage of the factors of production, fixed capital and variable labour. Equation (4.2) also makes clear that total cost is intimately related to the characteristics of the underlying production technology. As we will see, concepts such as total cost (TC), average total cost (ATC), average variable cost (AVC), and marginal cost (MC) are defined by their production counterparts, total physical product, average physical product, and marginal physical product of both labour and capital.

To begin with, let us assume that the prices of labour and capital are determined in perfectly competitive factor markets. The short-run total economic cost of production is given as

$$TC = P_K K_0 + PL_L \tag{4.3}$$

where P_K is the rental price of capital, PL is the rental price of labour, K_0 is a fixed amount of capital, and L is variable labour input. The most common example of the rental price of labour is the wage rate. An example of the rental price of capital might be what a construction company must pay to lease heavy equipment, such as a bulldozer or a backhoe. If the construction company already owns the heavy equipment, the rental price of capital may be viewed as the forgone income that could have been earned by leasing its own equipment to someone else. In either case, both P_K and P_L are assumed to be market determined and are thus parametric to the output decisions of the firm's management. Thus, Equation (4.3) may be written

$$TC(Q) = TFC + TVC(Q) \tag{4.4}$$

where TFC and TVC represent total fixed cost and total variable cost, respectively.

Total fixed cost is a short-run production concept. Fixed costs of production are associated with acquiring and maintaining fixed factors of production. Fixed costs are incurred by the firm regardless of the level of production. Fixed costs are incurred by the firm even if no production takes place at all. Examples often include continuing expenses incurred under a binding contract, such as rental payments on office space, certain insurance payments, and some legal retainers.

Total variable costs of production are associated with acquiring and maintaining variable factors of production. In stages I and II of production, total variable cost is an increasing function of the level of output. Total cost is the sum of total fixed and total variable cost.

KEY RELATIONSHIPS: AVERAGE TOTAL COST, AVERAGE FIXED COST, AVERAGE VARIABLE COST, AND MARGINAL COST

The definitions of average fixed cost, average variable cost, average total cost, and marginal cost are, appropriately, as follows:

Average fixed cost:

$$AFC = \frac{TFC}{Q} \tag{4.5}$$

Average variable cost:

$$AVC = \frac{TVC}{Q} \tag{4.6}$$

Average total cost:

$$ATC = \frac{TC}{Q} = \frac{TFC + TVC}{Q} = AFC + AVC \tag{4.7}$$

Marginal cost:

$$MC = \frac{dTC}{dQ} = \frac{dTVC}{dQ} \tag{4.8}$$

Average total cost is the total cost of production per unit. It is the total cost of production divided by total output. Average total cost is a short-run production concept if total cost includes fixed cost. It is a long-run production concept if all costs are variable costs. Average fixed cost, which is a short-run production concept, is total fixed cost per unit of output. It is total fixed cost divided by total output. Average variable cost is total variable cost of production per unit of output. Average variable cost is total variable cost divided by total output.

Marginal cost is the change in the total cost associated with a change in total output. Contrary to conventional belief, this is not the same thing as the cost of producing the "last" unit of output. Since it is total cost that is changing, the cost of producing the last unit of output is the same as the per-unit cost of producing any other level of output. More specifically, the marginal cost of production for a profit-maximizing firm is equal to average total cost plus the per-unit change in total cost, multiplied by total output. Equation (4.8) shows that marginal cost is the same as marginal variable cost, since total fixed cost is a constant.

Related to marginal cost is the more general concept of incremental cost. While marginal cost is the change in total cost given a change in output, incremental cost is the change in the firm's total costs that result from the implementation of decisions made by management, such as the introduction of a new product or a change in the firm's advertising campaign. By contrast, sunk costs are invariant with respect to changes in management decisions. Since sunk costs are not recoverable once incurred, they should not be considered when one is determining, say, an optimal level of output or product mix. Suppose, for example, that a textile manufacture purchases a loom for Rs.1 million. If the firm is able to dispose of the loom in the resale market for only Rs.750,000, the firm, in effect, has permanently lost Rs.250,000. In other words, the firm has incurred a sunk cost of Rs.250,000.

Related to the concept of sunk cost is the analytically more important concept of total fixed cost. Total fixed cost, which represents the cost of a firm's fixed inputs, is invariant with respect to the profit-maximizing level of output. This is demonstrated in Equation (4.8). Changes in total cost with respect to changes in output are the same as changes in total variable cost with respect to changes in output. In other words, marginal variable cost is identical to marginal cost.

The distinction between sunk and fixed cost is subtle. Suppose that when the firm operated the loom to produce cotton fabrics, the rental price of the loom was Rs.100,000 per year. This rental price is invariant to the firm's level of production. In other words, the firm would rent the loom for Rs.100,000 per year regardless of whether it produced 5,000 or 100,000 yards of cloth during that period. A sunk cost is essentially the difference between the purchase price of the loom and its salvage value.

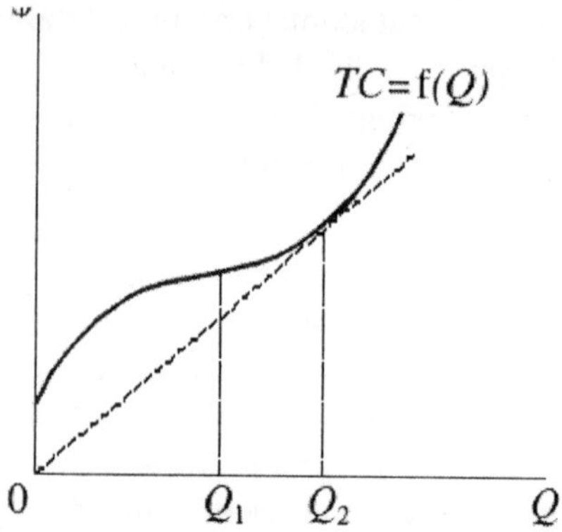

Figure: Total cost curve exhibiting increasing then diminishing marginal product.

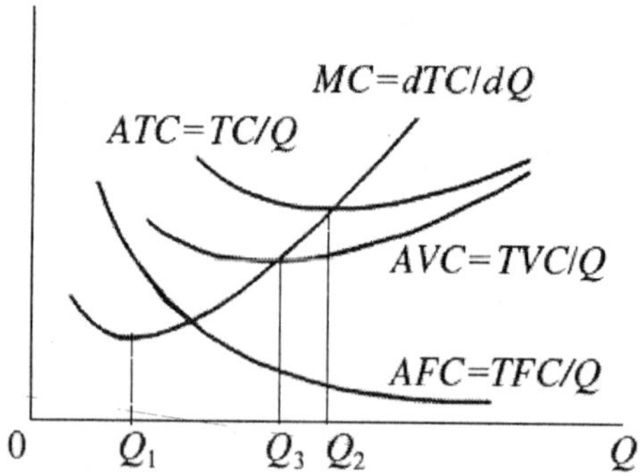

Figure: Marginal, average total, average variable, and average fixed cost curves.

Additional insights into the relationship between total cost and production may be seen by examining Equation (4.8). Recalling that Q = f(K, L) and applying the chain rule we obtain

$$MC = \frac{dTC}{dQ} = \left(\frac{dTC}{dL}\right)\left(\frac{dL}{dQ}\right)$$

Recalling from Equation (4.3) that TC = $P_K K_0 + PL_L$, then marginal cost may be written as

$$MC = \frac{dTC}{dQ} = \left(\frac{dTC}{dL}\right)\left(\frac{dL}{dQ}\right) \qquad (4.9)$$

where P_L is the rental price of homogeneous labour input and MP_L is the marginal product of labour. Equation (4.9) establishes a direct link between marginal cost and the marginal product of labour, which was discussed in previous chapter. Since P_L is a constant, it is easily seen that MC varies inversely with MP_L. The shapes of the TC, ATC, AVC, and MC curves may easily be explained. When MP_L is rising (falling), for example, MC will be falling (rising). These relationships are illustrated in figures above.

Equation (4.9) indicates clearly the relation between the theory of production and the theory of cost. The cost curves are shaped as they are because the production function exhibits the properties it does, especially the law of diminishing marginal product. In other words, underlying the short-run cost functions are the short-run production functions.

THE FUNCTIONAL FORM OF THE TOTAL COST FUNCTION

Figure above illustrated a short-run total cost function exhibiting both increasing and diminishing marginal product. In the diagram, increasing marginal product occurs over the range of output from 0 to Q_1, while diminishing marginal product characterizes output levels greater than Q_1. The inflection point, which occurs at output level Q_1, corresponds to minimum marginal cost. The short-run total cost function in Figure above may be characterized by a cubic function of the form

$$TC(Q) = b_0 \_ b_1Q + b_2Q^2 + b_3Q^3 \tag{4.10}$$

For Equation (4.10) to make sense, the values of the coefficients (b_i s) must make economic sense. The value of the constant term, for example, must be restricted to some positive value, $b_0 > 0$, since total fixed cost must be positive.

To determine the restrictions that should be placed on the remaining coefficient values, consider again Figure above. Note that as illustrated in Figure above, in which marginal cost is always positive, total cost is an increasing function of output. Since the minimum value of MC is positive, it is necessary to restrict the remaining coefficients so that the absolute minimum value of the marginal cost function is also positive. These restrictions are $b_0 > 0; b_1 > 0; b_2 < 0; b_3 > 0; 3b_3b_1 > b_2{}^2 > 0$

Equation (4.10) is the most general form of the total cost function because it reflects both increasing marginal product and diminishing marginal product. But, as we saw in last chapter, while the production function may exhibit increasing marginal product at low levels of output, this is not guaranteed. The only thing of which we may be certain is that in the short run, at some level of output (and this may occur as soon as the firm commences operations), total cost will begin to increase at an increasing rate. For firms that experience only diminishing marginal product, the total cost equation may be written as

$$TC(Q) = b_0 + b_1Q^2 \tag{4.11}$$

As before, positive total fixed cost guarantees that $b_0 > 0$. Increasing marginal cost requires that $dMC/dQ = d^2TC/dQ^2 > 0$. From Equation (4.11), the reader will verify that $MC = 2b_1Q$ and $dMC/dQ = 2b_1$. Increasing marginal cost also requires, therefore, that $b_1 > 0$.

MATHEMATICAL RELATIONSHIP BETWEEN ATC AND MC

An examination of Figure above indicates that the marginal cost (MC) curve intersects the average total cost (ATC) curve and average variable cost (AVC) curve from below at their minimum points. The relation between total, marginal, and average functions were discussed in last chapters. This section will extend that discussion to the specific relation between MC and ATC. The approach is to minimize the average total cost function and determine if the condition observed in Figure above is satisfied. Consider, again, the definition of average total cost

$$ATC = \frac{TC}{Q} \tag{4.12}$$

Minimizing Equation (4.7) by taking the first derivative with respect to output and setting the results equal to zero yields

$$\frac{dATC}{dQ} = \frac{Q(dTC/dQ) - TC}{Q^2} = 0 \tag{4.12}$$

Since $Q^2 > 0$, then, from Equation (4.12),

$$\frac{dTC}{dQ} = \frac{TC}{Q}$$

That is, the first-order condition for a minimum ATC is

$$MC = ATC \tag{4.13}$$

The second-order condition for minimum is that the second derivative of Equation (4.7) is positive. Taking the derivative of Equation (4.12) yields

$$\frac{d^2ATC}{dQ^2}$$

$$= \frac{Q^2\left[Q\left(d^2TC/dQ^2 + dTC/dQ - dTC/dQ\right)\right] - \left[Q\left(dTC/dQ\right) - TC\right](2Q)}{Q^4}$$

$$= \frac{\left(d^2TC/dQ^2\right)}{Q} - \frac{\left(2dTC/dQ\right)}{Q^2} + \frac{2TC}{Q^3}$$

Substituting the first-order condition Q(dTC/dQ) – TC yields

$$\frac{d^2ATC}{dQ^2} = \frac{\left(d^2TC/dQ^2\right)}{Q} - \frac{\left(2dTC/dQ\right)}{Q^2} + \frac{2Q\left(dTC/dQ\right)}{Q^3}$$

$$= \frac{\left(d^2TC/dQ^2\right)}{Q} = \frac{\left(dMC/dQ\right)}{Q} > 0$$

for a minimum ATC. Since Q > 0, at a minimum ATC the second-order condition requires that marginal cost is increasing. As indicated in Figure above, at the point at which ATC is minimized, ATC = MC, and the MC curve intersects the ATC curve from below.

It is also easy to demonstrate that the marginal cost curve also intersects the minimum point on the average variable cost (AVC) curve from below. From Equation (4.4)

$$TC(Q) = TFC + TVC(Q) \tag{4.14}$$

Dividing both sides of Equation (4.4) by output, and rearranging, we obtain

$$AVC(Q) = ATC(Q) - AFC \tag{4.15}$$

Taking the derivative of Equation (4.15) with respect to output yields

$$\frac{AVC(Q)}{dQ} = \frac{dATC(Q)}{dQ} \tag{4.16}$$

Since AFC is a constant. Thus, minimizing average variable cost with respect to output is equivalent to minimizing average total cost with respect to output, and generates identical conclusions.

It should be pointed out that although the MC curve intersects both the ATC and AVC curve at their minimum points that minimum AVC occurs at a lower output level than minimum ATC. To see why this is the case, refer again to Equation (4.15). For any output level, including the output level that minimizes ATC and AVC, ATC exceeds AVC by the amount of AFC. In Figure above, since the marginal cost curve is upward sloping, the MC curve cannot intersect both the AVC and ATC curves at their minimum points unless it does so at different output levels as long as AFC > 0 (otherwise ATC = AVC).

Since ATC > AVC, the output level corresponding to the minimum point on the ATC curve must be above and to the right of the output level that corresponds to the minimum point on the AVC curve. Finally, referring again to Figure above, from Equation (4.15), AFC must equal the vertical distance between the ATC and the AVC curves at any output level. Since AFC falls as Q increases, the ATC and AVC curves must be asymptotic vertically.

LEARNING CURVE EFFECT

The discussion in previous chapter noted that the profit-maximizing firm will operate in stage II of production. It will be recalled that in stage II the marginal product of a factor, say labour, is positive, but declining at an increasing rate. The phenomenon is a direct consequence of the law of diminishing marginal product. At constant factor prices this relationship implies that as output is expanded, the marginal cost of a variable factor increases at an increasing rate.

An important assumption implicit in the law of diminishing marginal product is that the quality of the variable input used remains unchanged.

In the case of labour, for example, the "productivity" of labour is assumed to remain unchanged regardless of the level of production. In fact, this restriction is an oversimplification: it is reasonable to expect that as output expands over time, the typical labourer "gets better" at his or her job. In other words, it is reasonable to assume that workers become more productive as they gain experience. This would suggest that over some range of production, per-unit labour input might, in fact, fall. At constant labour prices, this implies that per-unit labour costs may in fact fall.

We are not, of course, talking about stage I of production, where per-unit costs fall because of increased specialization as additional units of, say, labour are added to underutilized amounts of capital. On-the-job training and experience will make workers more productive, which has important implications for the cost structure of the firm. It is precisely the expectation of greater productivity that compels many firms to underwrite on-site employee training and off-site continuing education programs. The relationship between increased per-worker productivity and reduced perworker cost at fixed labour prices associated with an increase in output and experience is called the learning curve effect.

Definition: The learning curve effect measures the relation between an increase in per-worker productivity (a decrease in per-unit labour cost at fixed labour prices) associated with an improvement in labour skills from on-the-job experience.

One measure of the learning curve effect is Γ

$$= \text{Per-unit labour cost} = \varphi Q^{\beta} \tag{4.17}$$

where φ is the per-unit cost of producing the first unit of output, Q is the level of output, $\beta = (\ln m)/(\ln \lambda)$, m is the learning factor, and λ is a factor of output proportionality. In fact, β is a measure of the learning curve effect. It determines the rate at which per-unit labour requirements fall given the rate at which workers "learn" (m) following a scalar (proportional) increase in production (λ). The value of m varies from zero to unity ($0 \leq m \leq 1$). As the value of m approaches zero, the learning curve effect on lowering perunit labour costs becomes more powerful.

The reader will note that the lower the learning factor (i.e., the quicker the learning process), the more rapidly per-unit labour costs fall as output expands. Since the wage rate in this example is constant at Rs.10 per hour, the learning curve effect implies that fewer labour units per unit of output are required as output increases. The extreme cases are m = 1 and m = 0. When m = 1, no learning whatsoever takes place, and $\beta = (\ln 1/ \ln \lambda) = 0$. In this case, there are no learning curve effects, and the per-unit labour cost remains unchanged. On the other hand, when m = 0, then $\beta = -\infty$. In this case, learning is so complete and production so efficient that the per-unit labour cost reduces to zero, which implies that at a constant wage rate no labour is required at all. In the two-input case, this suggests that all production technology is embodied in the amount of capital employed.

Learning curve effects are usually thought to result from the development of labour skills, especially for tasks of a repetitive nature, over time. More broadly, however, incremental reductions in per-unit labour costs may result from a variety of factors, such as the adoption of new production, organizational, and managerial techniques, the replacement of higher cost with lower cost materials, an new product design. Consideration of these additional factors has given rise to the broader term experience curve effects.

Definition: The experience curve effect is a measure of the relationship etween an increase in per-worker productivity (a decrease in per-worker cost at fixed labour prices) associated with an improvement in labour skills from on-the-job experience, the adoption of new production, organizational and managerial techniques, the replacement of higher cost with lower cost materials, new product design, and so on.

Problem: Suppose that the labour cost to a firm of producing a single unit of output is Rs.5,000.

a. If the learning factor is 0.74 and the factor of proportionality is 2.5, estimate the per-unit labour cost of producing 120 units of output.

b. If the wage rate is constant at Rs.15 per hour, how many labour hours are required to produce the first unit of output? How many labour hours are required per unit of output when 120 units are produced?

Solution:

a. From Equation (4.17),

Per-unit labour cost

$$= \varphi Q^{\beta} = 5{,}000(120)^{\ln 0.74/\ln 2.5} = \$1{,}037 \text{ per unit}$$

b. first unit will require Rs.5,000/Rs.15 = 333.33 labour hours. When 120 units are produced, the per-unit labour requirement is Rs.1,037/Rs.15 = 69.13 labour hours.

LONG-RUN COST

In the long run all factors of production are assumed to be variable. Since there are no fixed inputs, there are no fixed costs. All costs are variable. Unlike the short-run production function, however, there is little that can be said about production in the long run. There is no long-run equivalent of the law of diminishing marginal product.

As in the case of the firm's short-run cost functions, long-run cost functions are intimately related to the long-run production function. In particular, the firm's long-run cost functions are related to the concept of returns to scale. In general, economists have theorized that an increase in the firm's scale of operations (i.e., a proportional increase in all inputs), is likely to be accompanied by increasing, constant, and decreasing returns to scale. The relation between total output and all inputs, the long-run total product curve (LRTP) is illustrated in figure below.

It will be recalled from previous chapter that the coefficient of output elasticity for increasing returns to scale, constant returns to scale, and decreasing returns to scale, which is the sum of the output elasticities of each input, is greater than unity, equal to unity, and less than unity, respectively. Although the shapes of the long-run and short-run total product curves are similar, the reasons are quite different. The short-run total product curve derives its shape from the law of diminishing marginal product.

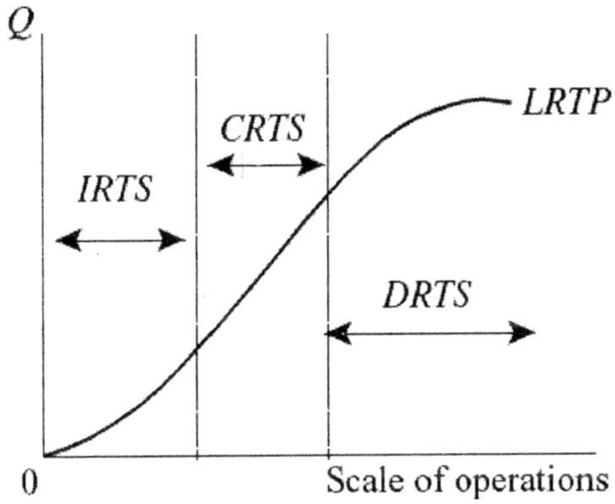

Figure: Long-run total product curve: the increase in total output from a proportional increase in all inputs.

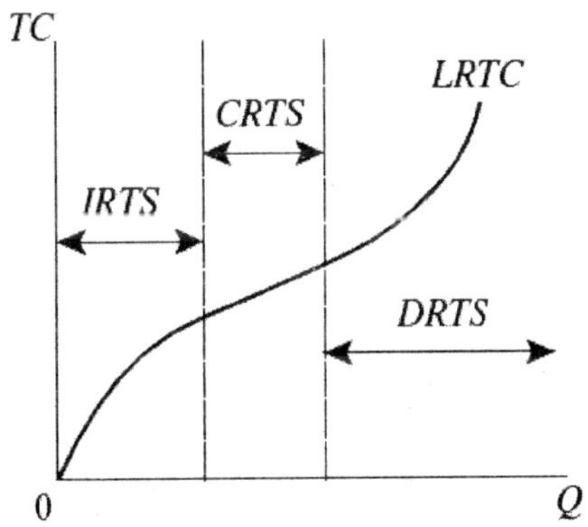

Figure: Long-run total cost curve.

The long-run total product curve derives its shape from quite different considerations. To begin with, firms might experience increasing returns to scale during the early stages of production because of the opportunity for increased specialization of both human and nonhuman factors, which would lead to gains in efficiency. Only large firms, for example, can rationalize the use of in-house lawyers, accountants, economists, and so on. Another reason is that equipment of larger capacity may be more efficient than mochinery of smaller capacity.

Eventually, as the firm gets larger, the efficiencies from increased size may be exhausted. As a firm grows larger, so too do the demands on management. Increased administrative layers may become necessary, resulting in a loss of efficiency as internal coordination of production processes become more difficult. At some large level of output, factors of production may become overworked and diminishing returns to management may set in. Problems of interdepartmental and interdivisional coordination may become endemic. The result would be decreasing returns to scale.

Since there are no fixed costs in the long run, the firm's corresponding long-run total cost curve (LRTC), which is similar in appearance to the shcrt-run total cost curve, intersects TC at the origin. This is illustrated in Figure above.

ECONOMIES OF SCALE

Scale refers to size. What is the effect on the firm's per-unit cost of production following an increase in all factors of production? In other words, does the size of a firm's operations affect its per-unit cost of production? The answer to the second questions is that it may. Regardless of what we have learned about the short-run production function and the law of diminishing marginal product, it is difficult to make generalizations about the effect of size on per-unit cost of production, although we may speculate about the most likely possibilities.

Economies of scale are intimately related to the concept of increasing returns to scale. If per-unit costs of production decline as the scale of a firm's operations increase, the firm is said to experience economies of scale. The reason is simple. If we assume constant factor prices, while the firm's total cost of production rises proportionately with an increase in total factor usage, per-unit cost of production falls because output has increased more than proportionately. In other words, an increase in the firm's scale of operations results in a decline in long-run average total cost (LRATC).

Conversely, diseconomies of scale are intimately related to the concept of decreasing returns to scale. Once again, the explanation is straightforward. Assuming constant factor prices, the firm's total cost of production rises proportionately with an increase in total factor usage, but the per-unit cost of production increases because output increases less than proportionately. In other words, an increase in the firm's scale of operations results in an increase in the firm's long-run average total cost.

Finally, in the case of constant returns to scale, per-unit cost of production remains constant as production increases or decreases proportionately with an increase or decrease in factor usage. In other words, an increase or decrease in the firm's size will have no effect on the firm's long-run average total cost.

Definition: Assuming constant factor prices, economies of scale occur when per-unit costs of production decline following a proportional increase in all factors of production.

Definition: Assuming constant factor prices, diseconomies of scale occur when per-unit costs of production increase following a proportional increase in all factors of production.

Assume that Q = f(L, K), where Q is output, L is variable labour, and K is fixed capital. Figure below illustrates several possible short-run average total cost curves (SRATC), each corresponding to a different level of capital usage. Here, $SRATC_2$ represents the short-run average total cost curve of the firm utilizing a higher level of fixed capital input than $SRATC_1$, $SRATC_3$ represents the short-run average total cost curve of the firm utilizing a higher level of fixed capital input than $SRATC_2$, and so on.

We can see that the firm may produce a given level of output with one or more short-run production functions: for example, the firm may produce output level Q_1 along $SRATC_1$ (point A) or $SRATC_2$ (point B).

If the firm believes that the demand for its product in the foreseeable future is Q_1, it will choose to employ a level of capital consistent with $SRATC_2$ to realize lower per-unit cost of production. As the demand for the firm's output increases, the firm will choose that production technology such that its per-unit costs are minimized. All such points are illustrated by the "envelope" of the short-run average total cost curves.

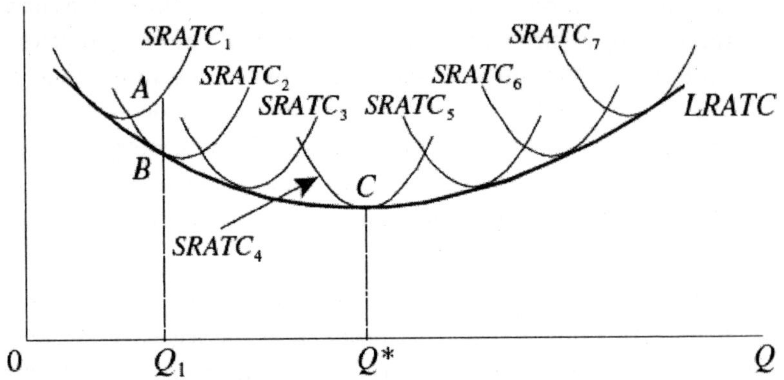

Figure: Long-run average total cost curve as the "envelope" of the short-run average total cost curves.

This curve is called the long-run average total cost curve, which is labelled LRATC in Figure above.

Unlike the short-run average total cost curves, which derive their shape from the law of diminishing returns, the long-run average total cost curve derives its shape from the returns to scale characteristics of the underlying production function. In Figure above, the range of output levels 0 to Q* corresponds to the underlying production characteristic of increasing returns to scale. Over this range of output, LRATC is downward sloping (i.e., $dLRATC/dQ < 0$). Output levels greater than Q* reflect decreasing returns to scale. Over this range of output LRATC is upward sloping (i.e., $dLRATC/dQ > 0$). Where the long-run average total cost curve is neither rising nor falling, $dLRATC/dQ = 0$, the underlying production function exhibits constant returns to scale.

The output level that corresponds to minimum long-run ATC is commonly referred to as the minimum efficient scale (MES). Minimum efficient scale is the level of output that corresponds to the lowest per-unit cost of production in the long run.

The shape of the long-run average total cost curve will vary from industry to industry. There is, in fact, no a priori reason for the LRATC curve to be U shaped. Figures above through 6.9 illustrate three other possible shapes of the long-run average total cost curve.

REASONS FOR ECONOMIES AND DISECONOMIES OF SCALE

As firms grow larger, economies of scale may be realized as a result of specialization in production, sales, marketing, research and development, and other areas. Specialization may increase the firm's productivity in greater proportion than the increase in operating cost associated with greater size. Some types of machinery, for example, are more efficient for large production runs. Examples include large electrical-power generators and large blast furnaces that generate greater output than smaller ones. Large companies may be able to extract more favourable financing terms from creditors than small companies.

Large size, however, does not guarantee that improvement in efficiency and lower per-unit costs. Large size is often accompanied by a disproportionately great increase in specialized management. Coordination and communication between and among departments becomes more complicated, difficult, and time-consuming. As a result, time that would be better spent in the actual process of production declines and overhead expenses increase disproportionately. The result is that diminishing returns to scale set in, and per-unit costs rise. In other words, growth usually is accompanied by diseconomies of scale.

MULTIPRODUCT COST FUNCTIONS

We have thus far discussed manufacturing processes involving the production of a single output. Yet, many firms use the same production facilities to produce multiple products. Automobile companies, such as Ford Motor Company, produce both cars and trucks at the same production facilities. Chemical and pharmaceutical companies, such as Dow Chemical and Merck, use the same basic production facilities to produce multiple different products. Computer companies, such as IBM, produce monitors, printers, scanners, modems and, of course, computers. Consumer product companies, such as General Electric, produce a wide range of household durables, such refrigerators, ovens, and light-bulbs. In each of these examples it is reasonable to suppose that total cost of production is a function of more than a single output. In the case of a firm producing two products, the multiproduct cost function may be written as

$$TC = TC(Q_1, Q_2) \tag{4.18}$$

where Q_1 and Q_2 represent the number of units produced of goods 1 and 2, respectively.

Definition: A multiproduct cost function summarizes the cost of efficiently using the same production facilities to produce two or more products.

The multiproduct cost function summarized in Equation (4.18) has the same basic interpretation as a single product cost function, although the specific relationship depends on the manner in which these goods are produced. Two examples of multiproduct cost relationships are economies of scope and cost complementarities.

ECONOMIES OF SCOPE

Economies of scope exist when the total cost of using the same production facilities to produce two or more goods is less than that of producing these goods at separate production facilities. In the case of a firm that produces two goods, economies of scope exist when

$$TC(Q_1,0)+TC(0,Q_2)>TC(Q_1,Q_2) \tag{4.19}$$

It may be less expensive, for example, for Ford Motor Company to produce cars and trucks by more intensively utilizing a single assembly plant than to produce these products at two separate, less intensively utilized, manufacturing facilities. It is less expensive for the restaurants in the Olive Garden chain to use the same ovens, tables, refrigerators, and so on to produce both pasta and parmigiana meals than to duplicate the factors of production.

Definition: Economies of scope in production exist when the total cost of producing two or more goods is lower when the same production facilities are used than when separate production facilities are used to produce the goods.

COST COMPLEMENTARITIES

Cost complementarities exist when the marginal cost of producing Q_1 is reduced by increasing the production of Q_2. From Equation (4.18), the marginal cost of producing Q_1 may be written as

$$MC_1(Q_1,Q_2)=\frac{\partial TC}{\partial Q_1}$$

The multiproduct cost function exhibits cost complementarities if the cross-second partial derivative of the multiproduct cost function is negative, that is,

$$\frac{\partial MC_1(Q_1,Q_2)}{\partial Q_2}=\frac{\partial^2 TC}{\partial Q_1 \partial Q_2}<0 \tag{4.20a}$$

$$\frac{\partial MC_2(Q_1,Q_2)}{\partial Q_1}=\frac{\partial^2 TC}{\partial Q_2 \partial Q_1}<0 \tag{4.20b}$$

Equations (4.20) says that an increase in the production of Q_2 reduces the marginal cost of producing Q_1.

Definition: Cost complementarities exist when the marginal cost of producing one good is reduced by increasing the production of another good.

Examples of cost complementarities include the simultaneous production of beef and leather, and doughnuts and doughnut "holes." Slaughtering cattle for beef without considering the potential usefulness of leather by-products, and vice versa, is not only poor business but wasteful. Producing doughnuts and doughnut holes is certainly more cost efficient when these snacks are produced together than when they are produced separately.

Note: Navistar International (NIC) is a holding company that operates through its principal operating subsidiaries, Navistar and Navistar Financial (NFC). The company is engaged in the manufacture and distribution of trucks, busses and engines. It is headquartered in Warrenville, Illinois and employs 17,800 people. For a very good case study regarding this topic, reader can visit company's website www.navistar.com

5

Profit and Revenue Maximization

Firms transform factors of production into goods and services for sale in the market. In last chapter, we discussed several important production relationships at length. We saw, for example, that firms produce in the short run, but plan in the long run. The short run in production was defined at that period of time during which at least one factor of production is held constant. In the short run, firms are subject to the law of diminishing marginal product with respect to the variable inputs. We also saw that in is generally possible to produce a given level of output with several different input combinations.

In other words, generally, but not always, factors of production are substitutable. The substitutability of the factors of production was illustrated diagrammatically with the use of an isoquant map, with each isoquant corresponding to a different level of output. By contrast, the long run in production was defined as the period of time in which all factors of production are variable. When all factors of production are variable, the optimal scale of the firm's future operations becomes an important managerial decision-making consideration.

Last chapter left a number of important short-run production questions unanswered. For one thing, what is the firm's "optimal" level of output? Not surprisingly, the optimal level of output is defined by the firm's organizational objective.

The output level that maximizes the firm's profits, for example, will generally be different from the output level that maximizes the firm's sales revenues or market share. Once the firm's organizational objective has been defined, management must determine the least-cost combination of inputs necessary to achieve that target output level. Clearly, this will depend not only on the firm's operating budget, but also on the market prices of the factors of production. As we saw in previous chapter, many of the most important cost relationships confronting managers are reflections of the firm's underlying production technology.

In this chapter we develop a general framework for finding optimal solutions to managerial decision-making problems. This framework will be expanded in subsequent chapters to take into consideration alternative market structures and operating environments. This chapter will consider the decision-making process with respect to two organizational objectives: profit maximization and total revenue maximization. We begin by considering profit maximization from two perspectives. At a more practical level, management will attempt to maximize profits by employing just the right amount of each factor of production subject to a predefined budget constraint. At a much more general level, profit maximization may be viewed as an unconstrained or constrained optimization problem in which the decision variable is the firm's level of output.

PROFIT MAXIMIZATION

Although discussion of the production function developed in last chapter has intuitive appeal in its own right, its usefulness to the business manager is in its application to profit maximization. It was demonstrated, for example, that with precise specification of the production function and a given output level, infinite input combinations are at least theoretically possible. The specific combination of inputs used to produce that output level, however, will be that which can be produced at least cost. Alternatively, given the firm's operating budget and the prices of productive resources, the perfectly competitive firm will choose that combination of resources that generates the greatest output level.

OPTIMAL INPUT COMBINATION

ISOCOST LINE

Given the prices of productive resources and the firm's operating budget, and assuming only two factors of production, labour and capital, the various combinations of inputs that a firm can employ in the production process may be summarized as

$$TC_0 = P_L L + P_K K \tag{5.1}$$

where TC_0 is the firm's operating budget, or total cost, P_L is the rental price of labour (or the wage rate), and P_K is the rental price of capital (or the interest rate). Equation (5.1) is known as the isocost equation. This expression is also known as the firm's cost constraint in the two-variable input case. Suppose, for example, that the firm's weekly operating budget is Rs.1,000, the weekly per worker wage rate is Rs.100, and the weekly rental price of capital is Rs.150. Expression (5.1), therefore, becomes

$$1{,}000 = 100L + 150K \tag{5.2}$$

Equation (5.2) may be solved for K to yield the firm's isocost line,

$$K = 6.67 - 0.67L \tag{5.3}$$

The negative slope coefficient indicates that more capital may be hired only at the expense of fewer units of labour. In this example, when zero labour is employed, at a rental price of capital of Rs.150, the total amount of labour that can be hired is 6.67 units (per operating period). Similarly, if no units of capital are employed, then 10 units of labour may be hired. In general, from Equation (5.1) the isocost line may be written as

$$K = \frac{TC_0}{P_K} - \left(\frac{P_L}{P_K}\right)L \tag{5.4}$$

Equation (5.4) indicates that the rate at which a unit of labour may be substituted for a unit of capital is given by the ratio of the input prices. In summary, the isocost line denotes the various combinations of inputs that a firm may hire at a given cost.

Equation (5.4) is illustrated diagrammatically in Figure below, where the isocost line (given an operating budget of TC_0 and labour and capital prices of P_L and P_K, respectively) is denoted by the line RAS. Consider, for example, point A on the RAS isocost line. At a total operating budget of TC_0,0K units of capital and 0L units of labour may be hired.

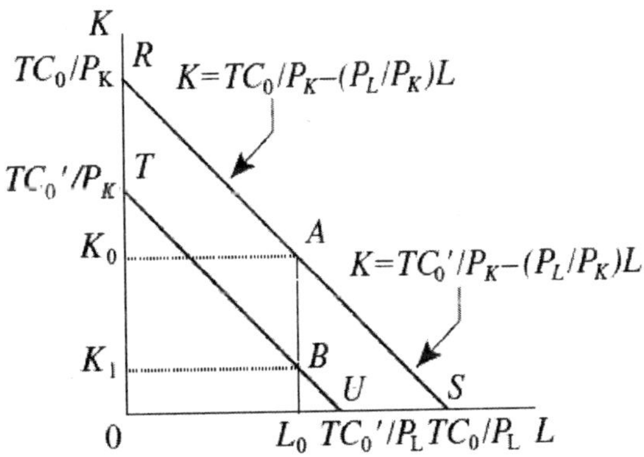

Figure: Isocost line and a budget increase.

Now suppose that there is a change in the operating budget from TC_0 to $TC_{0'}$, where $TC_0 > TC_{0'}$ and with unchanged resource prices. In Figure above this is illustrated by a parallel shift from RAS to TBU, where the vertical intercept has declined from TC_0 /P_K to $TC_0¢/P_K$. Since input prices are unchanged, the slope of the isocost line is unaffected. If the firm chooses to hire the same amount of labour as before ($0L_0$), then the new combination of capital and labour hired given the new, lower budget is illustrated by the movement from point A to point B. Here, the number of units of capital hired will fall from $0K_0$ to $0K_1$ because there is less money in the budget. Of course, any combination of labour and capital is possible along the TBU isocost line.

Suppose, on the other hand, that the operating budget remains the same but there is a change in the price of one of the productive factors. Suppose, for example, that the price of labour increases to $P_{L'}$ (i.e., $P_{L'} > P_L$). The result of this change is illustrated in Figure below.

Note that in Figure below, line RAS is the isocost line before the change in the wage rate. An increase in the wage rate from P_L to $P_{L'}$, however, results in a change in the slope of the isocost line from $-P_L/P_K$ to $-P_{L'}/P_K$; that is, the RBU line is steeper than the RAS line because $|P_{L'}/P_K| > |P_L/P_K|$. The result of this change is that the isocost line "rotates" clockwise. Assuming, as before, that the level of labour input usage remains unchanged at $0L_0$,the amount of capital that may now be hired falls from $0K_0$ to $0K_1$. This is because labour has become more expensive and there is less money in the budget to hire capital. Note also that since the wage rate does not appear in the vertical intercept term, the maximum amount of capital that may be hired remains TC_0/P_K, although the maximum amount of labour that may be hired falls from TC_0/P_L to $TC_0/P_{L'}$.

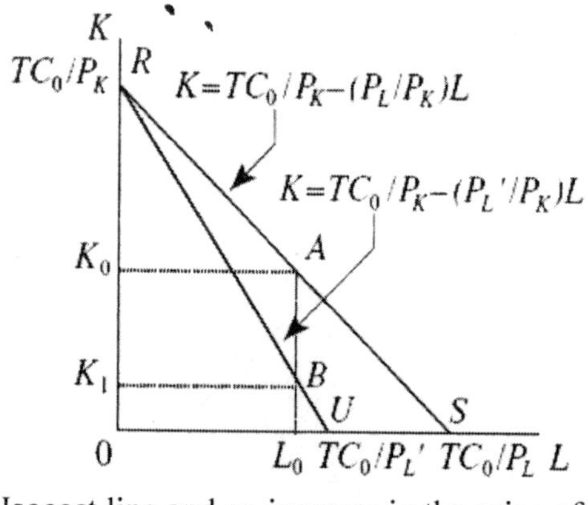

Figure: Isocost line and an increase in the price of labour.

Problem: Suppose that the wage rate (P_L) is Rs.25 and the rental price of capital (P_K) is Rs.40. In addition, suppose that the firm's operating budget is Rs.2,500.

a. What is the isocost equation for the firm?

b. If capital is graphed on the vertical axis, what happens to the isocost line if the wage rate increases?

c. If capital is graphed on the vertical axis, what happens to the isocost line if the rental price of capital falls?

d. If the wage rate and the rental price of capital remain unchanged, what happens to the isocost line if the firm's operating budget falls?

e. If the firm's operating budget remains unchanged, what happens to the isocost line if the wage rate and the rental price of capital fall by the same percentage?

Solution:

a. The firm's isocost line is given by the expression

$$TC_0 = P_L L + P_K K$$

Substituting into this expression we obtain

$$2,500 = 25L + 40K$$

b. Solving the isocost line for K yields

$$K = \frac{TC_0}{P_K} - \left(\frac{P_L}{P_K}\right)L$$

From this expression, if the wage rate increases, the isocost line will rotate clockwise. In other words, the K intercept will remain unchanged while the L intercept will move to the left.

c. If the rental price of capital falls, the solution of the isocost line for K shows that the isocost line will rotate clockwise. In other words, the L intercept will remain unchanged while the K intercept will move up.

d. If the operating budget falls, the isocost line will experience a parallel shift to the left. In other words, the K intercept will move down, the L intercept will move to the left, and the slope of the isocost line will remain unchanged.

e. If the wage rate and the rental price of capital fall by the same percentage, the isocost line will experience a parallel shift to the right. In other words, the K intercept will move up, the L intercept will move to the right, and the slope of the isocost line will remain unchanged.

FINDING THE OPTIMAL INPUT COMBINATION

We are, at last, in a position to answer the fundamental question facing the firm. That is, given fixed input prices and a known production function, what is the optimal combination of labour and capital. The term "optimal" in this context can be considered from two perspectives. We may consider it to mean maximizing output subject to a fixed operating budget. Somewhat equivalently, we may interpret it is the minimizing of total cost subject to a predetermined level of output. As we will see, both approaches represent the first-order conditions for profit maximization.

The optimal combination of labour and capital is illustrated diagrammatically in Figure below, which combines the isocost line, illustrated in Figure above with the isoquant map introduced in last chapter.

Three of the infinite number of possible isoquants are illustrated in Figure below. The isoquant furthest from the origin represents the combinations of labour and capital that generate the highest constant output level. Also illustrated in Figure below is an isocost line representing the different combinations of labour and capital that may be hired at the fixed input prices L and P_K, and the fixed operating budget TC_0. Graphically, it is not difficult to understand why this particular firm will operate at point B on isoquant labeled Q_1. Clearly, as we move from left to right from the horizontal axis along the isocost line, we move to successively higher and higher isoquants. At point C, for example, we are only able to produce an output of Q_0 with an operating budget of TC_0. On the other hand, as we move closer to point B, substituting labour for capital, total output rises.

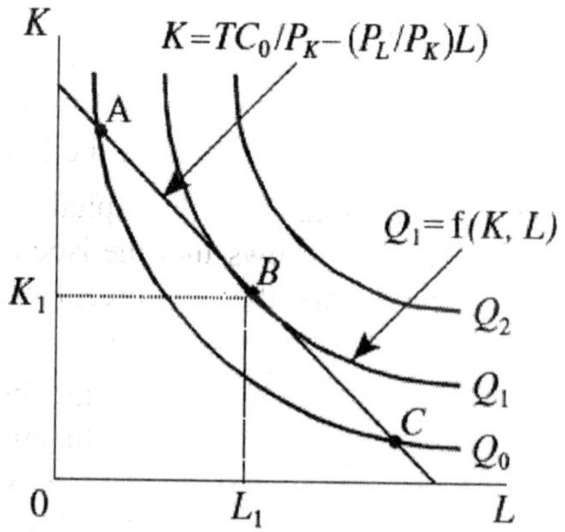

Figure: Optimal input combination: output maximization.

Beyond point B, however, output levels steadily decline as we move to lower isoquants. To understand why this is so, consider what is happening algebraically.

From last chapter recall that the slope of the isoquant is given by the marginal rate of technical substitution, or

$$\frac{dK}{dL} = -\frac{MP_L}{MP_K} = MRTS_{KL} < 0 \tag{5.21}$$

Likewise, the slope of the isocost line is given by the expression

$$\frac{dK}{dL} = \frac{P_L}{P_K} < 0 \tag{5.5}$$

At point C on the diagram we note that the absolute value of the slope of the isoquant is less than of the isocost line. That is

$$\frac{MP_L}{MP_K} < \frac{P_L}{P_K}$$

Rearranging, this expression becomes

$$\frac{MP_L}{P_L} < \frac{MP_K}{P_K} \tag{5.6}$$

Equation (5.6) says that at point C, the marginal product of labour per Rupee spent on labour is less than the marginal product of capital per Rupee spent on capital. It should be clear, therefore, that by reallocating a Rupee from the fixed operating budget from labour into capital, we should generate a net increase in output. Similarly, at point A in the diagram we have

$$\frac{MP_L}{MP_K} > \frac{P_L}{P_K}$$

Rearranging, this expression becomes

$$\frac{MP_L}{P_L} > \frac{MP_K}{P_K} \tag{5.7}$$

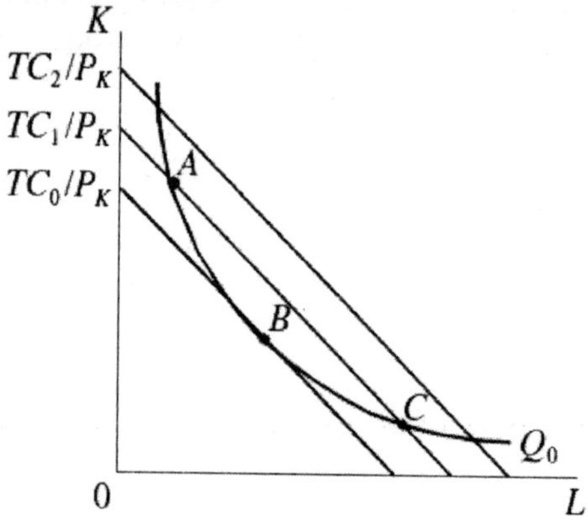

Figure: Optimal input combination: cost minimization.

Equation (5.7) says that reallocating a Rupee from capital to labour should generate an increase in output. The only point at which no gain in output will result by reallocating the firm's fixed operating budget Rupees is point B, where

$$\frac{MP_L}{MP_K} = \frac{P_L}{P_K} \tag{5.8}$$

In other words, only where the isocost line is just tangent to the isoquant will the firm be hiring the proper combination of labour and capital to generate the most output possible from its fixed operating budget. Of course, rearranging this expression yields

$$\frac{MP_L}{P_L} = \frac{MP_K}{P_K} \tag{5.9}$$

The same optimization conditions apply to the slightly different problem of minimizing the firm's total cost of production subject to a fixed level of production. This situation is illustrated in Figure above.

In above figure we have one isoquant and three isocost lines representing the different operating budgets TC_0, TC_1, and TC_2, where $TC_0 < TC_1 < TC_2$. Clearly, by the reasoning just outlined, total production costs will be minimized at point B in the diagram where, as before, $MP_L/P_L = MP_K/P_K$.

In general, to minimize total production costs subject to a fixed level of output, or to maximize total output subject to a fixed operating budget, the marginal product per last Rupee spent on each input must be the same for all inputs. That is, efficient production requires that the isoquant be tangent to the isocost line.

EXPANSION PATH

Note that Equations (5.8) and (5.9) are perfectly general in the sense that they represent the optimal combinations of productive resources independent of the budget or output constraint. In fact, Equations (5.8) and (5.9) are sometimes referred to as the expansion path of the firm because they represent the locus of all efficient input combinations. Figure below might be taken to represent one such expansion path.

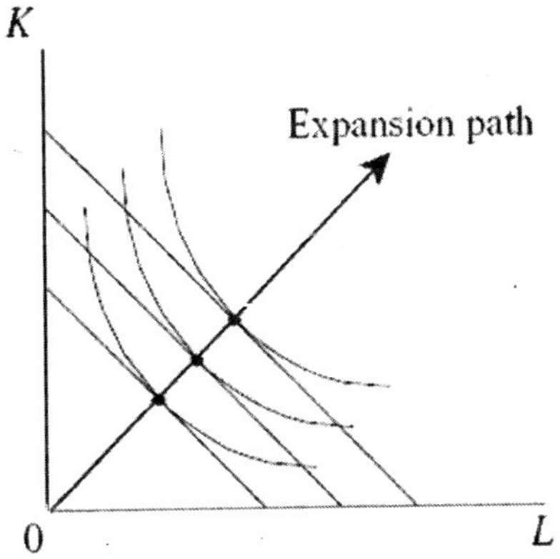

Figure: Expansion path.

Definition: The expansion path is the locus of points for which the isocost and isoquant curves are tangent. It represents the cost-minimizing (profit-maximizing) combinations of capital and labour for different operating budgets.

The expansion path, which represents the optimal combination of capital and labour used in the production process for different operating budgets, is characterized by Equations (5.8) and (5.9). In particular, Equation (5.9) says that a profit-maximizing firm will allocate its budget in such a way that the last Rupee spent on labour will yield the same additional output as the last Rupee spent on capital.

UNCONSTRAINED OPTIMIZATION: THE PROFIT FUNCTION

The objective of profit maximization facing the decision maker may, of course, be dealt with more directly. The optimality conditions just discussed are all by-products of this more direct approach. The problem confronting the decision maker is to choose an output level that will maximize profit. We will begin by defining profit as the difference between total revenue and total cost.

$$\pi(Q) = TR(Q) - TC(Q) \tag{5.10}$$

where TR(Q) represents total revenue and TC(Q) represents total cost, both of which are assumed to be functions of output. Equation (5.10) is an unconstrained objective function in which the object is to maximize total profit, which in this case is a function of the output level.

As we have already discussed, to meet the first-order and second-order conditions for a maximum, the first derivative must be equal to zero and the second derivative must be negative. In this case, the first- and second order conditions, respectively, are $d\pi / dQ = 0$ and $d^2\pi / dQ^2 < 0$. Applying these conditions to Equation (5.10), we obtain

$$\frac{d\pi}{dQ} = \frac{dTR}{dQ} - \frac{dTC}{dQ} = 0 \tag{5.11}$$

or

$$\text{MR} = \text{MC} \tag{5.12}$$

Equation (5.12) simply says that the first-order condition for the firm to maximize profits is to select an output level such that marginal revenue (MR = dTR/dQ) equals marginal cost (MC = dTC/dQ). Alternatively, a firstorder condition for the firm to maximize profits is to select an output level for which marginal profit $(M\pi = d\pi / dQ)$ is zero.

To ensure that the solution value for Equation (5.10) maximizes profit, the second-order condition must also be satisfied. Differentiating Equation (5.10) with respect to Q, we obtain

$$\frac{d^2\pi}{dQ^2} = \frac{d^2TR}{dQ^2} - \frac{d^2TC}{dQ^2} < 0 \tag{5.13}$$

$$\frac{d^2TR}{dQ^2} < \frac{d^2TC}{dQ^2} \tag{5.14}$$

In economic terms, Equation (5.14) simply says that to ensure that profit is maximized given that the first-order condition is satisfied, the rate of change in marginal revenue must be less than the rate of change in marginal cost. Diagrammatically, at the profit-maximizing level of output, where marginal revenue equals marginal cost, the marginal cost curve would intersect the marginal revenue curve from below. Alternatively, from Equation (5.13) the second-order condition for profit maximization requires that at the profit-maximizing level of output Q*, not only must marginal profit be zero but the slope of the profit function must be falling. Diagrammatically this would be illustrated as a profit "hill," where profit is maximized at an output level (Q*) that corresponds to the top of the profit "hill."

In two common illustrations of the foregoing concepts, which will be discussed at greater length in subsequent chapters, the selling price Q is taken to be parametric ($P = P_0$) or is assumed to be a function of output [$P = f(Q)$]. The first instance is typical of the market structure known as perfect competition. The second instance is typical of the market structure known as monopoly.

PERFECT COMPETITION

As before, assume that total cost is an increasing function of output [i.e., TC = TC(Q)]. If we assume that the selling price per unit of Q is given, the total revenue function becomes

$$TR = P_0Q \tag{5.15}$$

Substituting Equation (5.15) into Equation (5.10) yields

$$\pi(Q) = P_0Q - TC(Q) \tag{5.16}$$

The first-and second-order conditions for Equation (5.16) are, respectively,

$$\frac{d\pi}{dQ} = P_0 - \frac{dTC}{dQ} = 0 \tag{5.17}$$

or

$$P_0 = MC \tag{5.18}$$

and

$$d^2\pi/dQ^2 - \frac{d^2TC}{dQ^2} < 0 \tag{5.19}$$

or

$$\frac{d^2TC}{dQ^2} = \frac{dMC}{dQ} > 0 \tag{5.20}$$

Equation (5.18) says that at the profit-maximizing level of output, the fixed selling price is equal to marginal cost, while Equation (5.20) says that at the profit-maximizing level of output, total cost is increasing at an increasing rate (i.e., marginal cost is rising). Equation (5.19) says that at the profit-maximizing output level, marginal profit is zero and falling. These concepts are illustrated in Figure below.

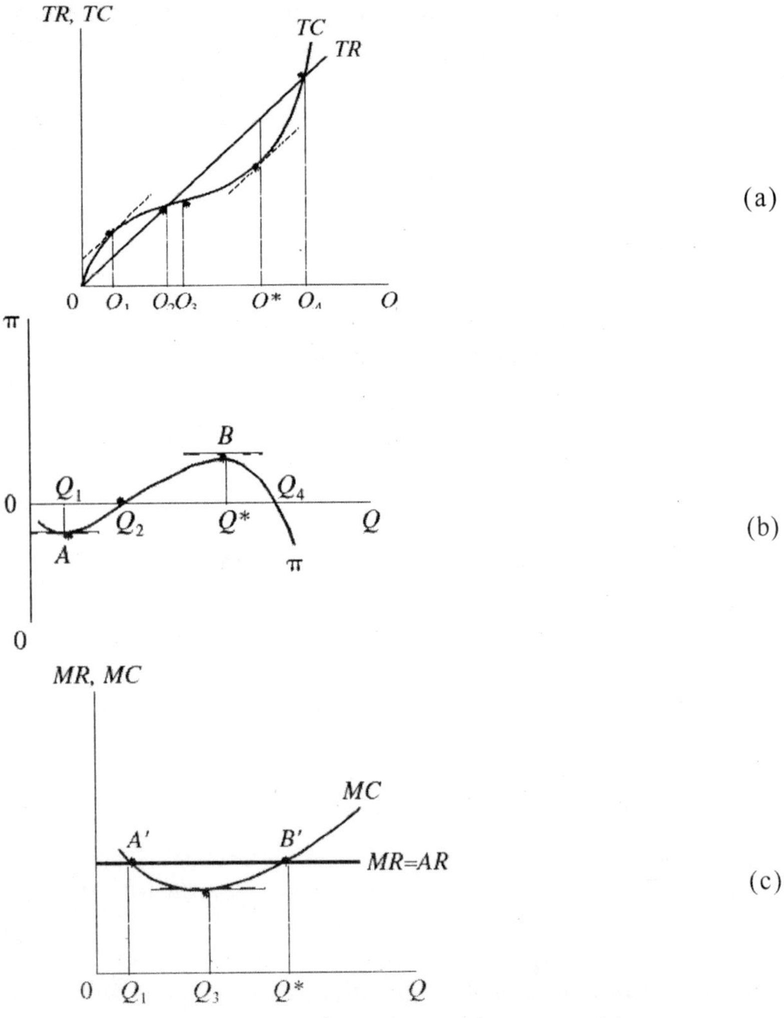

Figure: Profit maximization: perfect competition.

The shape of the total cost curve (TC) Figure (a) was discussed in last chapter and justified largely on the basis of the law of diminishing marginal product. The total revenue curve in Figure (a) is a straight line through the origin. The slope of the total revenue curve is equal to the fixed price of the product, P_0. In Figure (a) total profit (π) is illustrated by the vertical distance between the TR and TC curves. Total profit is also illustrated separately in Figure (b).

Total profit is maximized at output levels Q_1 and Q*, where $d\pi/dQ = 0$. This is the first-order condition for profit maximization. At both Q_1 and Q* the first-order conditions for profit maximization are satisfied, however only at Q* is the second-order condition for profit maximization satisfied. In the neighborhood around point B in Figure (b), the slope of the profit function is falling (i.e., $d^2\pi/dQ^2 < 0$. At point A, $d^2\pi/dQ^2 > 0$, which is a second-order condition for a local minimum. In other words, it is evident from the Figure (a) and (b) that total profit reaches a minimum at point A and a maximum at point B. Finally, note that at B' the profit-maximizing condition MC = MR, with MC intersecting the MR curve from below, is satisfied. At A', MC = MR but MC intersects MR from above, indicating that this point corresponds to a minimum profit level.

Note that the marginal cost curve in Figure (c) reaches its minimum value at output level Q_3, which corresponds to the inflection point on the total cost function.

MONOPOLY

We continue to assume that total cost is an increasing function of output [i.e., TC = TC(Q)]. Now, however, we assume that the selling price is a function of Q, that is,

$$P = P(Q) \tag{5.26}$$

where $dP/dQ < 0$. This is simply the demand function after applying the inverse-function rule. Substituting Equation (5.26) into Equation (5.10) yields

$$\pi(Q) = P(Q)Q - TC(Q) \tag{5.27}$$

For a profit maximum, the first- and second-order conditions for Equation (5.16) are, respectively,

$$d\pi/dQ = P + Q\left(\frac{dP}{dQ}\right) - \frac{dTC}{dQ} = 0 \tag{5.28}$$

$$\text{or } P + Q\left(\frac{dP}{dQ}\right) = MC \tag{5.29}$$

The term on the left-hand side of Equation (5.29) is the expression for marginal revenue. The second-order condition for a profit maximum is

$$\frac{d^2\pi}{dQ^2} - Q\left(\frac{d^2P}{dQ^2}\right) + 2\frac{dP}{dQ} - \frac{d^2TC}{dQ^2} < 0 \tag{5.30}$$

If we assume that the demand equation is linear, then Equation (5.26) may be written as

$$P = a + bQ \tag{5.31}$$

where b < 0. Substituting Equation (5.31) into (5.27) yields

$$\pi(Q) = (a + bQ)Q - TC(Q) = aQ + bQ^2 - TC(Q) \tag{5.32}$$

The first- and second-order conditions become

$$\frac{d\pi}{dQ} = a + 2bQ - \frac{dTC}{dQ} = 0$$

where

$$a + 2bQ = MR \tag{5.33}$$

Note that the marginal revenue equation is similar to the demand equation in that it has the same vertical intercept but twice the (negative) slope. Note also that, by definition, Equation (5.31) is the average revenue equation, that is,

$$AR = \frac{TR}{Q} = \frac{aQ + bQ^2}{Q} = a + bQ = P$$

The second-order condition for a profit maximum is

$$\frac{d^2\pi}{dQ^2} = 2b - \frac{d^2TC}{dQ^2} < 0 \tag{5.34}$$

The conditions for profit maximization assuming a linear demand curve are shown in Figure below. The cost functions displayed in figure (a) are essentially the same as those depicted in figure below. All of the cost functions represent the short run in production in which above, the prices of the factors of production are assumed to be fixed. The fundamental difference between the two sets of figures is that in the case of perfect competition the firm is assumed to be a "price taker," in the sense that the firm owner can sell as much product as required to maximize profit without affecting the market price of the product.

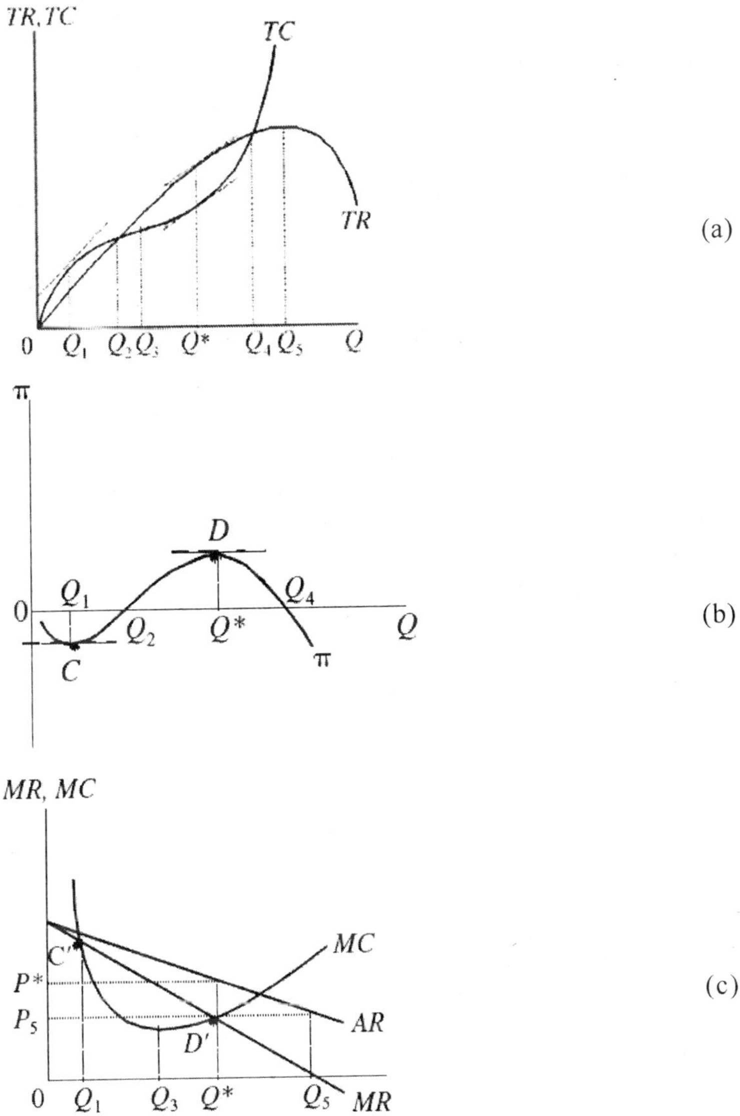

Figure: Profit maximization: monopoly.

In the case of monopoly, on the other hand, the firm is a "price maker," since increasing or decreasing output will raise or lower the market price. The simple explanation of this is that because the monopolist is the only firm in the industry, increasing or decreasing output will result in a right- or a left-shift in the market supply curve.

As always, the firm maximizes profit by producing at an output level where MR = MC, which in Figure above occurs at an output level of Q*. As before, total profit is optimized at output levels Q_1 and Q*, where $d\pi/dQ = 0$. At both Q_1 and Q* the first-order conditions for profit maximization are satisfied, however only at Q* is the second-order condition for profit maximization satisfied. In the neighborhood around point D in Figure (b), while the slope of the profit function is positive, it is falling (i.e., $d^2\pi/dQ^2 < 0$). At point C$d^2\pi/dQ^2 > 0$, which is the second-order condition for a local minimum. Again, note that at D' the profit-maximizing condition MC = MR, with MC intersecting the MR curve from below, is satisfied. At C', MC = MR but, MC intersects MR from above, indicating that this point corresponds to a minimum profit level.

Note that the marginal cost curve in Figure (c) reaches its minimum value at output level Q_3, which corresponds to the inflection point on the total cost function in Figure (a). Unlike the case of perfect competition, however, while the selling price is by definition equal to average revenue, in the case of monopoly the price is greater than marginal revenue. Once output has been determined by the firm, the selling price of the product will be defined along the demand curve. In fact, any market structure in which the firm faces a downward-sloping demand curve for its product will exhibit this characteristic. Only in the case of perfect competition, where the demand curve for the product is perfectly elastic, will the condition P = MR be satisfied for a profit-maximizing firm.

CONSTRAINED OPTIMIZATION: THE PROFIT FUNCTION

The preceding discussion provides valuable insights into the operations of a profit-maximizing firm. Unfortunately, that analysis suffers from a serious drawback. Implicit in that discussion was the assumption that the profit-maximizing firm possesses unlimited resources. No limits were placed on the amount the firm could spend on factors of production to achieve a profit-maximizing level of output. A similar solution arises when the firm's limited budget is nonbinding in the sense that the profit-maximizing level of output may be achieved before the firm's operating budget is exhausted. Such situations are usually referred to as unconstrained optimization problems.

By contrast, the operating budget available to management may be depleted long before the firm is able to achieve a profit-maximizing level of output. When this happens, the firm tries to earn as much profit as possible given the limited resources available to it. Such cases are referred to as constrained optimization problems. It is to this topic that the current discussion returns.

Consider, for example, a profit-maximizing firm that faces the following demand equation for its product

$$Q = \frac{20}{3} - \left(\frac{1}{3}\right)P + \left(\frac{10}{3}\right)A \tag{5.35}$$

where Q represents units of output, P is the selling price, and A is the number of units of advertising purchased by the firm.

The total cost of production equation for the firm is given as

$$TC = 100 + 2Q^2 + 500A \tag{5.36}$$

Equation (5.36) indicates that the cost per unit of advertising is Rs.500 per unit.

If there are no constraints placed on the operations of the firm, this becomes an unconstrained optimization problem. Solving Equation (5.35) for P and multiplying through by Q yields the total revenue equation

$$TR = 20Q + 10AQ - 3Q^2 \tag{5.37}$$

The total profit equation is

$$\pi = TR - TC = \left(20Q + 10AQ - 3Q^2\right) - \left(100 + 2Q^2 + 500A\right)$$

$$\pi = -100 + 20Q - 5Q^2 + 10AQ - 500A \tag{5.38}$$

The first-order conditions for profit maximization are

$$\frac{\partial \pi}{\partial Q} = 20 - 10Q + 10A = 0 \tag{5.39a}$$

$$\frac{\partial \pi}{\partial A} = 10Q - 500 = 0 \tag{5.39b}$$

Solving simultaneously Equations (5.39a) and (5.39b), and assuming that the second-order conditions for a maximum are satisfied, yields the profit maximizing solutions

P* = Rs.350; Q* = 50; A* = 48

In this example, profit-maximizing advertising expenditures are Rs. 500(48) =Rs.24,000. In other words, to achieve a profit-maximizing level of sales, the firm must spend Rs.24,000 in advertising expenditures. Suppose, however, that the budget for advertising expenditures is limited to Rs.5,000. What, then, is the profit-maximizing level of output. A formal statement of this problem is

$$\text{Maximize: } \pi(Q, A) = -100 + 20Q - 5Q^2 + 10AQ - 500A$$

$$\text{Subject to: } 500A = 5{,}000$$

SUBSTITUTION METHOD

One approach to this constrained profit maximization problem is the substitution method. Solving the constraint for A and substituting into Equation (5.38) yields

$$\pi = -100 + 20Q - 5Q^2 + 10(10)Q - 500(10)$$

$$= -5{,}100 + 120Q - 5Q^2 \quad (5.40)$$

Maximizing Equation (5.40) with respect to Q and solving we obtain.

$$\frac{d\pi}{dQ} = 120 - 10Q = 0$$

$$Q^* = 12$$

The second derivative of the profit function is

$$\frac{d^2\pi}{dQ^2} = -10 < 0$$

The negative value of the second derivative of Equation (5.40) guarantees that the second-order condition for a maximum is satisfied.

LAGRANGE MULTIPLIER METHOD

A more elegant solution to the constrained optimization is the Lagrange multiplier method. The elegance of this method can be found in the interpretation of the new variable, the Lagrange multiplier, which is usually designated as λ.

The first step in the Lagrange multiplier method is to bring all terms to right side of the constraint.

$$500A - 5{,}000 = 0 \tag{5.41}$$

Actually, it does not matter whether the terms are brought to the right or left side, although it will affect the interpretation of the value of λ. With Equation (5.41) we now form a new objective function called the Lagrange function, which is written as

$$\psi(Q, A, \lambda) = -100 + 20Q - 5Q^2 + 10AQ - 500A + \lambda(500A - 5{,}000) \tag{5.42}$$

It is important to note that the Lagrange function is equivalent to the original profit function, since the expression in the parentheses on the right is equal to zero. The first-order conditions for a maximum are

$$\frac{\partial \psi}{\partial Q} = 20 + 10A - 10Q = 0 \tag{5.43a}$$

$$\frac{\partial \psi}{\partial A} = 10Q - 500 - \lambda = 0 \tag{5.43b}$$

$$\frac{\partial \psi}{\partial \lambda} = 500A - 5{,}000 = 0 \tag{5.43c}$$

Note that, conveniently, Equation (5.43c) is the constraint. Equations (5.43) represent a system of three linear equations in three unknowns. Assuming that the second-order conditions for a maximum are satisfied, the simultaneous solution to Equations (5.43) yield

P* = Rs.84; Q* = 12; A* = 10; $\lambda^* = 380$

Note that these solution values are identical to the solution values in the unconstrained case. The Lagrange multiplier technique is a more powerful approach to the solution of constrained optimization problems because it allows us to solve for the Lagrange multiplier, λ. It can be demonstrated that the Lagrange multiplier is the marginal change in the maximum value of the objective function with respect to parametric changes in the value of the constraint. In the present example, the constraint is the firm's advertising budget. Defining the advertising budget as BA, the value of the Lagrange multiplier is

$$\lambda^* = \frac{\partial \psi}{\partial B_A} = \frac{\partial \pi^*}{\partial B_A} = 380 \qquad (5.44)$$

In the present example, the value of the Lagrange multiplier says that, in the limit, an increase in the firm's advertising budget by Rs.1 will result in a Rs.380 increase in the firm's maximum profit. Note that, by construction, the optimization procedure guarantees that the firm's profit will always be maximized subject to the constraint. Changing the constraint simply changes the maximum value of π.

Problem: The total profit equation of a firm is

$$\pi(x, y) = -1,000 - 100x - 50x^2 - 2xy - 12y^2 + 50y$$

where x and y represent the output levels for the two product lines.

a. Use the substitution method to determine the profit-maximizing output levels of goods x and y subject to the side condition that the sum of the two product lines equal 50 units.

b. Use the Lagrange multiplier method to verify your answer to part a.

c. What is the interpretation of the Lagrange multiplier?

Solution:

a. The formal statement of this problem is

Maximize: $\pi(x, y) = -1,000 - 100x - 50x^2 - 2xy - 12y^2 + 50y$

Subject to: $x + y = 50$

Solving the side constraint for y and substituting this result into the objective function yields

$$\pi(x) = -1,000 - 100x - 50x^2 - 2x(50 - x) - 12(50 - x)^2 + 50(50 - x)$$

$$= -28,500 + 950x + 60x^2$$

The first-order condition for a profit maximization is

$$\frac{d\pi}{dx} = 950 - 120x = 0$$

$$x^* = 7.92$$

units of output.

The optimal output level of y is determined by substituting this result into the constraint, that is, $y^* = 50 - 7.92 = 42.08$

The second derivative of the profit equation is $\frac{d^2\pi}{dx^2} = -120 < 0$

which verifies that the second-order condition for profit maximization is satisfied.

b. Forming the Lagrangian expression

$$\psi(x, y) = -1{,}000 - 100x - 50x^2 - 2xy - 12y^2 + 50y + \lambda(50 - x - y)$$

The first-order conditions are

$$\frac{\partial \psi}{\partial x} = -100 - 100x - 2y - \lambda = 0$$

$$\frac{\partial \psi}{\partial y} = -2x - 24y + 50 - \lambda = 0$$

$$\frac{\partial \psi}{\partial \lambda} = 50 - x - y = 0$$

This is a system of three linear equations in three unknowns. Solving this system simultaneously yields the optimal solution values

$x^* = 792$; $y^* = 4208$; $\lambda^* = -975$

c. Denoting total combined output capacity of the firm as k, which in this case is $k = x + y = 50$, the value of the Lagrangian multiplier is given as $\lambda^* = \frac{\partial \psi}{\partial k} = \frac{\partial \pi^*}{\partial k} =$ –Rs 975

The Lagrange multiplier says that, in the limit, a decrease in the firm's combined output level by 1 unit will result in a Rs.975 increase in the firm's maximum profit level.

TOTAL REVENUE MAXIMIZATION

Although profit maximization is the most commonly assumed organizational objective, it is by no means the only goal of the firm. Firms that are not owner operated and firms that operate in an imperfectly competitive environment often adopt an organizational strategy that focuses on maximizing market share. Unit sales are one way of defining market share. Total revenue generated is another. In this section we will assume that the objective of the firm is to maximize total revenue. The first- and second-order conditions are, respectively,

$$\frac{dTR}{dQ} = 0 \tag{5.45}$$

and

$$\frac{d^2TR}{dQ^2} < 0 \tag{5.46}$$

In Figure (a), (c) the profit-maximizing and revenue-maximizing levels of output are Q* and Q_5, respectively. If we assume that firms are price takers in resource markets (the price of labour and capital are fixed) because price and output are always positive, it can be easily demonstrated that the output level that maximizes total revenue will always be greater than the output level that maximizes total profit. This is because of the law of diminishing marginal product guarantees that the rate of increase in marginal cost is greater than the rate of increase in marginal revenue.

Note that in figure above total revenue is maximized where MR = 0, which occurs at an output level of Q_5. As before, in the case of a monopolist facing a downward-sloping demand curve, once output has been determined, the selling price of the product is determined along the demand curve. In Figure above, the revenue-maximizing price is P_5. Of course, revenue maximization is not possible in the perfectly competitive case, since the selling price of the product is fixed and parametric. The total revenue function is linear and revenue maximization, therefore, is not possible.

Note: Navistar International (NIC) is a holding company that operates through its principal operating subsidiaries, Navistar and Navistar Financial (NFC). The company is engaged in the manufacture and distribution of trucks, busses and engines. It is headquartered in Warrenville, Illinois and employs 17,800 people. For a case study visit company's site www.navistar.com

6

Perfect Competition and Monopoly

One of the most important decisions made by a manager is how to price the firm's product. If the firm is a profit maximizer, the price charged must be consistent with the realities of the market and economic environment within which the firm operates. Remember, price is determined through the interaction of supply and demand. A firm's ability to influence the selling price of its product stems from its ability to influence the market supply and, to a lesser extent, on its ability to influence consumer demand, as, say, through advertising.

One important element in the firm's ability to influence the economic environment within which it operates is the nature and degree of competition. A firm operating in an industry with many competitors may have little control over the selling price of its product because its ability to influence overall industry output is limited. In this case, the manager will attempt to maximize the firm's profit by minimizing the cost of production by employing the most efficient mix of productive resources. On the other hand, if the firm has the ability to significantly influence overall industry output, or if the firm faces a downward-sloping demand curve for its product, the manager will attempt to maximize profit by employing an efficient input mix and by selecting an optimal selling price.

Definition: Market structure refers to the environment within which buyers and sellers interact.

CHARACTERISTICS OF MARKET STRUCTURE

There are, perhaps, as many ways to classify a firm's competitive environment, or market structure, as there are industries. Consequently, no single economic theory is capable of providing a simple system of rules for optimal output pricing. It is possible, however, to categorize markets in terms of certain basic characteristics that can be useful as benchmarks for a more detailed analysis of optimal pricing behaviour. These characteristics of market structure include the number and size distribution of sellers, the number and size distribution of buyers, product differentiation, and the conditions of entry into and exit from the industry.

NUMBER AND SIZE DISTRIBUTION OF SELLERS

The ability of a firm to set its output price will largely depend on the number of firms in the same industry producing and selling that particular product. If there are a large number of equivalently sized firms, the ability of any single firm to independently set the selling price of its product will be severely limited. If the firm sets the price of its product higher than the rest of the industry, total sales volume probably will drop to zero. If, on the other hand, the manager of the firm sets the price too low, then while the firm will be able to sell all that it produces, it will not maximize profits. If, on the other hand, the firm is the only producer in the industry (monopoly) or one of a few large producers (oligopoly) satisfying the demand of the entire market, the manager's flexibility in pricing could be quite considerable.

NUMBER AND SIZE DISTRIBUTION OF BUYERS

Markets may also be categorized by the number and size distribution of buyers. When there are many small buyers of a particular good or service, each buyer will likely pay the same price. On the other hand, a buyer of a significant proportion of an industry's output will likely be in a position to extract price concessions from producers. Such situations refer to monopsonies (a single buyer) and oligopsonies (a few large buyers).

PRODUCT DIFFERENTIATION

Product differentiation is the degree that the output of one firm differs from that of other firms in the industry. When products are undifferentiated, consumers will decide which product to buy based primarily on price. In these markets, producers that price their product above the market price will be unable to sell their output. If there is no difference in price, consumers will not care which seller buy from. A given grade of wheat is an example of an undifferentiated good. At the other extreme, firms that produce goods having unique characteristics may be in a position to exert considerable control over the price of their product. In the automotive industry, for example, product differentiation is the rule.

CONDITIONS OF ENTRY AND EXIT

The ease with which firms are able to enter and exit a particular industry is also crucial in determining the nature of a market. When it is difficult for firms to enter into an industry, existing firms will have much greater influence in their output and pricing decisions than they would if they had to worry about increased competition from new comers, attracted to the industry by high profits.

In other words, managers can make pricing decisions without worrying about losing market share to new entrants. Thus if a firm owns a patent for the production of a good, this effectively prohibits other firms from entering the market. Such patent protection is a common feature of the pharmaceutical industry.

Exit conditions from the industry also affect managerial decisions. Suppose that a firm had been earning below-normal economic profit on the production and sale of a particular product. If the resources used in the production of that product are easily transferred to the production of some other good or service, some of those resources will be shifted to another industry. If, however, resources are highly specialized, they may have little value in another industry.

In this and the next two chapters we will examine four basic market structures: perfect competition, monopoly, oligopoly, and monopolistic competition. For purposes of our analysis we will assume that the firms in each of these market structures are price takers in resource markets and that they are producing in the short run. The result of these assumptions is that the cost curves of each firm in these industries will have the same general shape.

Firms differ in the proportion of total market demand that is satisfied by the production of each. This is illustrated in Figure below. At one extreme is perfect competition, in which the typical firm produces only a very small percentage of total industry output. At the other extreme is monopoly, where the firm is responsible for producing the entire output of the industry.

The percentage of total industry output produced is critical in the analysis of profit maximization because it defines the shape of the demand curve facing the output of each individual firm. The market structures that will be examined in this and the next chapter can be viewed as lying along a spectrum, with the position of each firm defined by the percentage of the market satisfied by the typical firm in each industry—from perfect competition at one extreme to monopoly at the other.

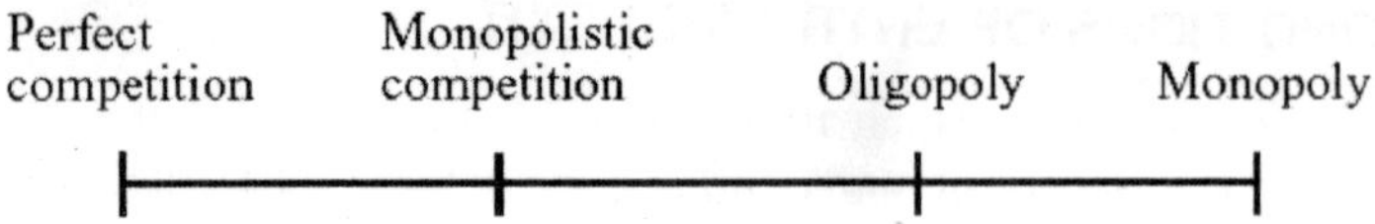

Figure: Market structure is defined in terms of the proportion of total market demand that is satisfied by the output of each firm in the industry.

PERFECT COMPETITION

The expression "perfect competition" is somewhat misleading because overt competition among firms in perfectly competitive industries is nonexistent. The reason for this is that managers of perfectly competitive firms do not take into consideration the actions of other firms in the industry when setting pricing policy. The reason for this is that changes in the output of each firm are too small relative to the total output of the industry to significantly affect the selling price. Thus, the selling price is parametric to the decision-making process.

The characteristics of a perfectly competitive market may be identified by using the criteria previously enumerated. Perfectly competitive industries are characterized by a large number of more or less equally sized firms. Because the contribution of each firm to the total output of the industry is small, the output decisions of any individual firm are unlikely to result in a noticeable shift in the supply curve. Thus, the output decisions of any individual firm will not significantly affect the market price. Thus, firms in perfectly competitive markets may be described as price takers. The inability to influence the market price through output changes means that the firm lacks market power.

Definition: Market power refers to the ability of a firm to influence the market price of its product by altering its level of output. A firm that produces a significant proportion of total industry output is said to have market power.

Definition: A firm is described as a price maker if it has market power. A price maker faces a downward-sloping demand curve for its product, which implies that the firm is able to alter the market price of its product by changing its output level.

Definition: Perfect competition refers to the market structure in which there are many utility-maximizing buyers and profit-maximizing sellers of a homogeneous good or service in which there is perfect mobility of factors of production and buyers, sellers have perfect information about market conditions, and entry into and exit from the industry is very easy.

Definition: A perfectly competitive firm is called a price taker because of its inability to influence the market price of its product by altering its level of output. This condition implies that a perfectly competitive firm should be able to sell as much of its good or service at the prevailing market price.

A second requirement of a perfectly competitive market is that there also be a large number of buyers. Since no buyer purchases a significant proportion of the total output of the industry, the actions of any single buyer will not result in a noticeable shift in the demand schedule and, therefore, will not significantly affect the equilibrium price of the product.

A third important characteristic of perfectly competitive markets is that the output of one firm cannot be distinguished from that of another firm in the same industry. The purchasing decisions of buyers, therefore, are based entirely on the selling price. In such a situation, individual firms are unable to raise their prices above the market-determined price for fear of being unable to attract buyers. Conversely, price cutting is counterproductive because firms can sell all their output at the higher, market-determined, price. Remember, the market clearing price of a product implies that there is neither a surplus nor a shortage of the commodity.

A final characteristic of perfectly competitive markets is that firms may easily enter or exit the industry. This characteristic allows firms to easily reallocate productive resources to be able to exploit the existence of economic profits. Similarly, if profits in a given industry are below normal, firms may easily shift productive resources out of the production of that particular good into the production of some other good for which profits are higher.

THE EQUILIBRIUM PRICE

As we have already discussed, the market-determined price of a good or service is accepted by the firm in a perfectly competitive industry as datum. Moreover, the equilibrium price and quantity of that good or service are determined through the interaction of supply and demand. The relation between the market-determined price and the output decision of a firm is illustrated in figure below.

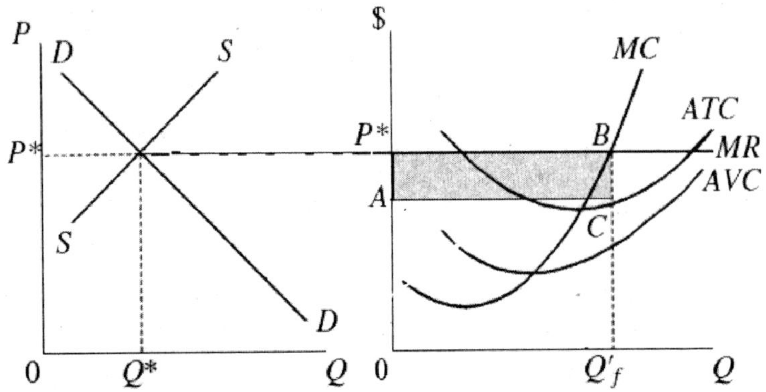

Figure: Short-run competitive equilibrium with positive (above-normal) economic profit.

The market demand for a good or service is the horizontal summation of the demands of individual consumers, while the market supply curve is the sum of individual firms' marginal cost (above-average variable cost) curves. As discussed earlier, if the prevailing price is abovc the equilibrium price (P*), a condition of excess supply forces producers to lower the selling price to rid themselves of excess inventories. As the price falls, the quantity of the product demanded rises, while the quantity supplied from current production falls (QF). Alternatively, if the selling price is below P* a situation of excess demand arises. This causes consumers to bid up the price of the product, thereby reducing the quantity available to meet consumer demands, while compelling producers to increase production. This adjustment dynamic will continue until both excess demand and excess supply have been eliminated at P*.

Problem: Suppose that a perfectly competitive industry comprises 1,000 identical firms. Suppose, further, that the market demand (Q_D) and supply (Q_S) functions are

$$Q_D = 170,000,000 - 10,000,000P$$

$$Q_S = 70,000,000 + 15,000,000P$$

a. Calculate the equilibrium market price and quantity?

b. Given your answer to part a, how much output will be produced by each firm in the industry?

c. Suppose that one of the firms in the industry goes out of business. What will be the effect on the equilibrium market price and quantity?

Solution:

a. Equating supply and demand yields

$$170,000,000 - 10,000,000P_S = 70,000,000 + 15,000,000P$$

P*= Rs. 4.00

Substituting the equilibrium price into either the market supply or demand equation yields

$$Q^* = 170,000,000 - 10,000,000(4)$$

$$= 70,000,000 + 15,000,000(4) = 130,000,000$$

b. Since there are 1,000 identical firms in the industry, the output of any individual firm Q_i is

$$Q_i = \frac{Q^*}{1,000} = \frac{130,000,000}{1,000} = 130,000$$

c. The supply equation of any individual firm in the industry is

$$Q_i = \frac{Q^*}{1,000} = 70,000 + 15,000P$$

Subtracting the supply of the individual firm from market supply yields

$$Q^* - Q_i = (70,000,000 + 15,000,000P) - (70,000 + 15,000P)$$

$$= 69,930,000 + 14,985,000P$$

Equating the new market demand and supply equations yields

$$170,000,000 - 10,000,000P = 69,930,000 + 14,985,000P$$

P*= Rs. 4.0052

$$Q^* = 170,000,000 - 10,000,000(4.0052)$$

$$= 69,930,000 + 14,985,000(4.0052) = 129,948,000$$

This problem illustrates the virtual inability of an individual firm in a perfectly competitive industry, which is characterized by a large number of firms, to significantly influence the market equilibrium price of a good or service by changing its level of output. For this reason, it is generally assumed that the market price for a perfectly competitive firm is parametric.

SHORT-RUN PROFIT MAXIMIZATION PRICE AND OUTPUT

If we assume that the perfectly competitive firm is a profit maximizer, the pricing conditions under which this objective is achieved are straightforward. First, define the firm's profit function as:

$$\pi(Q) = TR(Q) - TC(Q) \tag{6.1}$$

To determine the optimal output level that is consistent with the profit maximizing objective of this firm, the first-order condition dictates that we differentiate this expression with respect to Q and equate the resulting expression to zero. This procedure yields the following results

$$\frac{d\pi(Q)}{dQ} = \frac{dTR'(Q)}{dQ} - \frac{dTR(Q)}{dQ} = 0 \tag{6.2}$$

$$MR - MC = 0 \tag{6.3}$$

That is, the profit-maximizing condition for this firm is to equate marginal revenue with marginal cost, MR = MC.

To carry this analysis a bit further, recall that the definition of total revenue is TR = PQ. The preceding analysis of a perfectly competitive market reminds us that the selling price is determined in the market and is unaffected by the output decisions of any individual firm. Therefore,

$$\frac{dTR(Q)}{dQ} = MR = P_0$$

where the selling price is determined in the market and parametric to the firm's output decisions. Thus, the profit-maximizing condition for the perfectly competitive firm becomes

$$P_0 = MC \tag{6.5}$$

To maximize its short-run (and long-run) profits, the perfectly competitive firm must equate the market-determined selling price of its product with the marginal cost of producing that product. This condition was illustrated in Figure above.

Assuming that the firm has U-shaped average total and marginal cost curves, Figure above illustrates that the perfectly competitive firm maximizes profits by producing 0Qf units of output, that is, the output level at which P* = MC. The economic profit earned is illustrated by the shaded area AP*BC in the figure. This can be seen when we remember that

$$\pi = TR - TC = P^*Qf - ATC\left(Q_f\right) \tag{6.6}$$

This is illustrated in figure above as

$$\text{Area}\left\{AP^*BC\right\} = \text{Area}\left\{0P^*BQ_f\right\} - \text{Area}\left\{0ACQ_f\right\}$$

It should be remembered that the cost curves of figure above include a normal rate of profit. As a consequence, any time the firm has an average revenue greater than average cost, it is earning an economic profit.

Definition: A firm earns economic (above-normal) profit when total revenue is greater than total economic cost.

Problem: Consider the firm with the following total monthly cost function, which includes a normal profit.

$$TC = 1{,}000 + 2Q + 0.01Q^2$$

The firm operates in a perfectly competitive industry and sells its product at the market-determined price of Rs.10. To maximize total profits, what should be the firm's monthly output level, and how much economic profit will the firm earn each month?

Solution: First, determine the firm's marginal cost function by taking the first derivative of the total cost function with respect to Q.

$$\frac{dTC}{dQ} = MC = 2 + 0.02Q$$

As discussed earlier, profit is maximized by setting

MC = P*

thus

$$10 = 2 + 0.02Q \quad Q = 400$$

Economic profit is given by the expression

$$\pi = TR - TC = P^*Q - 1{,}000 - 2Q - 0.01Q^2$$

Rs. 10 $=(400) - 1{,}000 - 2(400) - 0.01(4002)$= Rs. 600

Problem: A perfectly competitive industry consists of 300 firms with identical cost structures. The respective market demand (Q_D) and market supply (Q_S) equations for the good produced by this industry are

$$Q_D = 3,000 - 60P$$

$$Q_S = 500 + 40P$$

a. What are the profit-maximizing price and output for each individual firm?

b. Assume that each firm is in long-run competitive equilibrium. Determine each firm's total revenue, total economic cost, and total economic profit.

Solution:

a. Firms in a perfectly competitive industry are characterized as "price takers." The profit-maximizing condition for firms in a perfectly competitive industry is P = MC, where the price is determined in the market. The market equilibrium price and quantity are determined by the condition

$$Q_D = Q_S$$

$$3,000 - 60P = 500 + 40P$$

P* = Rs. 25

$$Q^* = 500 + 40(25) = 500 + 1,000 = 1,500$$

The market equilibrium price, which is the price for each individual firm, is P* = Rs.25. The market equilibrium output is Q = 1,500. Since there are 300 firms in the industry, each firm supplies Q_i = 1,500/300 =5 units.

b. The total revenue of each firm in the industry is

$$TR = P^*Q_i = 25(5) = \text{Rs. } 125$$

In long-run competitive equilibrium, each firm earns zero economic profit. Since economic profit is defined as the difference between total revenue and total economic cost, then the total economic cost of each firm is $TC_{economic}$ = Rs. 125

Problem: The market-determined price in a perfectly competitive industry is P = Rs.10. Suppose that the total cost equation of an individual firm in the industry is given by the expression $TC = 100 + 5Q + 0.02Q^2$

a. What is the firm's profit-maximizing output level?

b. Given your answer to part a, what is the firm's total profit?

c. Diagram your answers to parts a and b.

Solution:

a. The profit-maximizing condition for a firm in a perfectly competitive industry is

$P_0 = MC$

The firm's marginal cost equation is

$$MC = \frac{dTC}{dQ} = 5 + 0.04Q$$

Substituting these results into the profit-maximizing condition yields

$$10 = 5 + 0.04Q$$

$$0.04Q = 5$$

$$Q^* = 125$$

b. The perfectly competitive firm's profit at

P* = Rs.10 and Q* = 125 is $\pi^* = TR - TC$

$$= P^*Q^* - \left(100 + 5Q^* + 0.02Q^{*2}\right)$$

$$= 10(125) - \left[100 + 5(125) + 0.02(125)^2\right]$$

$$= 1{,}250 - 1{,}037.50 = \$212.50$$

LONG-RUN PROFIT MAXIMIZATION PRICE AND OUTPUT

The shaded area in figure above represents the firm's total economic profit, that is, the excess of total revenue over total cost of production after a normal rate of return (normal profit) has been taken into consideration. In a perfectly competitive industry, however, this situation will not long persist.

We have already mentioned that a key characteristic of a perfectly competitive industry is ease of entry and exit by potentially competing firms. The existence of economic profits in an industry will attract productive resources into the production of that particular good or service. This transfer of resources will not, however, be instantaneous. It takes time for new firms to build production facilities and for existing firms to increase output. Nevertheless, in the long run all inputs are variable, and the increased output by new and existing firms will result in a right-shift of the market supply curve. Consider Figure above.

In Figure below, a right-shift of the industry supply function has resulted in a fall of the equilibrium price from P* to P' and an increase in the equilibrium output from Q* to Q'. But note what has happened to the typical firm in this perfectly competitive industry. The decline in the market equilibrium price has reduced the economic profit to the firm to the shaded area A'P'B'C'. In fact, because of the upward sloping marginal cost function, not only has the selling price of the firm's product fallen but the output of the typical firm has dropped as well.

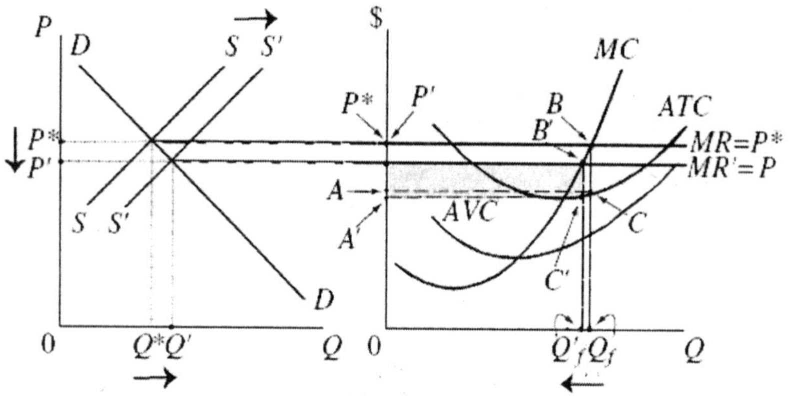

Figure: A price decline, short-run competitive equilibrium, and a reduction in economic (above-normal) profit.

It should, of course, be noted that this result holds only for the "typical" firm. In fact, there is no a priori reason to suppose that all firms in a perfectly competitive industry are of equal size. Some existing firms after all will have increased their output by expanding operations in response to the existence of economic profits. If we assume that all firms in this industry are approximately the same size, then the output of each firm will decline, although industry output will increase because there are a larger number of firms.

The situation depicted in figure above is not, however, stable in the long run, since the area A'P'B'C' still represents a situation in which the firm is earning economic profits. The continued existence of economic profits will continue to attract resources to the production of the particular good or service in question. The situation of long-run competitive equilibrium is illustrated in figure below.

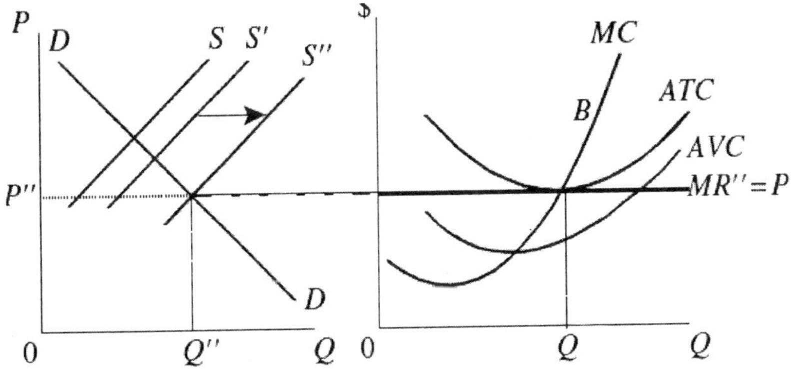

Figure: Long-run competitive equilibrium: zero economic (normal) profit.

Figure above represents a break-even situation for the firm. Since normal profit is included in total cost, at the point where MR'' = P'' = P = MC, total revenues equal total costs. In above figure, P and Q represent the break-even price and output level for the individual firm, respectively. In this situation, the firm described in Figure above is no longer earning an economic profit, and thus there is no further incentive for firms outside the industry to transfer productive resources into this industry to earn above-normal profits. In a sense, economic profits have been "competed" away. Since there is no further incentive for firms to enter, or for that matter exit, this industry, it may be said that the firm is in a position of long-run competitive equilibrium.

Definition: The break-even price is the price at which total revenue is equal to total economic cost.

Definition: Economic cost is the sum of the firm's total explicit and implicit costs.

Unfortunately, the process of adjustment to long-run competitive equilibrium may not be as smooth as described in connection with figure above.

If uncertainty and incomplete information lead managers to miscalculate, too many firms will enter the industry. This situation is depicted in Figure below: this firm is earning an economic loss (below-normal profit), illustrated by the area $P^{\dagger}A^{\dagger}B^{\dagger}C^{\dagger}$. This can be seen when we remember that

$$\pi = TR - TC = P^{\dagger}Q_f^{\dagger} = ATC \times Q_f^{\dagger} \tag{6.8}$$

This is illustrated in Figure below as

$$\text{Area}\left\{P^{\dagger}A^{\dagger}B^{\dagger}C^{\dagger}\right\} = \text{Area}\left\{0A^{\dagger}B^{\dagger}Q_f^{\dagger}\right\} - \text{Area}\left\{0P^{\dagger}C^{\dagger}Q_f^{\dagger}\right\} < 0 \tag{6.9}$$

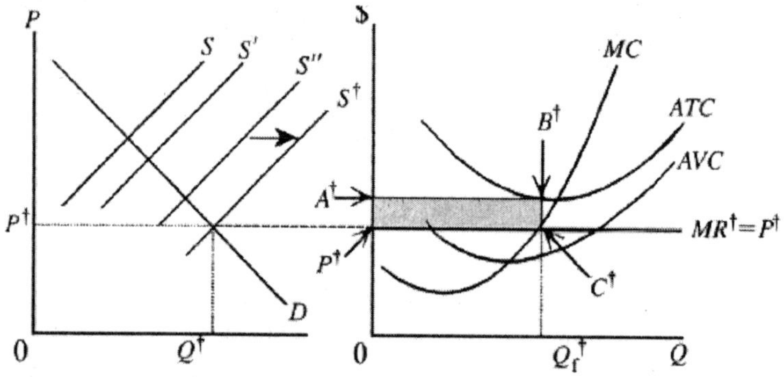

Figure: Short-run competitive equilibrium: economic loss (below-normal profit).

In this situation, firms in this industry are earning below-normal profits.

Under such circumstances, productive resources are transferred out of the production of this particular good or service, and output declines, resulting in a left-shift in the market supply function. Eventually, the selling price will rise and long-term competitive equilibrium will be reestablished.

Definition: A firm earns an economic loss when total revenue is less than total economic cost.

ECONOMIC LOSSES AND SHUTDOWN

For firms earning economic profits, the only meaningful decision facing management is the appropriate level of output. When firms are posting economic losses, however, the manager must decide whether it is in the long-run interests of the shareholders to continue producing that particular product. The course of action to be adopted by the manager will be based on a number of alternatives. The manager may decide, for example, to continue producing at the least unprofitable rate of output in the hope that prices will rebound, or the manager might decide to shut down operations completely. In the short run, the consequences of shutting down are illustrated in figure below.

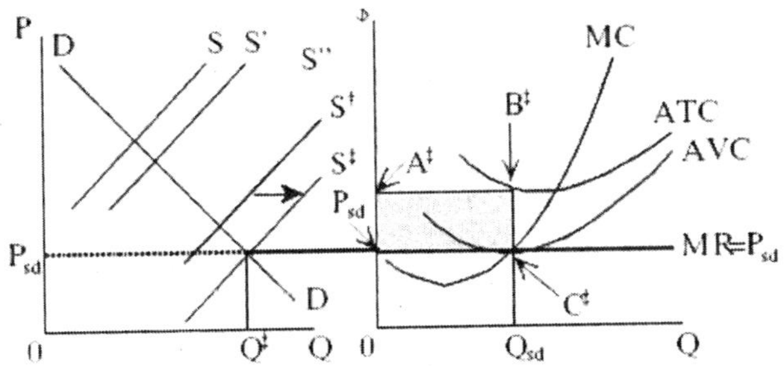

Figure: Shutdown price and output level.

TC = TFC + TVC

Definition: Total fixed cost refers to the firm's expenditures on fixed factors of production.

Definition: Total variable cost refers to the firm's expenditures on variable factors of production.

Dividing total cost by the level of output, we get

ATC = AFC + AVC

or

AFC = ATC – AVC

Diagrammatically, average fixed cost is measured by the vertical distance between the average total cost and average variable cost curves. It follows, therefore, that if the firm in figure above produces at $Q_f^{\dagger}$ it will recover all of its variable costs and at least some of its fixed costs.

The essential element in the manager's decision is the discrepancy between the selling price of the product and average variable cost. As long as price is greater than average variable cost, the firm minimizes its loss by continuing to produce. Otherwise, the firm will suffer larger short-run losses, since it is still responsible for its fixed costs. On the other hand, when the price falls below average fixed cost, it will be in the firm's best interest to shut down operations, since to continue to produce would result in losses greater than its fixed cost obligations. This concept is illustrated in figure above.

In figure below, P_{sd} and Q_{sd} represent the firm's shutdown price and output level, respectively. A profit-maximizing firm that produces at all will produce Q_{sd}, where MR = P_{sd} = MC. In fact, the firm is indifferent to producing Q_{sd}, since the firm's economic loss, which is given by the area of the rectangle P_{sd}A‡B‡C‡ is equivalent to the firm's total fixed costs (i.e., the firm's economic loss if it shuts down). Below the price Psd, however, the optimal decision by the firm's manager is to cease production, since the firm's total economic loss is greater than its total fixed cost.

Diagrammatically, it is often argued that the portion of the marginal cost curve that lies the average variable cost curve represents the firm's supply curve. The reason for this is that a profit-maximizing firm will produce at an output level at which P = MC. Since the marginal cost curve is upward sloping, then an increase in price essentially traces out the firm's supply curve.

In a previous chapter it was asserted that the market supply curve is the horizontal summation of the individual firms' supply curves. This assertion, however, is correct only as long as input prices remain unchanged. It is entirely possible that a simultaneous increase in the demand for inputs resulting from an increase in industry output will cause input prices to rise. When this occurs, the industry supply curve will be less price elastic than if input prices remained constant.

Definition: Shutdown price is equal to the minimum average variable cost of producing a good or service. Below this price the firm will shut down because the firm's loss, which will equal the total fixed cost, will be less than if the firm continues to stay in business.

We have mentioned that the optimal rule for the manager of the firm in the short run is to shut down when the selling price of the product falls below P_{sd}. This decision rule is subject to two qualifications. First, the firm will not shut down every time P < AVC. In many cases, the firm will incur substantial costs when a production process is shut down or restarted, as in the case of a blast furnace for manufacturing steel, which may require several days to bring up to operating temperature. Similarly, a firm that shuts down and then reopens may find that its customers are buying from other suppliers. The decision to shut down operations, therefore, is made only if in the opinion of the manager the price will stay below average variable cost for an extended period of time.

The second qualification involves the distinction between the short run and the long run. The decision to shut down depends on whether the firm can make a contribution to its fixed cost by continuing to produce. In the long run, however, there are no fixed costs. Buildings are sold, equipment is auctioned off, contracts expire, and so on. Thus, in the long run, as long as price is expected to remain below average variable cost, the firm will shut down. This decision rule applies in both the short and the long run.

Problem: A perfectly-competitive firm faces the following total variable cost function where Q is quantity. Below what price should the firm shut down its operations?

$$TVC = 150Q - 20Q^2 + Q^3$$

Solution: Find the output level that corresponds to the minimum average variable cost. First, calculate average variable cost

$$TVC = \frac{TVC}{Q} = 150 - 20Q + Q^2$$

Next, take the first derivative, equate the result to zero, and solve.

$$\frac{dAVC}{dQ} = -20 + 2Q = 0$$

$$Q = 10$$

Since the firm operates at the point where P = MC, substitute this result into the marginal cost function to yield

$$P = MC = \frac{dTVC}{dQ} = 150 + 40Q + 3Q^2$$

$$= 150 - 40(10) + 3(102) = \text{Rs. } 50$$

Thus, if the price falls below Rs.50 per unit, then the firm should shut down.

Problem: Hale and Hearty Limited (HH) is a small distributor of B&Q Food stores, Inc., in the highly competitive health care products industry. The market-determined price of a 100-tablet vial of HH's most successful product, papaya extract, is Rs.10. HH's total cost (TC) function is given as

$$TC = 100 + 2Q + 0.01Q^2$$

a. What is the firm's profit-maximizing level of output? What is the firm's profit at the profit-maximizing output level? Is HH in short-run or longrun competitive equilibrium? Explain.

b. At P =Rs.10, what is HH's break-even output level?

c. What is HH's long-run break-even price and output level?

d. What is HH's shutdown price and output level? Does this price–output combination constitute a short-run or a long-run competitive equilibrium? Explain.

Solution:

a. Total profit is defined as the difference between total revenue (TR) and total cost, that is,

$$\pi = TR - TC = PQ - TC = 10Q - \left(100 + 2Q + 0.01Q^2\right)$$

$$= -100 + 8Q - 0.01Q^2$$

Differentiating this expression with respect to Q and setting the result equal to zero (the first-order condition for a local maximization) yields

$$\frac{d\pi}{dQ} = 8 - 0.02Q = 0$$

$$Q^* = 400$$

b. To verify that this output constitutes a maximum, differentiate the marginal profit function (take the second derivative of the total profit function). A negative value for the resulting expression constitutes a second-order condition for a local maximum.

$$\frac{d^2\pi}{dQ^2} = -0.02 < 0$$

Total profit at the profit-maximizing output level is

$$\pi^* = -100 + 8(400) - 0.01(400)^2$$

$$= -100 + 3,200 - 1,600 = \text{Rs. } 1,500$$

HH is in short-run competitive equilibrium. In perfectly competitive markets, individual firms earn no economic profit in the long run. HH, however, is earning an economic profit of Rs.1,500, which will attract new firms into the industry, which will increase supply and drive down the selling price of papaya extract (assuming that the demand for the product remains unchanged).

c. The break-even condition is defined as

TR = TC

Substituting into this definition gives

$$10Q = 100 + 2Q + 0.01Q^2$$

$$100 - 8Q + 0.01Q^2 = 0$$

This equation, which has two solution values, is of the general form

$$aQ^2 + bQ + c = 0$$

The solution values may be determined by factoring this equation, or by applying the quadratic formula, which is given as

$$Q_{1,2} = \frac{-b \pm \sqrt{b^2 - 4ac}}{2a}$$

$$= \frac{-(-8) \pm \sqrt{\left[(-8)^2 - 4(0.01)(100)\right]}}{2(0.01)}$$

$$= \frac{8 \pm \sqrt{(64 - 4)}}{0.02} = \frac{8 \pm 7.746}{0.02}$$

$$Q_1 = \frac{8 + 7.746}{0.02} = 787.3$$

$$Q_2 = \frac{8 - 7.746}{0.02} = 12.7$$

These results indicate that there are two break-even output levels at P = Rs.10. Consider Figure above.

d. In long-run competitive equilibrium, no firm in the industry earns an economic profit. It is an equilibrium in that while each firm earns a "normal" profit, there is no incentive for new firms to enter the industry, nor is there an incentive for existing firms to leave. The break-even price is defined in terms of the output level of which price is equal to minimum average total cost (ATC), that is, $P_{be} = ATC_{\min}$

ATC is given by the expression

$$ATC = \frac{TC}{Q} = \frac{100 + 2Q + 0.01Q^2}{Q} = 100Q^{-1} + 2 + 0.01Q$$

Minimizing this expression yields

$$\frac{dATC}{dQ} = -100Q^{-2} + 0.01 = 0$$

which is a first-order condition for a local minimum.

$$0.01Q^2 = 100$$

$$Q^2 = 10,000$$

$$Q_{be} 100$$

$$\frac{d^2ATC}{dQ^2} = 200Q^{-3} = \frac{200}{(100)^3 > 0}$$

which is a second-order condition for a local minimum.

Substituting this result into the preceding condition yields

$$P_{be} = ATC_{\min} = 100Q^{-1} + 2 + 0.01Q = \frac{100}{100} + 2 + 0.01(100) = 4$$

e. The firm's shutdown price is defined in terms of the output level of which price is equal to minimum average variable cost (AVC), that is, $P_{sd} = ATC_{\min}$

AVC is given by the expression

$$AVC = \frac{TVC}{Q} = \frac{2Q + 0.01Q^2}{Q} = 2 + 0.01Q$$

Since this expression is linear, AVC is minimized where $Q_{sd} = 0$. Substituting this result into the preceding condition we get

$$P_{sd} = AVC_{min} = 2 + 0.01Q = 2 + 0.01(0) = \$2$$

This result is a short-run competitive equilibrium. At a price below Rs.2, the firm's loss will exceed its fixed costs. Under these circumstances, it will pay the firm to go out of business, in which case its short-run loss will be limited to its fixed costs. Because the firm is earning an economic loss for P < ATC, there will be an incentive for firms to exit the industry, which will reduce supply. If the demand for papaya extract is constant, the result will be an increase in price. Firms will continue to exit the industry until economic losses have been eliminated, as illustrated in Figure below.

MONOPOLY

We now turn out attention to the other market extreme, monopoly. Monopolies may be described in terms of the same characteristics used to discuss perfect competition.

In the case of a monopoly, the industry is dominated by a single producer. The most obvious implication of this is that the demand curve faced by the monopolist is the same downward-sloping market demand curve. Unlike the perfectly competitive firm, which produces too small a proportion of total industry output to significantly affect the market price, the output of the monopolist, is total industry output. Thus, for the monopolist, market prices are no longer parametric. An increase or decrease in the output will lower or raise the market price of the monopolist's product. For this reason, monopolists may be characterized as price makers.

Definition: The term "monopoly" is used to describe the market structure in which there is only one producer of a good or service for which there are no close substitutes and entry into and exit from the industry is impossible.

In the case of a monopoly, the number and size distribution of buyers is largely irrelevant, since the buyers of the firm's output have no bargaining power with which to influence prices. Such bargaining power is usually manifested through the explicit or implicit threat to obtain the desired product from a competing firm, which is nonexistent in a market sewed by a monopoly.

Goods and services produced by monopolies are unique. That is, the output of a monopolist has no close substitutes. In one respect, monopolies are diametrically opposed to perfectly competitive firm in that they do not have to compete with other firms in the industry. The output level of individual firms in perfectly competitive industries is so small relative to total industry output that each firm may effectively ignore the output decisions of other firms. A monopolist, on the other hand, is the only seller in an industry and, therefore, has no competitors.

For the firm to continue as a monopolist in the long run, there must exist barriers that prevent the entry of other firms into the industry. Such restrictions may be the result of the monopolist's control over scarce productive resources, patent rights, access to unique managerial talent, economies of scale, location, and so on. Another significant barrier to entry is found when a firm has a government franchise to be the sole provider of a good or service.

CONTROLLING SCARCE PRODUCTIVE RESOURCES

Until the 1940s, the Aluminum Company of America owned or controlled nearly 100% of the world's bauxite deposits. Since bauxite is needed to manufacture aluminum, that company, now known as Alcoa, was the sole producer and distributor of aluminum. Clearly, a firm that controls the entire supply of a vital factor of production will control production for the entire industry.

Patient rights

A legal barrier to the entry of new firms into an industry is the patent. A patent, which is granted by a national government, is the exclusive right to a product or process by its inventor.2 In the United States, patent protection is granted by Congress for a period of 20 years. Of course, during that period, the owner of the patent has the sole authority to produce for sale in the market the commodity protected by the patent.

Definition: A patent is the exclusive right granted to an inventor by government to a product or a process.

The rationale behind the granting of patents is that they provide an incentive for product research, development, invention, and innovation.

Without such protection, investors are less likely to incur the often substantial development costs and risks associated with bringing a new product to market. On the other hand, the existence of patents discourages competition, which promotes product innovation, the development of more efficient, less costly production techniques, and lower prices. It is for these reasons that patents are not granted in perpetuity.

Arguments for and against patents have recently taken center stage in the United States in the debate over the escalating cost of health care. A frequently cited culprit has been the high price of prescription drugs. Pharmaceutical companies have been granted thousands of patents for a wide range of new prescription medicines, for which they have been able to charge monopoly prices.

While recognizing that the high price of prescription medicines places a financial burden on some consumers, particularly the elderly, these companies nonetheless argue that the high prices are necessary as compensation for the millions of Rupees in research and development costs. The companies also argue that these profits are necessary as compensation for the risks incurred in developing new products that are never brought to market or do not receive approval by the U.S. Food and Drug Administration.

GOVERNMENT FRANCHISE

Perhaps the most common example of a monopoly in the United States is the government franchise. Many firms are monopolies because the government has granted them the sole authority to supply a particular product within a given region. Public utilities are the most recognizable of government franchises. Government-franchised monopolies are usually justified on the grounds that it is more efficient for a single firm to produce, say, electricity because of the large economies of scale involved and the desire to eliminate competing power grids. In exchange for this franchise, public utilities have agreed to be regulated. In principle, public utility commissions regulate the rates charged to ensure that the firm does not abuse its monopoly power.

Definition: A government franchise is a publicly authorized monopoly. Fairness is another reason frequently cited in defense of government regulation. In many states, local telephone service is subject to regulation to ensure that consumers have access to affordable service. In fact, the profits earned by telephone companies from business users subsidize private household use, which is billed to individual consumers at below cost.

LAWSUITS

Monopolists can attempt to protect exclusive market positions by filing lawsuits against potential competitors claiming patent or copyright infringement. Start-up companies typically need to get their products to market as quickly as possible to generate cash flow. Regardless of the merits of lawsuits that may be brought against them, such cash-poor companies are financially unprepared to weather these legal challenges. In the end, the companies may be forced out of business, or may even be acquired by the monopolist.

SHORT-RUN PROFIT-MAXIMIZING PRICE AND OUTPUT

The case of the monopolist is illustrated in figure below. In the diagram we note that the monopolist faces the downward-sloping market demand curve, and the usual U-shaped marginal and average total cost curves. As in the case of a perfectly competitive firm, the profit-maximizing monopolist will adjust its output level up to the point at which the marginal cost of producing an addition unit of the good is just equal to the marginal revenue from its sale. This condition is satisfied at point E in Figure above, at output level Q_m.

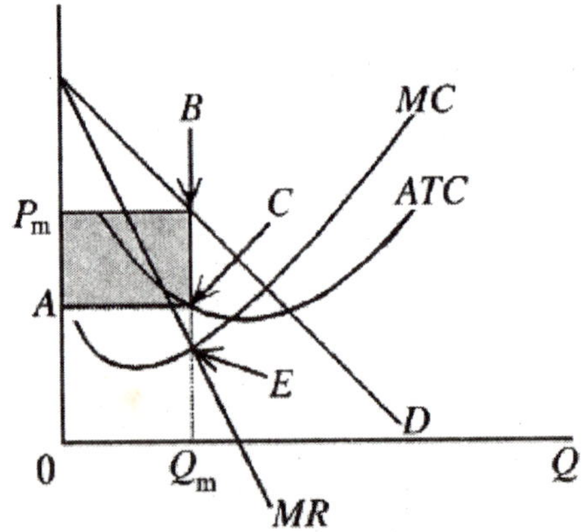

Figure: Monopoly: short-run and long-run profit-maximizing price and output.

The selling price of the monopolist output is determined along the market demand function at Pm. At this price–quantity combination, the economic profit earned by the firm is illustrated by the shaded area AP_mBC.

If entry into this industry were relatively easy, the existence of such economic profits would attract scarce productive resources into the production of the monopolist's product. As new firms entered the industry, the demand function facing the monopolist at any given price would become more elastic (flatter), with economic profit being dissipated as a result of increase competition. Eventually, the industry might even approach the perfectly competitive market structure.

If, on the other hand, the monopolist's position in the industry is secure, economic profits could persist indefinitely. Thus, figure above may depict both short-run and long-run profit-maximizing price and output.

Problem: Suppose that the total cost (TC) and demand equations for a monopolist is given by the following expressions:

$$TC = 500 + 20Q^2$$

$$P = 400 - 20Q$$

What are the profit-maximizing price and quantity?

Solution: The total revenue function for the firm is

$$TR = OQ = 400Q - 20Q^2$$

Define total profit as

$$\pi = TR - TC = 400Q - 20Q^2 - 500 - 20Q^2$$

Taking the first derivative, and setting the resulting expression equal to zero, yields the profit-maximizing output level.

$$\frac{d\pi}{dQ} = 400 - 80Q = 0$$

$$Q^* = 5$$

Substituting this result into the demand equation yields the selling price of the product

$$P^* = 400 - 20(5) = \text{Rs. } 300$$

LONG-RUN PROFIT-MAXIMIZING PRICE AND OUTPUT

The long-run profit-maximizing price and output for a monopolist in the long run are the same as the short-run profit-maximizing price and output. The reason for this is that in the absence of changes in demand, profits to the monopolist will continue because restrictions to entry into the industry guarantee that these profits will not be competed away.

Problem: Suppose that an industry is dominated by a single producer and that the demand for its product is

$$Q_D = 3,000 - 60P$$

Suppose further that the total cost function of the firm is

$$TC = 100 + 5Q + \frac{1}{480}Q^2$$

a. What is the monopolist's profit-maximizing price and output?

b. Given your answer to part a, what is the firm's economic profit?

Solution:

a. The profit-maximizing condition for a monopolist is

MR = MC

The monopolist's total revenue equation is

RT = PQ

Solving the demand equation for P yields

$$P = 50 - \frac{1}{60}Q$$

Substituting this result into the total revenue equation yields

$$TR = \left[50 - \left(\frac{1}{60}\right)Q\right]Q = 50Q - \left(\frac{1}{60}\right)Q^2$$

The monopolist's marginal revenue equation is

$$MR = \frac{dTR}{dQ} = 50 - \left(\frac{1}{30}\right)Q$$

The monopolist's marginal cost equation is

$$MC = \frac{dTC}{dQ} = 5 + \left(\frac{1}{240}\right)Q$$

Substituting these results into the profit-maximizing condition yields the profit-maximizing output level

$$50-\left(\frac{1}{30}\right)Q=5+\left(\frac{1}{240}\right)Q$$

$$Q^*=1,200$$

To determine the profit-maximizing price, substitute this result into the demand equation:

$$P^*=50-\left(\frac{1}{60}\right)1,200=50-20=\text{Rs. }30$$

b. The monopolists profit at P* = Rs.30 and Q* = 1,200 is

$$\pi^*=TR-TC=P^*Q^*-\left(100+5Q^*+\left(\frac{1}{480}\right)Q^{*2}\right)$$

$$=30(1,200)-\left[100+5(1,200)+\left(\frac{1}{480}\right)(1,200)^2\right]=\$26,900$$

Problem: Explain why a profit-maximizing monopolist would never produce at an output level (and charge a price) that corresponded to the inelastic portion of a linear market demand curve.

Solution: In the case of a linear market demand curve, when demand is elastic ε_p (<-1), marginal revenue is positive (MR $>$ 0) and total revenue is increasing. When the price elasticity of demand is unitary ε_p $(=-1)$, marginal revenue is zero (MR = 0) and total revenue is maximized. Finally, when the price elasticity of demand is inelastic $(-1<\varepsilon_p<0)$, marginal revenue is negative (MR $<$ 0) and total revenue is decreasing. Thus, if the monopolist were to produce at an output level corresponding to the inelastic portion of the demand curve, the corresponding marginal revenue would be negative. Since profit is maximized where MR = MC, this would imply that MC $<$ 0, which is false by assumption. In other words, since total cost is assumed to be an increasing function of total output, then marginal cost cannot be negative, and a profit-maximizing monopolist would not produce where MC = MR.

MONOPOLY AND THE PRICE ELASTICITY OF DEMAND

Consider the relationship between the price charged by a profit-maximizing monopolist and the price elasticity of demand. From Equation

$$\frac{d\pi(Q)}{dQ} = \frac{dTR(Q)}{dQ} - \frac{dTC(Q)}{dQ} = 0 \tag{6.2}$$

Recall that because the monopolist faces a downward-sloping demand curve, price is functionally related to output. Thus, Equation (6.2) may be rewritten as

$$\frac{d\pi(Q)}{dQ} = P + Q\left(\frac{dP}{dQ}\right) - MC = 0 \tag{6.10}$$

Rearranging the right-hand side of Equation (6.10) we obtain

$$-Q\left(\frac{dP}{dQ}\right) = P - MC \tag{6.11}$$

Dividing both sides of Equation (6.11) by P, we write

$$\left(-\frac{Q}{P}\right)\left(\frac{dP}{dQ}\right) = \frac{P - MC}{P}$$

$$\frac{-1}{\varepsilon_p} = \frac{P - MC}{P} \tag{6.12}$$

The profit-maximizing monopolist produces where MR = MC. Since marginal cost is normally positive, the left-hand side of Equation (6.12) implies that $-1 \leq \varepsilon_p < -\infty$; that is, demand is price elastic. Thus, a monopolist will produce, and price, along the elastic portion of the demand curve.

LERNER INDEX

Equation (6.12) is referred to as the Lerner index. The Lerner index, which is simply the negative of the inverse of the price elasticity of demand, is a measure of monopoly power and takes on values between 0 and 1. The greater the difference between price and marginal cost (marginal revenue) for a profit-maximizing firm, the greater the value of the Lerner index, and thus the greater the monopoly power of the firm. This result also suggests that the more elastic (flatter) the demand curve, the smaller will be the firm's proportional markup over marginal cost. A special case of the Lerner index is the case of a profit-maximizing, perfectly competitive firm where P = MC. The reader will verify that in this case the value of the Lerner index is 0 (i.e., no monopoly power).

Definition: The Lerner index is a measure of the monopoly power of a firm.

Problem: The market-determined price in a perfectly competitive industry is P = Rs.10. The total cost equation of an individual firm in this industry is

$TC = 100 + 6Q + Q^2$

Calculate the value of the Lerner index for this firm.

Solution: The profit equation for this firm is

$$\pi = TR - TC = 10Q - \left(100 + 6Q + Q^2\right)$$

$$= -100 + 4Q - Q^2$$

Assuming that the second-order condition is satisfied, the profit-maximizing output level is found by taking the first derivative of the total profit function, setting the results equal to zero, and solving for Q.

$$\frac{d\pi}{dQ} = 4 - 2Q = 0$$

$$Q^* = 2$$

Marginal cost of this firm at $Q^* = 2$ is

$$MC = \frac{dTC}{dQ} = 6 + 2Q = 6 + 2(2) = 10$$

Thus, the value of the Lerner index is

$$\frac{-1}{\varepsilon_p} = \frac{P - MC}{P} = \frac{10 - 10}{10} = \frac{0}{10} = 0$$

Thus, this perfectly competitive firm has no monopoly power. The firm's proportional mark-up over marginal cost is zero; that is, the firm is earning zero economic profit.

Problem: The demand equation for a product sold by a monopolist is

$P = 10 - Q$

The total cost equation of the firm is

$TC = 100 + 6Q + Q^2$

Calculate the value of the Lerner index for this firm.

Solution: The profit equation for this firm is

$$\pi = TR - TC = PQ - TC = (10 - Q)Q - (100 + 6Q + Q^2)$$

$$= -100 + 4Q - 2Q^2$$

Assuming that the second-order condition is satisfied, the profit-maximizing output level is found by taking the first derivative of the total profit function, setting the results equal to zero, and solving for Q.

$$\frac{d\pi}{dQ} = 4 - 4Q = 0$$

$$Q^* = 1$$

Substituting this into the demand equation gives the profit-maximizing price

$P^* = 10 - Q = 10 - 1 = 9$

Marginal cost of this firm at $Q^* = 1$ is

$$MC = \frac{dTC}{dQ} = 6 + 2Q = 6 + 2(1) = 8$$

Thus, the value of the Lerner index is

$$\frac{-1}{\varepsilon_p} = \frac{P - MC}{P} = \frac{9-8}{8} = \frac{1}{8} = 0.125$$

Thus, this firm enjoys monopoly power. The firm's proportional mark-up over marginal cost is 11.1%; that is, the firm is earning positive economic profit.

EVALUATING PERFECT COMPETITION AND MONOPOLY

In closing this chapter a few words are in order about the societal implications of a market structure that is characterized as perfectly competitive versus one that is dominated by a monopolist. In the case of a perfectly competitive output market, the equilibrium price and quantity are determined through the interaction of supply and demand forces. In

Figure below, the equilibrium price and quantity are determined at point E. At that point the equilibrium price and quantity in a perfectly competitive market are P_{pc} and Q_{pc}, respectively. In the case of a market dominated by a single producer, however, the equilibrium price and quantity are determined where MC = MR. In Figure below the equilibrium price and quantity are P_m and Q_m, respectively. From society's perspective, perfect competition is clearly preferable to monopoly because it results, even in the short run, in greater output and lower prices. This is not, however, the end of the story.

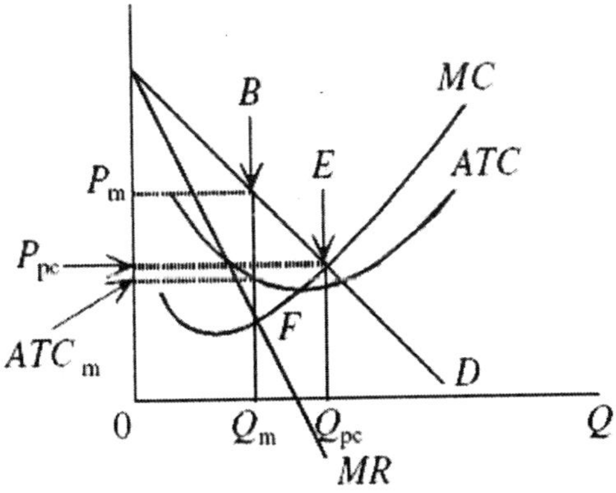

Figure: Evaluating monopoly and perfect competition.

In Figure above both the monopolist and the perfectly competitive firm are making economic profits. Unlike the case of an industry comprising a single producer, however, this situation will set into motion competitive forces that will eventually drive down prices and increase output further in markets that are characterized as perfectly competitive. Consider Figure below.

As the lure of economic profit attracts new firms into the perfectly competitive industry, the market supply curve shifts to the right. As discussed earlier, long-run competitive equilibrium will be established where demand equals supply at point E'. At this point the typical firm in a perfectly competitive industry is making only normal profits. Since firms will no longer be attracted into the industry or compelled to leave it, the long-run competitive equilibrium price and quantity are P_{pc}' and Q_{pc}', respectively. For the monopolist, however, since new firms may neither enter nor exit the industry, equilibrium continues to be determined at point F and the longrun (and short-run) price and quantity remain P_m and Q_m, respectively. Clearly in this idealized case, society is better off when output is generated by perfectly competitive industries.

Monopolists are also less efficient than perfectly competitive firms, as an examination of Figure below illustrates. In long-run competitive equilibrium, the selling price of the product is equal to minimum cost per unit (i.e., $P_{pc'} = ATC_{min}$). In the case of an industry dominated by a monopolist, however, this is clearly not the case. At the profit-maximizing output level Q_m, the cost per unit of output is ATC_m. This solution is clearly inefficient and represents a misallocation of society's productive resources in the sense that not enough of the product is being produced. These results have profound implications for government-franchised monopolies, such as public utilities. At what price should the output of these firms be regulated? This question will be taken up in a later chapter. However, considerations of public welfare and efficiency should be central to regulators' concerns.

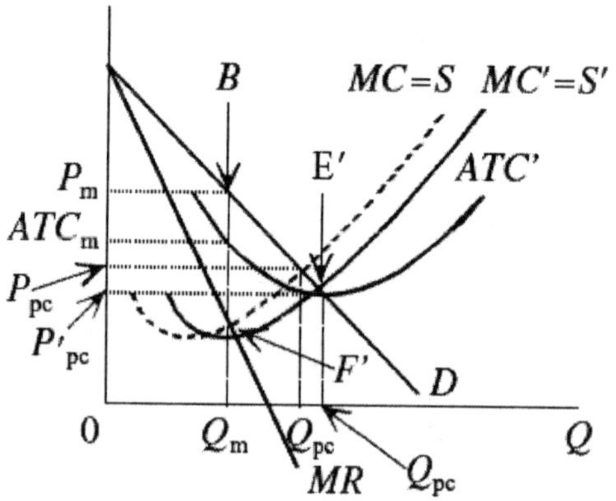

Figure: Long-run competitive equilibrium: perfect competition and monopoly.

WELFARE EFFECTS OF MONOPOLY

Another approach to evaluating the relative merits of firms in perfectly competitive industries against those of a monopoly is by employing the concepts of consumer surplus and producer surplus.

CONSUMER SURPLUS

Consider figure below, which depicts the case of the perfectly competitive market. The area of the shaded region in the diagram 0AEQ* represented the total benefits derived by consumers in competitive equilibrium. Total expenditures on Q* units, however, is given by the area 0P*EQ*. The difference between the total net benefits received from the consumption of Q* units of output and total expenditures on Q* units of output is given by the shaded area 0AEQ* – 0P*EQ* = P*AE. Consumer surplus is given by the shaded area P*AE.

Consumer surplus is the difference between what consumers would be prepared to pay for a given quantity of a good or service and the amount they actually pay. The idea of consumer surplus is a derivation of the law of diminishing marginal utility. The law of diminishing marginal utility says that individuals receive incrementally less satisfaction from the consumption of additional units of a good or service and thus pay less for those additional units. Thus, in Figure above, consumers are willing to pay more than P* for the first unit of Q, but are prepared to pay just P* for the Q*th unit.

Definition: Consumer surplus is the difference between what consumers are willing to pay for a given quantity of a good or service and the amount that they actually pay. Diagrammatically, consumer surplus is illustrated as the area below a downward-sloping demand curve but above the selling price.

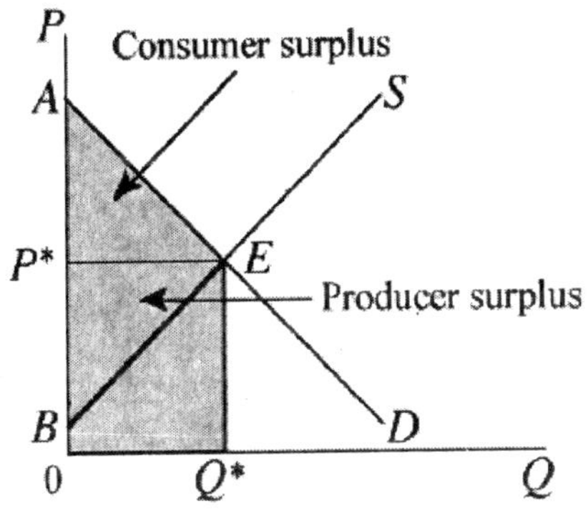

Figure: Consumer and producer surplus.

PRODUCER SURPLUS

Consider, again, Figure above Recalling that the firm's supply curve is the marginal cost curve above minimum average variable cost, the total cost of producing Q* units of output is given by the area 0BEQ*. Total revenues (consumer expenditures) earned from the sale of Q* units of output is given by the area 0P*EQ*. The difference between the total revenues from the sale of Q* and the total cost of producing Q* (total economic profit) is given by the shaded area 0BEQ* – 0P*EQ* = BP*E. The shaded area BP*E is referred to as producer surplus. Producer surplus is the difference between the total revenues earned from the production and sale of a given quantity of output and what the firm would have been willing to accept for the production and sale of that quantity of output.

Definition: Producer surplus is the difference between the total revenues earned from the production and sale of a given quantity of output and what the firm would have been willing to accept for the production and sale of that quantity of output.

PERFECT COMPETITION

It is often suggested in the economic literature that perfect competition is the "ideal" market structure because it guarantees that the "right" amount of a good or service is being produced. This is because the profit maximizing firm will increase production up to the point at which marginal revenue (price) equals marginal cost. In this context, the demand curve for a good or service is society's marginal benefit curve. In a perfectly competitive market, output will expand until the marginal benefit derived by consumers, as evaluated along the demand function, is just equal to the marginal opportunity cost to society of producing the last unit of output. This is illustrated at point E in figure above. A voluntary exchange between consumer and producer will continue only as long as both parties benefit from the transaction. In the long run, perfectly competitive product markets guarantee that productive resources have been efficiently allocated and that production occurs at minimum cost.

Another way to evaluate a perfectly competitive market structure is to examine the relative welfare effects. Point E in Figure above also corresponds to the point at which the sum of consumer and producer surplus is maximized. The reader will note that no attempt is made to moralize about the relative virtues of consumers and producers. Perfect competition is considered to be a superior market structure precisely because perfect competition maximizes total societal benefits.

MONOPOLY

If it is, indeed, true that perfect competition is the "ideal" market structure because it results in the "right" amount of the product being produced, how are we to assess alternative market structures? It is, of course, tempting to condemn monopolies as avaricious, self-serving, or immoral, but are these characterizations justified? After all, profit-maximizing, perfectly competitive firms follow precisely the same decision criterion as the monopolist: that is, MR = MC. Viewed in this way, it is difficult to sustain the argument that the evils of monopolies reside in the hearts of monopolists.

To evaluate the relative societal merits of perfect competition versus monopoly, a more objective standard must be employed. We may infer, for example, that a monopolist earning economic profit benefited at the expense of consumers. We have already noted that consumers are made worse off because monopolists charge a higher price and produce a lower level of output than would be the case with perfect competition. We have also noted that monopolies are inherently inefficient because monopolists do not produce at minimum per unit cost.

The real issue is whether the gain by monopolists in the form of higher profits is greater than, less than, or equal to the loss to consumers paying a higher price from a lower level of output. If the gain by monopolists is equal to the loss by consumers, it will be difficult to objectively argue that society is worse off because of the existence of monopolies. After all, monopolists are people too.

There are a number of reasoned economic arguments favouring perfect competition over monopoly. One such argument involves the application of the concepts of consumer and producer surplus. Consider figure below, which illustrates the situation of a profit-maximizing monopolist. For ease of exposition, the marginal cost curve is assumed to be linear.

In the case of perfect competition, equilibrium price and quantity are determined by the intersection of the supply (marginal cost) and demand (marginal benefit) curves. In figure below this occurs at point E. The equilibrium price and quantity are P* and Q*, respectively. As in Figure above, consumer surplus is given by the area P*AE and producer surplus is given by the area BP*E. The sum of consumer and producer surplus is given by the area BAE.

Suppose that the industry depicted in Figure below is transformed into a monopoly. A monopolist will maximize profits by producing at the output level at which MR = MC. The monopolist in figure below will produce Q_m units of output and charge a price of P_m. The reader will verify that under monopoly the consumer is paying a higher price for less output. The reader will also verify that consumer surplus has been reduced from P*AE to

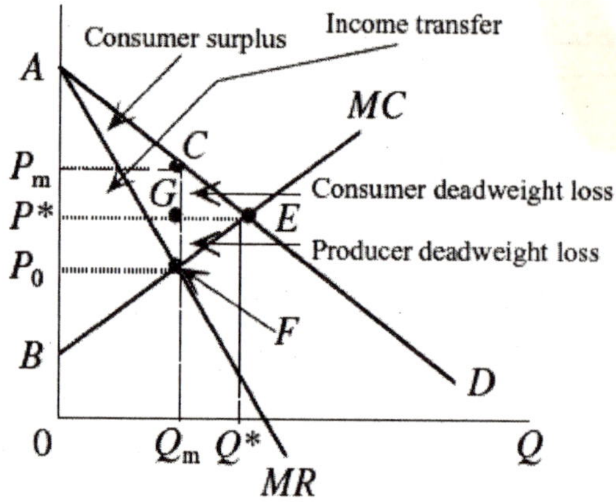

Figure: Consumer and producer deadweight loss.

P_mAC. Clearly, the consumer has been made worse off as a result of the monopolization of this industry by the area P^*P_mCE. To what extent has the monopolist benefited at the expense of the consumer?

An examination of Figure below clearly indicates that producer surplus has changed from the area BP^*E to BP_mCF. The net change in producer surplus is $P^*P_mCG - FGE$. The portion of lost consumer surplus P^*P_mCE captured by the monopolist (P^*P_mCE) represents an income transfer from the consumer to the producer. If the net change in producer surplus is positive, then the producer has been made better off as a result of the monopolization of the industry. Certainly, in terms of Figure above, this appears to be the case, but is society better off or worse off? To see this we must compare the sums of consumer and producer surpluses before and after monopolization of the industry.

Before the monopolization of the industry, net benefits to society are given by the sum of consumer and producer surplus, $P^*AE + BP^*E = BAE$. After monopolization of the industry the net benefits to society are given by the sum of consumer and producer surplus $P_mAC + BP_mCF = BACF$. Since $BACF < BAE$, society has been made worse off as a result of monopolization of the industry.

DEADWEIGHT LOSS

The reader should note that in Figure above the portion of lost consumer and producer surplus is given by the area $GCE + FGE = FCE$. The area FCE is referred to as total deadweight loss. The area GCE is referred to as consumer deadweight loss. Consumer deadweight loss represents the reduction in consumer surplus that is not captured as an income transfer to a monopolist. The area FGE is referred to as producer deadweight loss. Producer deadweight loss arises when society's resources are inefficiently employed because the monopolist does not produce at minimum per-unit cost. No assumptions about the relative merits of consumers or producers or the distribution of income are required to assess this outcome. Clearly, the loss of consumer and producer surplus represents a net loss to society.

Definition: Consumer deadweight loss represents the reduction in consumer surplus that is not captured as an income transfer to a monopolist.

Definition: Producer deadweight loss arises when society's resources are inefficiently employed because the monopolist does not produce at minimum per-unit cost.

Definition: Total deadweight loss is the loss of consumption and production efficiency arising from monopolistic market structures. Total deadweight loss is the sum of the losses of consumer and producer surplus for which there are no offsetting gains.

The importance of the foregoing analysis of the welfare effects of monopoly for public policy cannot be underestimated. Demands by public interest groups for remedies against the "abuses" of monopolies are seldom framed in terms of total deadweight loss, and indeed focus on the unfairness of the transfer, with monopoly pricing of income from consumer to producer, (i.e., the net loss of consumer surplus). But as we have seen, part of this loss of consumer surplus is captured by the monopolist in the form of an income transfer. It is important, however, to question the disposition of income transfers before categorically condemning monopolistic pricing and output practices.

Monopolistic market structures that result in increased research and development, such as product invention and innovation, may be considered to be socially preferable to the rough-and-tumble of perfect competition. An example of this is monopolies arising from patent protection that results in the development of lifesaving pharmaceuticals. Another example of a monopoly that is considered to be socially desirable is that of the government franchise, which was also discussed earlier. The static analysis of the welfare effects of monopoly ignores the dynamic implications of monopolistic market structures. The dynamic implications must also be considered when one is evaluating the relative benefits of perfect competition versus monopoly.

Problem: Consider the monopolist that faces the following market demand and total cost functions:

$$Q = 22 - \frac{P}{5}$$

$$TC = 100 - 10Q + Q^2$$

a. Find the profit-maximizing price (P_m) and output (Q_m) for this firm. At this price–quantity combination, how much is consumer surplus?

b. How much economic profit is this monopoly earning?

c. Given your answer to part a, what, if anything, can you say about the redistribution of income from consumer to producer?

d. Suppose that government regulators required the monopolist to set the selling price at the long-run, perfectly competitive rate. At this price, what is consumer surplus?

e. Relative to the perfectly competitive long-run equilibrium price, what is the deadweight loss to society at Pm?

Solution:

a. The total revenue function for the monopolist is

$$TR = PQ = 110Q - 5Q^2$$

The monopolist's total profit function is therefore

$$\pi = -100 + 120Q - 6Q^2$$

Taking the first derivative of this expression yields the profit maximizing output level

$$\frac{d\pi}{dQ} = 120 - 12Q = 0$$

$$Q_m = 10$$

The profit-maximizing price is, therefore

$$P_m = 110 - 5Q_m = 110 - 5(10) = 60$$

Consumer surplus may be determined from the following expression:

$$\text{Consumer surplus} = 0.5(110 - P_m)Q_m$$

where 110 is the price according to the demand function when Q = 0. Utilizing this expression yields

Consumer surplus $=0.5(110-60)10$ = Rs. 250

b. The monopolist economic profit is $\pi=-100+120Q-6Q^2$

$=-100+120(10)-6(102)$ = Rs. 500

which is the amount of the income transfer from consumer to producer.

c. Unfortunately, economic theory provides no insights about whether this income transfer is an improvement in society's welfare. Such an analysis would require an assumption about the appropriate distribution for the society in question, and this cannot be evaluated by using efficiency criteria.

d. The perfectly competitive long-run equilibrium price is defined as

P = MC = ATC

Marginal cost is equal to average total cost at the output level where average total cost is minimized. Define average total cost as

$ATC = 100Q^{-1} - 10 + Q$

Taking the first derivative and setting the results equal to zero yields

$$\frac{dATC}{dQ}=-100Q^{-2}+1=0$$

$$Q^*=10$$

Alternatively, setting MC =ATC yields

$$-10+2Q=100Q^{-1}-10+Q$$

$$Q^2=100$$

$$Q=10$$

At this output level, the long-run, perfectly competitive price is

$$P_{pc}=-10+2Q=-10+2(10)=10$$

with an output level of

$$Q_{pc} = 22 - \frac{P}{5} = 22 - \frac{10}{5} = 20$$

In this case, consumer surplus may be determined from the following expression:

$$\text{Consumer surplus} = 0.5(110 - P_{pc})Q_{pc}$$

$$= 0.5(110 - 10)20 = \text{Rs. } 1{,}000$$

e. Finally, the deadweight loss to society is

$$\text{Deadweight loss} = 0.5[(P_m - P_{pc})(Q_{pc} - Q_m)]$$

$$= 0.5[(60 - 10)(20 - 10)] = \text{Rs. } 250$$

This solution is illustrated in Figure below.

NATURAL MONOPOLY

At the beginning of the discussion about the existence of monopolies, the focus was on such barriers to entry as control over scarce productive resources, patent rights, and government franchises. In each instance, monopoly power was based on exclusive access or special privilege. It is conceivable, however, that a firm may come to dominate a market based on the underlying production technology. In particular, if a single firm is able to realize sufficiently large economies of scale such that alone it can satisfy total market demand at a per-unit cost that is less than an industry consisting of two or more firms, then that firm is referred to as natural monopoly.

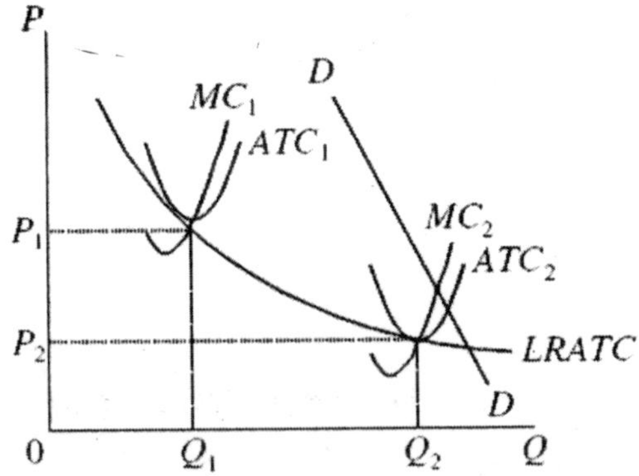

Figure: Natural monopoly and economies of scale.

Definition: A natural monopoly is a firm that is able to satisfy total market demand at a per-unit cost of production that is less than an industry comprising two or more firms.

The case of a natural monopoly is illustrated in Figure above, where the MC_1 and ATC_1 curves designate a small-scale plant and MC_2 and ATC_2 a large-scale plant. Suppose that Q_2 represents an output level of 250,000 units and Q_1 represents an output level of 50,000 units. Clearly, it would be more efficient, less costly, and in the public interest for one firm to operate a single large-scale plant than for five firms to operate several small-scale plants. This is, in fact, one rationale underlying the granting of government franchises of public utilities.

COLLUSION

Suppose that an industry initially comprised several firms, which decided to coordinate their pricing and output decisions to limit competition and maximize profits for the group. Such an arrangement is referred to as collusion. Analytically, the impact on the consumer would be the same as in the case of a monopoly.

Definition: Collusion refers to a formal agreement among producers in an industry to coordinate pricing and output decisions to limit competition and maximize collective profits.

Note: Navistar International (NIC) is a holding company that operates through its principal operating subsidiaries, Navistar and Navistar Financial (NFC). The company is engaged in the manufacture and distribution of trucks, busses and engines. It is headquartered in Warrenville, Illinois and employs 17,800 people. For further knowledge regarding this chapter reader can visit www.navistar.com

7

Monopolistic Competition

Although the conditions necessary for the existence of perfect competition and monopoly, which were discussed in last chapter, are unlikely to be found in the real world, an analysis of these market structures is important because it provides insights into more commonly encountered industry types. These insights provide guidance in the formulation of public policy to promote the general economic welfare. We saw in previous chapter, for example, that unlike monopolies, perfectly competitive firms produce at minimum per-unit cost. Thus, perfectly competitive market structures efficiently allocate society's scarce productive resources and tend to maximize consumer and producer surplus. For these reasons, economists tend to favour policies that move industries closer to the perfectly competitive paradigm.

Despite the unlikelihood encountering the conditions that define perfect competition in reality, the insights gleaned from an analysis of this market structure yield important insights into real-world phenomena. As Milton Friedman (1981) observed: "I have become increasingly impressed with how wide is the range of problems and industries for which it is appropriate to treat the economy as if it were competitive" (p. 120). What is important is not that the characteristics that define perfect competition are religiously satisfied, but that in large measure the interactions of market participants simulate the competitive model.

Although models of perfect competition and monopoly are useful, it is important analytically to bridge the gap between these two extreme cases. The first significant contributions in this direction were provided by Edward Chamberlin and Joan Robinson. These economists observed that in many intensely competitive markets individual firms were able to set the market price of their product. Since these firms exhibit characteristics of both perfect competition and monopoly, this market structure is referred to as monopolistic competition.

The market power of monopolistically competitive firms, such as fast food restaurants, is derived from product differentiation and market segmentation. Through subtle and not-so-subtle distinctions, each firm in a monopolistically competitive industry is a sort of minimonopolist. But, unlike monopolists, these firms are severely constrained in their ability to set the market price for their product by the existence of many close substitutes.

Thus, the demand for the output of monopolistically competitive firms is much more price elastic (flatter) than the demand curve confronting the monopolist. A firm in a perfectly competitive industry faces a perfectly elastic (horizontal) demand curve because its output is a perfect substitute for the output of other firms in the industry. Unlike monopolies and monopolistically competitive firms, which may be described as price makers, perfectly competitive firms are price takers.

CHARACTERISTICS OF MONOPOLISTIC COMPETITION

Monopolistic competition has characteristics in common with both perfect competition and monopoly. The most salient features of monopolistically competitive markets are as follows.

NUMBER AND SIZE DISTRIBUTION OF SELLERS

As in perfect competition, a monopolistically competitive industry is assumed to have a large number of firms, each producing a relatively small percentage of total industry output. As in perfect competition, the actions of any individual firm are unlikely to influence the actions of its competitors.

NUMBER AND SIZE DISTRIBUTION OF BUYERS

Also as in perfect competition, monopolistic competition assumes that there are a large number of buyers for its output and that resources are easily transferred between alternative uses.

PRODUCT DIFFERENTIATION

Unlike perfect competition, while each firm in a monopolistically competitive industry produces essentially the same type of product, each firm produces a product that is considered by consumers to be somewhat different from those of its competitors. The products of each firm in the industry are close, albeit not perfect, substitutes. Monopolistic competition is frequently encountered in the retail and service industries. Examples of product differentiation are most frequently encountered in the same industries and include such products as clothing, soft drinks, beer, cosmetics, gasoline stations, and restaurants.

Product differences may be real or imagined. For example, regular (87 octane) gasoline has a precise chemical composition. Many consumers, however, believe brand-name gasoline stations, such as Exxon and Mobile, sell better gasoline than little-known vendors. Firms often reinforce these perceived differences by introducing real or cosmetic additives into their product. Monopolistically competitive firms commit substantial sums in advertising expenditures to reinforce real and perceived product differences.

These efforts are intended not only to attract new buyers but also to create brand-name recognition and solidify customer loyalty. By segmenting the market in this manner, these producers are able to charge higher prices. Within each segment of the market, the individual firm is a monopolist that is able to exercise market power.

CONDITIONS OF ENTRY AND EXIT

Finally, as in perfect competition, it is relatively easy for new firms to enter the industry, or for existing firms to leave it. Definition: Monopolistic competition is a market structure that is characterized by buyers and sellers of a differentiated good or service and in which it is relatively easy to enter the industry or to leave it.

SHORT-RUN MONOPOLISTICALLY COMPETITIVE EQUILIBRIUM

Clearly, then, the one condition that differentiates the perfectly competitive firm from the monopolistically competitive firm is that the latter faces a downward-sloping demand curve for its product, which implies that, like a monopolist, the firm has some control over the selling price of its product. This market power stems from consumers' belief that each firm in the industry produces a somewhat different product, with different qualities and different customer appeal.

The typical firm's ability to affect the selling price of its product implies that the firm is able, within bounds, to raise the price of its product without completely losing its customer base. This situation is illustrated in Figure below, which assumes the usual U-shaped marginal and average total cost curves.

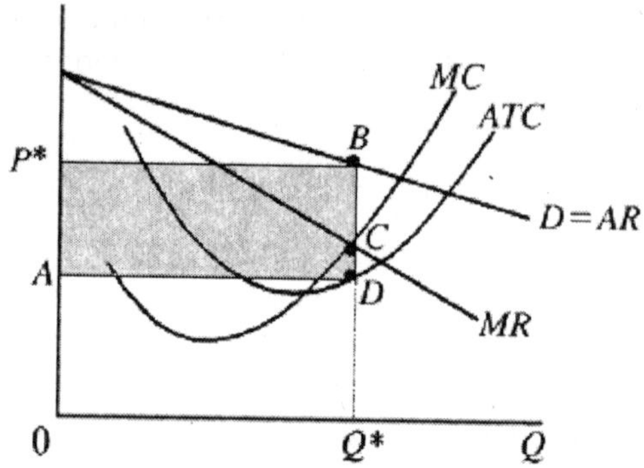

Figure: Short-run monopolistically competitive equilibrium and positive economic (above-normal) profit.

In Figure above, we observe that a typical monopolistically competitive firm maximizes its short-run profit by producing at the level of output at which marginal cost equals marginal revenue. This occurs at the output level Q*. At this output level, the firm charges a price of P*, which is determined along the demand (average revenue) curve. The firm's total revenue is illustrated by the area of the rectangle 0P*BQ*. The firm's total cost at output level Q* is illustrated by the area of the rectangle 0ADQ*. Since total profit is defined as the difference between total revenue and total cost, the firm's profit at output level Q* is illustrated by the area of the rectangle AP*BD.

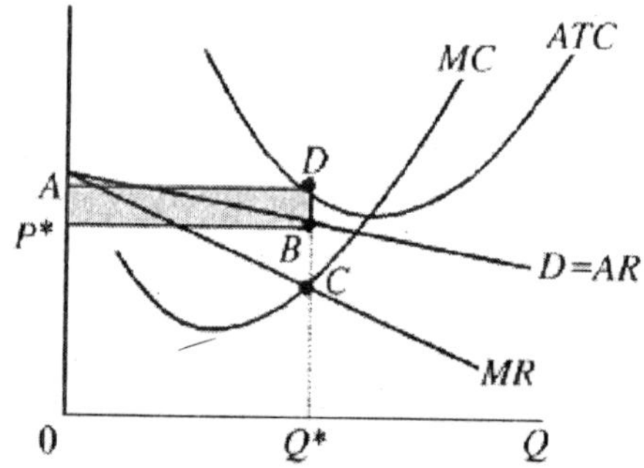

Figure: Short-run monopolistically competitive equilibrium and negative economic (below-normal) profit.

Of course, in the short run the monopolistically competitive firm might just as easily have generated an economic loss. This is illustrated by the area of the rectangle P*ADB in Figure above. Note, again, that profit is maximized at Q*, where marginal cost equals marginal revenue.

LONG-RUN MONOPOLISTICALLY COMPETITIVE EQUILIBRIUM

Each firm in a monopolistically competitive industry produces a somewhat different version of the same product. The objective of product differentiation is market segmentation. By producing a product that is perceived to be different from those produced by every other firm in the industry, firms in monopolistically competitive markets are able to carve out their own market niche. In doing so, each firm faces a downward-sloping demand curve for its product. Within a relatively narrow range of prices, each firm exercises a degree of market power by exploiting brand-name identification and customer loyalty.

There is, however, a limit to the ability of firms in a monopolistically competitive industry to exercise market power by exploiting customer loyalty. Since all firms produce fundamentally the same type of product, the demand for each firm's product is more price elastic because of the existence of many close substitutes. By contrast, there are not close substitutes for the output of a monopolist. Moreover, as more firms enter the market, the number of close substitutes increases, which not only reduces each firm's market share but also increases the price elasticity of demand for each firm's product.

The short-run analysis of the profit-maximizing, monopolistically competitive firm is similar to that of the monopolist, but that is where the similarity ends. Relatively easy entry into and exit from the industry guarantees that in the long run monopolistically competitive firms will earn zero economic profit. To see this, consider, again, the short-run monopolistically competitive equilibrium condition in Figure below.

The opportunity to obtain positive economic profits attracts new firms into the industry. Each firm offers for sale in the market a product that is somewhat different from those of its competitors, which results in increased market segmentation. As a result, the demand curve firm not only shifts to the left (because each firm has a smaller market share), but also becomes more price elastic (because of an increase in the number of close substitutes). Conversely, as firms exit the industry in the face of economic losses, the market share of each firm increases and the demand curve shifts to the right and becomes less price elastic (because fewer substitutes are available to the consumer).As in the case of perfect competition, this process will continue until each firm earns zero economic (normal) profit. This final, long-run monopolistically competitive equilibrium, is illustrated in figure below.

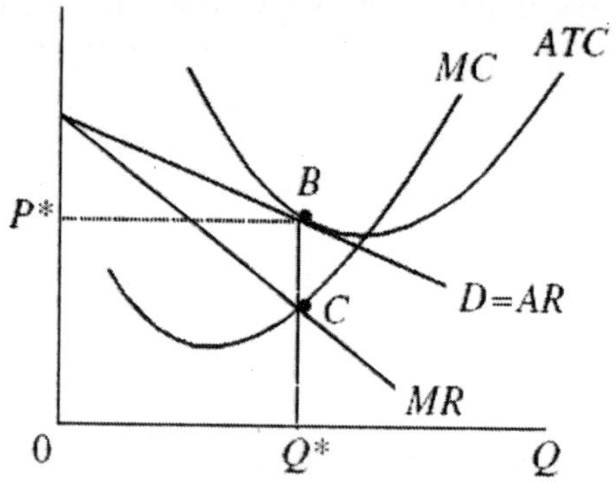

Figure: Long-run monopolistically competitive equilibrium and zero economic (normal) profit.

In the long run, the demand curve of the monopolistically competitive firm is tangent to the average total cost curve at the profit-maximizing output level Q*. At this output level, total revenue (P* × Q*) is just equal to total economic cost (ATC* × Q*). This result is similar to the long-run equilibrium solution for the perfectly competitive industry, where P* = ATC* at the profit-maximizing output level. Unlike the perfectly competitive firm, where P* = MR, profit-maximizing, monopolistically competitive firms produce at an output level at which P* > MR, which is the same as that for monopolies.

The long-run competitive equilibrium for a monopolistically competitive industry can also be demonstrated as follows. By definition, total profit is defined as $\pi = TR - TC = P^*Q^* - TC$

Average profit is defined as

$$A\pi = \frac{\pi}{Q^*} = \frac{TC}{Q^*} - \frac{TC}{Q^*} = AR - ATC^*$$

$$= \frac{P^*Q^*}{Q^*} - ATC^*$$

Since

$\pi = 0$, then A $\pi = 0$, then

P* = ATC*

This result is identical to the situation that arises in long-run perfectly competitive equilibrium.

The long-run monopolistically competitive equilibrium output level is to the left of the minimum point on its average total cost curve. Price equals average total cost, as in the case of long-run perfectly competitive equilibrium; however, price does not equal marginal revenue or marginal cost. Thus, output is lower and the price is higher than would be the case in a perfectly competitive industry. This result is similar to that found in the case of monopoly.

Problem: A typical firm in a monopolistically competitive industry faces the following demand and total cost equations for its product.

$$Q = 20 - \frac{P}{3}$$

$$TC = 100 - 5Q + Q^2$$

a. What is the firm's short-run, profit-maximizing price and output level?

b. What is the firm's economic profit?

c. Suppose that the existence of economic profit attracts new firms into the industry such that the new demand curve facing the typical firm in this industry is Q = 35/3 – P/3. Assuming no change in the firm's total cost function, find the new profit-maximizing price and output level.

d. Is the firm earning an economic profit?

e. What, if anything, can you say about the relationship between the firm's demand and average cost curves? Is this result consistent with your answer to part c?

Solution:

a. To maximize profit, the monopolistically competitive firm produces at the output level at which marginal cost equals marginal revenue. Price is determined along the demand curve. Solving the demand equation for price yields

P = 60 – 3Q

Substituting this result into the definition of total revenue yields

$$TR = PQ = (60 - 3Q)Q = 60Q - 3Q^2$$

Substituting this into the definition of total profit yields

$$\pi = TR - TC = 600Q - 3Q^2 - 100 + 5Q - Q^2$$

$= -100 + 65Q - 4Q^2$

Taking the first derivative of this expression with respect to Q and setting the resulting equation equal to zero yields

$$\frac{d\pi}{dQ} = 65 - 8Q = 0$$

The profit-maximizing output level is

$Q^* = 8.125$

Substituting this result into the demand equation results in

$P^* = 60 - 3(8.125) = 35.625$

b. The firm's economic profit is

$\pi = -100 + 65(8.125) - 4(8.125)^2 =$ Rs. 164.0625

These results are illustrated in the Figure below.

c. The firm's new profit equation is

$\pi = -100 + 40Q - 4Q^2$

Taking the first derivative of this expression and setting the results equal to zero yields

$$\frac{d\pi}{dQ} = 40 - 8Q = 0$$

$Q^* = 5$

Substituting this result into the demand equation yields

$P^* = 35 - 3(35) = 20$

d. The firm's economic profit is $\pi = -100 + 40(5) - 4(5)^2$

$= -100 + 200 - 100 = 0$

This result is consistent with the profit-maximizing condition that marginal revenue must equal marginal cost, that is, $MR = MC$ $35 - 6Q = -5 + 2Q$ $Q^* = 5$

e. The firm's average total cost equation is

$$ATC = \frac{TC}{Q} = \frac{100}{Q} - 5 + Q$$

The slope of this function is

$$\frac{dATC}{dQ} = \frac{-100}{Q^2} + 1$$

In long-run monopolistically competitive equilibrium, the slope of the ATC curve and the slope of the demand function are the same, therefore

$$\frac{-100}{Q^2} + 1 = -3$$

$$Q^* = 5$$

Moreover, at Q* = 5, ATC = 20 = P*. These results are consistent with the results in part c and are illustrated in Figure below.

Problem: The demand equation for a product sold by a monopolistically competitive firm is

The total cost equation of the firm is $TC = 225 + 5Q + 0.25Q^2$

a. Calculate the equilibrium price and quantity.

b. Is this firm in long-run or short-run equilibrium at the equilibrium price and quantity?

c. Diagram your answers to parts (a) and (b).

Solution:

a. The profit-maximizing condition is $MR = MC$

The total revenue equation is $TR = PQ$

Solving the demand equation for P yields $P = 50 - 2Q$

Substituting this result into the total revenue equation yields $TR = (50 - 2Q)Q = 50Q - 2Q^2$

The monopolist's marginal revenue equation is

$$MR = \frac{dTR}{dQ} = 50 - 4Q$$

The monopolist's marginal cost is

$$MC = \frac{dTC}{dQ} = 5 + 0.5Q$$

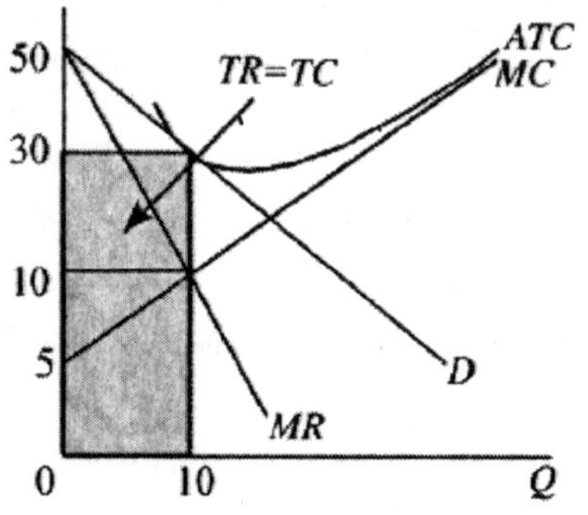

Figure: Diagrammatic solution

Substituting these results into the profit-maximizing condition yields the profit-maximizing output level:

$$50 - 4Q = 5 + 0.5Q$$

$$Q^* = 10$$

To determine the profit-maximizing (equilibrium) price, substitute this result into the demand equation:

$$P^* = 50 - 2(10) = \text{Rs. } 30$$

b. Long-run competitive equilibrium is defined as the condition under which $\pi = 0$. In the short run, $\pi \neq 0$. The profit for the monopolistically competitive firm at P* = Rs.30 and Q* = 10 is $\pi = TR - TC = P^*Q^* - (225 + 5Q + 0.25Q^{*2})$

$$= 30(10) - \left[225 + 5(10) + 0.25(10)^2\right] = 300 - 300 = \text{Rs. } 0$$

We can conclude from this result that the monopolistically competitive firm is in long-run competitive equilibrium.

Problem: The market equation for a product sold by a monopolistically competitive firm is $Q_D = 100 - 4P$

The total cost equation of the firm is $TC = 500 + 10Q + 0.5Q^2$

a. Calculate the equilibrium price and quantity.

b. Is this firm in long-run or short-run equilibrium at the equilibrium price and quantity?

Solution:

a. The profit-maximizing condition is $MR = MC$

The total revenue equation is $TR = PQ$

Solving the demand equation for P yields $P = 25 - 0.25Q$

Substituting this result into the total revenue equation yields

$TR = (25 - 0.25Q)Q = 25Q - 0.25Q^2$

The monopolist's marginal revenue equation is

$$MR = \frac{dTR}{dQ} = 25 - 0.5Q$$

The monopolist's marginal cost is

$$MC = \frac{dTC}{dQ} = 10 + Q$$

Substituting these results into the profit-maximizing condition yields the profit-maximizing output level:

$25 - 0.5Q = 10 + Q$

$Q^* = 10$

To determine the profit-maximizing (equilibrium) price, substitute this result into the demand equation:

$P^* = 25 - 0.25(10)$ = Rs. 22.5

b. Long-run competitive equilibrium is defined as the condition under which $\pi = 0$. In the short run, $\pi \neq 0$. The profit for the monopolistically competitive firm at P* = Rs.40 and Q* = 20 is $\pi = TR - TC = P^*Q^* - [500 + 10Q^* + 0.5Q^{*2}]$

$= 22.5(10) - \left[500 + 10(10) + 0.5(10)^2\right] =$ Rs. – 425

Since $\pi < 0$, we can conclude from this result that the firm is in short-run monopolistically-competitive equilibrium.

ADVERTISING IN MONOPOLISTICALLY COMPETITIVE INDUSTRIES

The importance of advertising in monopolistic industries is readily apparent. Advertising highlights real or perceived product differences between and among products of firms in the industry. Advertising creates

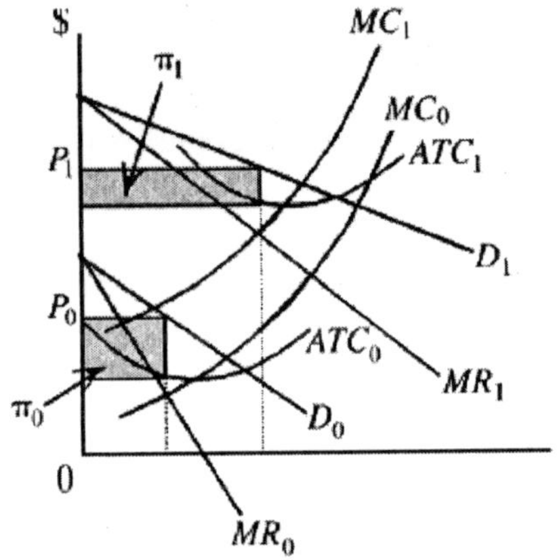

Figure: Successful advertising by a monopolistically competitive firm.

And reinforces customer loyalty, which gives the firm limited market power. The effect of successful advertising by firms in monopolistically competitive firms is illustrated in Figure above.

In above figure the demand curve for the firm's product shifts from D_0 to D_1 as a result of the firm's advertising expenditures. The costs of advertising are illustrated by the shifts in the marginal and average total cost curves from MC_0 to MC_1 and ATC_0 to ATC_1, respectively. These changes result in an increased unit sales and prices. In the situation depicted the figure above, the firm is clearly better off as a result of its presumably successful advertising campaign. This is seen by the increase in profits from π_0 to π_1.

How much advertising is optimal? In principle, the optimal level of advertising expenditure maximizes the firm's profits from having spent that money. As a general rule, the firm will maximize its profits from advertising by producing at an output level at which marginal production cost (including incremental advertising expenditures) equals marginal revenue.

EVALUATING MONOPOLISTIC COMPETITION

Many of the same criticisms of monopolistic market structures compared with perfect competition are applicable when one is evaluating monopolistic competition. As with monopoly, perfect competition may be considered to be a superior market structure because it results in greater output and lower prices than are obtained with monopolistic competition. This is because as with a monopolist, the demand curve confronting the monopolistically competitive firm is downward sloping. On the other hand, the demand curve confronting the monopolistically competitive firm is generally more elastic than that confronting the monopolist because of the existence of many close substitutes. Thus, the disparity between perfectly competitive and monopolistically competitive prices and output levels will generally be less than what is found for the pricing and output decisions of the monopolist.

Another criticism of monopolistic competition in comparison to perfect competition is that production in the long run does not occur at minimum per-unit cost. Thus, monopolistically competitive firms are inherently less efficient than firms in perfectly competitive industries. On the other hand, as with perfect competition, relatively easy entry into and exit from the industry ensures that in the long-run monopolistically competitive firms earn zero economic profits. Moreover, unlike monopolies, entry and exit are relatively easy, which encourage product innovation and development.

Can we say anything good about monopolistic competition? Indeed, we can. Although production is less efficient, the consumer is rewarded with the greater product variety. In fact, it might be argued that the cost to the consumer of increased product variety is somewhat higher per-unit cost of production. This, of course, differs significantly from monopolies from which, in the long run, the consumer receives nothing in return for sluggish product innovation, production inefficiency, and higher per-unit costs.

At a more general level, the model of monopolistic competition has been the subject of numerous criticisms since it was first proposed by Chamberlin and Robinson in the early 1930s. To begin with, the existence of monopolistically competitive industries has been difficult to identify empirically. Product differentiation in industries comprising a large number of firms has been found to be minimal, which implies that the demand curves facing individual firms in the industry are approximately perfectly elastic (horizontal). Thus, the model of perfect competition has been found to provide a reasonably accurate approximation of the behavior of firms in monopolistically competitive industries.

It has also been found that industries characterized by products with strong brand-name recognition typically consist of a few large firms that dominate total industry output. As we will see in next chapter, these industries are best classified as oligopolistic. Finally, as with perfect competition, monopolistic competition assumes that the pricing and output decisions of one firm in the industry are unrelated to the pricing and output decisions of its competitors. This assumption has been found to be unrealistic, since a change in product price by one firm, say a local gasoline station, will prompt price changes by neighboring firms. Interdependency of pricing and output decisions of firms is characteristic of oligopolistic market structures.

CONCLUSION

Monopolistic competition is an example of an imperfect competition. Firms in such industries exercise a degree of market power, albeit less than that exercised by a monopoly. As in the cases of perfect competition and monopoly, profit-maximizing monopolistically competitive and oligopolistic firms will produce at an output level at which MR = MC.

The characteristics of a monopolistically competitive industry are a large number of sellers acting independently, differentiated products, partial (and limited) control over product price, and relatively easy entry into and exit from the industry.

Product differentiation refers to real or perceived differences in goods or services produced by different firms in the same industry. Product differentiation permits market segmentation, which enables individual firms to set their own prices within limits. As in the case of a monopoly, each firm in a monopolistically competitive industry faces a downward-sloping demand curve, which implies that i > MR.

The short-run profit-maximizing condition for a monopolistically competitive firm is P > MR = MC. As in the case of perfect competition, the firm earns economic profit when P > ATC, which will attract new firms into the industry. As new firms enter the industry, existing firms lose market share. This is illustrated graphically by a shift to the left of each firm's demand curve. If P < ATC, the firm earns an economic loss, which will cause firms to exit the industry, resulting in an increase in market share and a shift to the right of the demand curve.

In the long run, the firm earns no economic profit because P = ATC. The demand curve for the firm's product is just tangent to the firm's average total cost curve.

The long-run competitive equilibrium in monopolistically competitive industries is P = ATC > MR = MC. As in the case of monopoly, since MC < ATC, per-unit cost is not minimized; that is, monopolistically competitive firms produce inefficiently in the long run.

Advertising is an important element of monopolistic competition because it reinforces customer loyalty by highlighting real or perceived product differences between and among products of firms in the industry. The optimal level of advertising expenditures maximizes the firm's profits; profit maximization occurs when the firm is produced at an output level at which marginal cost (which includes incremental advertising expenditures) equals marginal revenue.

When compared with the model of perfect competition, in many respects monopolistic competition is considered to be an inferior market structure. As in the case of monopoly, the demand curve confronting a monopolistically competitive firm is downward sloping. Thus, monopolistic competition results in lower output levels and higher prices than are characteristic of perfect competition.

Moreover, monopolistically competitive firms do not produce at minimum per-unit cost. On the other hand, although production is not as efficient as in perfect competition, the consumer is rewarded with the greater product variety. As in the case of perfect competition, relatively easy entry and exit encourage product innovation and development. In the long run, monopolistically competitive firms earn only a normal rate of return.

The model of monopolistic competition itself has been subjected to numerous criticisms. First, it has been empirically difficult to identify monopolistically competitive industries. Product differentiation in industries comprising a large number of firms has been found to be minimal. Industries characterized by strong brand-name recognition typically consist of a few large firms.

Such industries are best described as oligopolistic. Finally, the assumption that the pricing and output decisions of one firm are unrelated to the pricing and output decisions of its competitors is unrealistic.

Note: Oracle Corporation (Oracle) is one of the largest enterprise software companies in the world. The company develops, manufactures, markets, distributes and serves database and middleware software as well as applications software. It is headquartered in Redwood Shores, California and employs about 84,200 people. For detailed information related to this chapter reader can visit www.oracle.com

8

Duopoly and Oligopoly

Despite its shortcomings, the analysis of monopolistically competitive industries provides valuable insights into the operations of markets in general. We will next examine the cases of duopoly and oligopoly. An oligopoly is an industry comprising "a few" firms. What constitutes "a few" in this context, however, is somewhat debatable. A duopoly, which is a special case of oligopoly, is an industry comprising two firms.

The distinguishing feature of oligopolistic or duopolistic market structures, especially compared with perfect competition or monopoly, is not simply a matter of the number of firms in the industry. Rather, it is the degree to which the output, pricing, and other decisions of one firm affect, and are affected by, similar decisions made by other firms in the industry. What is important is the interdependence of the managerial decisions among the various firms in the industry.

The interdependence of firm behavior in duopolistic or oligopolistic industries contrasts with market structures encountered in earlier chapters. There was previously no need to consider the strategic behavior of rival firms, either because the output of each firm was very small relative to industry output (perfect competition) or because the firm had no competitors (monopoly) or because of some combination of the two (monopolistic competition).

In the United States, where collusion between and among firms is illegal, oligopolistic behavior may be modeled analytically as a noncooperative game in which the actions of one firm to increase market share will, unless countered, result in a reduction of the market share of other firms in the industry. Thus, action will be followed by reaction. This interdependence is the essence of an analysis of duopolistic or oligopolistic market structures.

CHARACTERISTICS OF DUOPOLY AND OLIGOPOLY

There are a number of approaches to the analysis of duopolistic and oligopolistic markets. Each of the models we discuss is developed for the duopolistic market but can easily be generalized to the case of oligopolies. Before examining these analytical approaches, we make some general statements about the basic characteristics of duopolies and oligopolies.

NUMBER AND SIZE DISTRIBUTION OF SELLERS

"Oligopoly" refers to the condition in which industry output is dominated by relatively few large firms. Although there is no precise definition attached to the word "few," two to eight firms controlling 75% or more of a market could be defined as an oligopoly. However an oligopolistic market structures is defined, its distinguishing characteristic is strategic interaction, which refers to the extent to which the pricing, output, and other decisions of one firm affect, and are affected by, the decisions of other firms.

The interdependence of firms in an industry is illustrated in figure below, which shows the demand curve faced by all firms in the industry, DD, and the demand curve faced by an individual firm, dd. The rationale behind the diagram is as follows. If all firms in the industry decide to lower their price, say from P_1 to P_2, then the quantity demanded by consumers will increase from Q_1 to Q_2.

Suppose, however, that a single firm in the industry decided to reduce price from P_1 to P_2 in the expectation that other firms would not respond in a similar manner. In this case, the firm could anticipate a substantial increase in its sales, say from Q_1 to Q_3. This implies that over this price range, the demand curve facing the individual firm is more price elastic than the demand curve faced by the entire industry. The decision by one firm to unilaterally lower its selling price will result in a substantially larger market

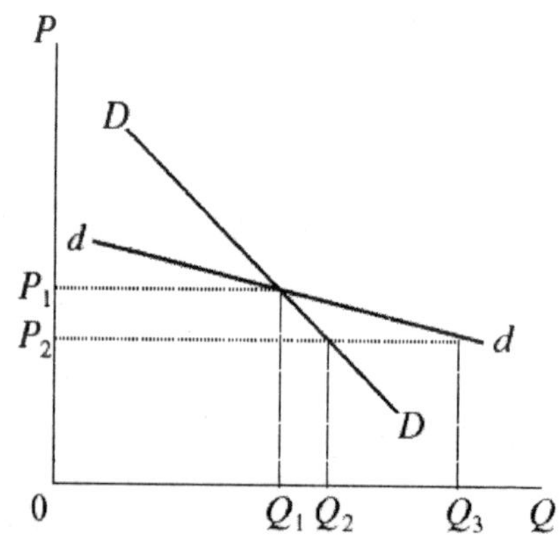

Figure: Oligopolistic industry and individual demand curves.

share, provided this price reduction is not matched by the firm's rivals—a dubious assumption, indeed.

NUMBER AND SIZE DISTRIBUTION OF BUYERS

The number and size distribution of buyers in duopolistic and oligopolistic is usually unspecified, but generally is assumed to involve a large number of buyers.

PRODUCT DIFFERENTIATION

Products sold by duopolies and oligopolies may be either homogeneous or differentiated. If the product is homogeneous, the industry is said to be purely duopolistic or purely oligopolistic. Examples of pure oligopolies are the steel and copper industries. Examples of industries producing differentiated products are the automobile and television industries.

CONDITIONS OF ENTRY AND EXIT

For either duopolies or oligopolies to persist in the long run, there must exist conditions that prevent the entrance of new firms into the industry. There is disagreement among economists over just what these conditions are.

Bain (1956) has argued that these conditions should be defined as any advantage that existing firms hold over potential competitors, while Stigler (1968) argues that these barriers to entry comprise any costs that must be paid by potential competitors that are not borne by existing firms in the industry.

Many of the barriers to entry erected by oligopolists are the same as those used by monopolists. Oligopolist also can control the industry supply of a product and enhance its market power through the control of distribution outlets, such as by persuading retail chains to carry only its product. Persuasion may take the form of selective discounts, longterm supply contracts, or gifts to management.

Devices such as product warranties also serve as an effective barrier to entry. New car warranties, for example, typically require the exclusive use of authorized parts and servicc. Such warranties limit the ability of potential competitors from offering better or less-expensive products.

Definition: A duopoly is an industry comprising two firms producing homogeneous or differentiated products; it is difficult to enter or leave the industry.

MEASURING INDUSTRIAL CONCENTRATION

It was demonstrated in a previous chapter that perfect competition results in an efficient allocation of resources. Perfect competition results in the production of goods and services that consumers want at least cost. As we move further away from the assumptions underlying the paradigm of perfect competition, with monopoly being the extreme case, firms acquire increasing levels of market power, which usually results in prices that are higher and output levels that are lower than socially optimal levels.

Oligopolies are characterized by a "few" firms dominating the output of an industry. In many respects, an oligopolistic industry is like art—you know it when you see it. But is it possible to measure the extent to which production is attributable to a select number of firms? Is it possible to gauge the degree of industrial concentration? To illustrate the concerns associated with industrial concentration, it is useful to review the historical development of antitrust legislation in the India, where the federal government has attempted to remedy the socially nonoptimal outcomes of imperfect competition either by enacting regulations to encourage competition and limit market power, or by regulating industries to encourage socially desirable outcomes.

CONCENTRATION RATIO

The concentration ratio compares the Rupee value of total shipments in an industry accounted for by a given number of firms in an industry. The Indian Narcotics Bureau, for example, calculates concentration ratios for the 4, 8, 20, and 50 largest companies, which are grouped according to a standardized industrial classification.

Definition: Concentration ratios measure the percentage of the total industry revenue or market share that is accounted for by the largest firms in an industry.

It is important not to read too much into the statistics. To begin with, standard industrial classifications are based on the similarity of production processes but ignore substitutability across products, such as glass versus plastic containers. Indian narcotics bureau data describe domestically produced goods and do not include import competing products.

Another weakness of concentration ratios is that they are not sensitive to differences within categories. The concentration ratio, for example, makes no distinction between industry A, in which the top four companies have 24% of the market, and industry B, in which the largest firm has 90% of the market, while the next three companies account for an additional 6%. In both industries the concentration ratio for the largest four companies is 96%.

MODELS OF DUOPOLY AND OLIGOPOLY

As mentioned earlier, the distinctive characteristic of duopolies and oligopolies is the interdependence of firms. It is difficult to formulate models of duopoly and oligopoly because of the many ways in which firms deal with this interdependence. Thus, there is no general theory to explain this interdependence. The models presented next are based on specific assumptions regarding the nature of this interaction.

SWEEZY MODEL

Although managers of oligopolistic firms are aware of the law of demand, they are also aware that their pricing and output decisions depend on the pricing and output decisions of their competitors. More specifically, such firms know that their pricing and output decisions will provoke pricing and output adjustments by their competitors.

Another notable characteristic of oligopolistic industries is the relative infrequency of price changes. Paul Sweezy (1939) attempted to explain this price rigidity by suggesting that oligopolists face a "kinked" demand curve, as illustrated in Figure below.

Definition: Price rigidity is characterized by the tendency of product prices to change infrequently in oligopolistic industries.

Definition: The "kinked" demand curve is a model of firm behavior that seeks to explain price rigidities in oligopolistic industries.

Figure below depicts the situation of a typical firm operating in an oligopolistic industry. The demand curve for the product of the firm really comprises two demand curves, D_1 and D_2.

Unlike a monopoly or monopolistically competitive firm that has a degree of market power along the length of a single demand curve, the oligopolist faces a demand curve characterized by a "kink," illustrated in Figure below as the heavily darkened portions of demand curves D_1 and D_2.

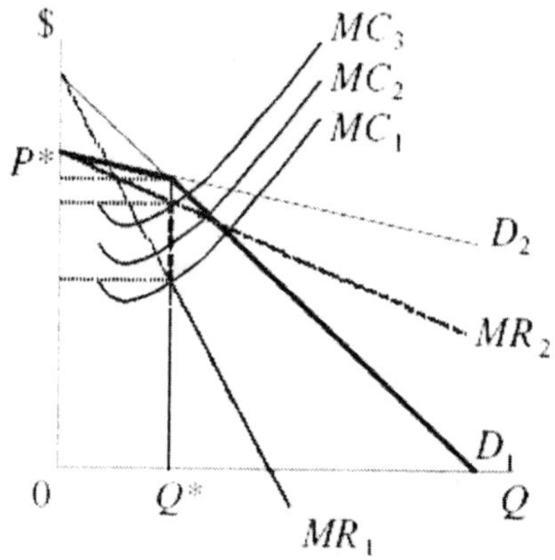

Figure: The "kinked" demand curve (Sweezy) model.

Suppose initially that the price of the oligopoly's product is P*. If the firm raises the price of its product above P* and its competitors do not follow the price increase, it will lose some market share. The firm realizes this and is reluctant to sacrifice its market position to its competitors. On the other hand, if the firm attempts to capture market share by lowering price, the price decrease will be matched by its rivals, who are not willing to cede their market share. The firm whose experience is depicted in figure above posts a small increase in sales as the inflation-adjusted purchasingpower by consumers increases following an industry-wide decrease in prices, but the increase in sales is considerably less than the loss of sales from a comparable increase in prices. In other words, demand for the oli-gopolist's product is relatively more elastic for price increases than for price decreases.

Figure above also illustrates why prices in oligopolistic industries change more infrequently than in market structures characterized by more robust competition. Assume that the few firms in this oligopolistic industry are of comparable size. The marginal revenue curve associated with the "kinked" demand curve is illustrated by the heavy dashed line in Figure above. Because of the "kink" at output level Q*, the marginal revenue curve is discontinuous.

Figure above also assumes the usual U-shaped marginal cost curves. As always, the firm maximizes its profit at the output level at which MR = MC. This occurs at Q*. Note, however, that because of the discontinuity of the marginal revenue curve, marginal cost can fluctuate from MC_1 to MC_3 without a corresponding change in the profit-maximizing price or output level. This result differs from cases considered thus for, in which an increase (decrease) in marginal cost will be matched by an increase (decrease) in price and a decrease (increase) in output. The importance of this result is that the adoption of more efficient production technologies, which results in lower marginal costs, may not result in significant reductions in the market price of the product. Conversely, an increase in marginal costs may not be immediately passed along to the consumer.

The "kinked" demand curve analysis has been criticized on two important points. While the analysis offers some explanation for price stability in oligopolistic industries, it offers no insights with respect to how prices are originally determined. Moreover, empirical research generally has failed to verify predictions of the model. Stigler (1947), for example, found that in oligopolistic industries price increases were just as likely to be matched as were price cuts.

Problem: Lightning Company is a firm in an oligopolistic industry. Lightning faces a "kinked" demand curve for its product, which is characterized by the following equations:

$$Q_1 = 82 - 8P$$

$$Q_2 = 44 - 3P$$

Suppose further that the firm's total cost equation is

$$TC = 8 + Q + 0.05Q^2$$

a. Give the price and output level for Lightning's product.

b. Based on your answer to part a, what is the firm's profit?

c. Determine the range of values within which Lightning's marginal cost may vary without affecting the prevailing price and output level.

d. Based on your answer to part a, what is the firm's marginal cost? Is it consistent with your answer to part c?

e. Suppose that Lightning's total cost equation changed to $TC = 12 + 5Q + 0.1Q^2$. Will the firm continue to operate at the same price and output level? If not, what price will the firm charge and how many units will it produce?

f. Based on your answer to part e, what is the Lightning's profit?

Solution:

a. $82 - 8P = 44 - 3P \quad P^* = 7.6 \quad Q^* = 82 - 8(7.6) = 21.2$

b. $\pi = TR - TC = 7.6(21.2) - 8 - 21.2 - 0.05(21.1)^2$

$= 161.21 - 8 - 21.2 - 22.47 = 109.45$

c. $P = 10.25 - \frac{1}{8}Q_1$

$TR_1 = 10.25Q_1 - \frac{1}{8}Q_1^2$

$MR_1 = 10.25 - \frac{1}{4}Q_1 = 10.25 - \frac{1}{4}(21.2) = 4.95$

$P = 14.67 - \frac{1}{3}Q_2$

$TR_2 = 14.67Q_2 - \frac{1}{3}Q_2^2$

$MR_2 = 14.67 - \frac{2}{3}Q_2 = 14.67 - \frac{2}{3}(21.2) = 0.54$

Marginal cost may vary between 0.54 and 4.95 without affecting the prevailing (profit-maximizing) price and output level.

d. $MC = \frac{dTC}{dQ} = 1 + 0.1Q = 1 + 0.1(21.2) = 3.12$

This result is consistent with the answer to part c, since it lies between 0.54 and 4.95.

e. The firm will maximize its profit where MC = MR. Marginal cost is

$$MC = \frac{dTC}{dQ} = 5 + 0.2Q$$

The relevant portion of the marginal revenue curve is

$$MR_1 = 10.25 - \frac{1}{4}Q_1$$

Equating marginal cost with marginal revenue yields

$$5 + 0.2Q_1 = 10.25 - 0.25Q_1$$

$$Q^* = 11.67$$

$$P^* = 10.25 - \frac{1}{8}(11.67) = 8.79$$

In other words, Lightning will not continue to produce at the original price and output level. Note that at the new output level Lightning's marginal cost is $MC = 5 + 0.2(11.67) = 7.32$ which falls outside the range of values calculated in part c.

f. $\pi = TR - TC = 8.79(11.67) - 12 - 5(11.67) - 0.1(11.67)^2$

$= 102.58 - 12 - 58.35 - 13.62 = 18.61$

Problem: Suppose that International Dynamo is a contractor in the oligopolistic aerospace industry. International Dynamo faces a "kinked" demand curve for its product, which is defined by the equations

$Q_1 = 200 - 2P$

$Q_2 = 60 - 0.4\ P$

Suppose further that International Dynamo has a constant marginal cost MC = Rs.50.

a. Give the price and output level for International Dynamo's product.

b. Based on your answer to part a, what is International Dynamo's profit?

c. Determine the range of values within which marginal cost may vary without affecting the prevailing market price and output level.

d. Diagram your answers to parts a, b, and c.

Solution:

a. We determine the price and output level for International Dynamo's product at the "kink" of the "kinked" demand curve, which occurs at the intersection of the two demand curves. Solving the two demand curves simultaneously yields $200 - 2P = 60 - 0.4P$ $P^* =$ Rs. 87.50

At P* = Rs.87.50, International's total output is

$Q^* = 200 - 2(87.50) = 50 - 175 = 25$ units

b. Since MC is constant, MC = ATC. By the definition of

ATC $ATC = \frac{TC}{Q}$ $TC = ATC \times Q = MC \times = 50(25) =$ Rs. 1,250

Total revenue is $TR = PQ = 87.50(25) = =$ Rs. 2,187.50

Total profit is, therefore,

$\pi = TR - TC = 2{,}187.50 - 1{,}250 =$ Rs. 937.50

c. To determine the range of values within which marginal cost may vary without affecting the price and output level, first derive the marginal revenue function for International Dynamo. Solving the demand equations for P yields

$P = 100 - 0.5Q_1$

$P = 150 = 2.5Q_2$

Total revenue is defined as $TR = PQ$

Applying this definition to the demand functions yields

$TR_1 = 100Q - 0.5Q^2$

$TR_2 = 150Q - 2.5Q_2$

The corresponding marginal revenue functions are

$$MR_1 = \frac{dTR_1}{dQ} = 100 - Q$$

$$MR_2 = \frac{dTR_2}{dQ} = 150 - 5Q$$

These marginal revenue functions, however, are not relevant for all positive values of Q; MR_1 is relevant only for values $0 \leq Q \leq 25$; MR_2 is relevant for values $Q \geq 25$. For the firm to maximize profit, MC must equal MR.

At Q = 25,

$MR_1 = 100 - 25 = 75$

$MR_2 = 150 - 5(25) = 25$

Thus, marginal cost may vary between 25 and 75 without affecting the prevailing (profit-maximizing) price and output level.

d. Consider Figure below.

COURNOT MODEL

A classic treatment of duopolies (and oligopolies) was first formulated by the French economist Augustin Cournot in the early nineteenth century. Cournot began by assuming that duopolies produce a homogeneous product. The critical assumption of the model deals with the firms' output decision-making process. In the Cournot model, each firm

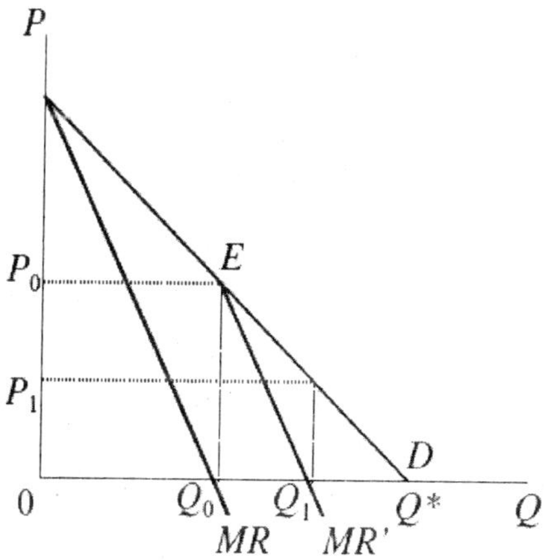

Figure: The Cournot model.

Decides how much to produce and assumes that its rival will not alter its level of production in response. Additionally, total output of both firms equals the output for the industry. The process whereby equilibrium is established in the Cournot model may be illustrated by considering Figure above.

Definition: The Cournot model is a theory of strategic interaction in which each firm decides how much to produce by assuming that its rivals will not alter their level of production in response.

To simplify matters, assume that the demand curve for the product is linear and that the marginal cost of production for each firm is zero. Cournot's example was that of a monopolist selling spring water produced at zero cost. Assume that firm A is the first to enter the industry. Thus, to maximize its profits (MC = MR), firm A will produce Q_0 = 1/2Q* units of output and charge a price of P0. With a linear demand curve and zero marginal cost of production, Q_0 is half the output, where P = 0, or Q*. The latter condition also assumes a perfectly competitive industry, where individual firms take the selling price as constant. Since MC = 0, maximizing profits is equivalent to maximizing total revenue, since P = MR = MC = 0.

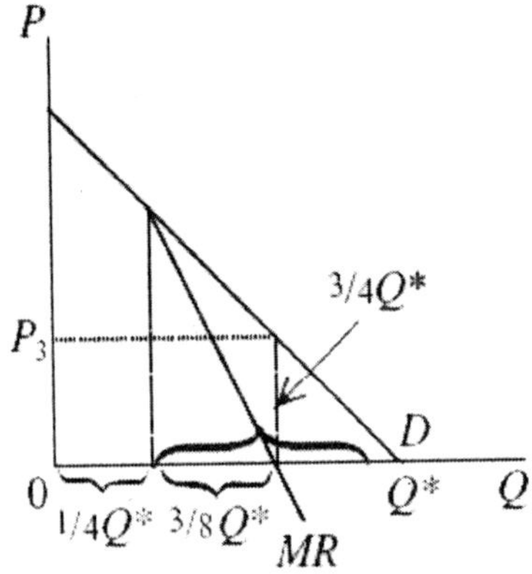

Figure: Determination of market shares in the Cournot model.

Since the barriers to entry into this industry are low, the existence of economic profit attracts firm B into production. firm B also sells spring water that is produced at zero cost. In the Cournot model, firm B takes the output of firm A (Q_0) as given. Thus, from the point of view of firm B the vertical axis has been shifted to Q_0. The demand curve relevant to firm B is the line segment ED. To maximize its profits, firm B will produce such that marginal revenue is equal to zero marginal cost, which occurs at an output level of $Q_1 - Q_0$, which is $\frac{1}{2}Q_0$ or $\frac{1}{4}Q^*$.

The combined output of the industry is now $\frac{1}{2}Q^* + \frac{1}{4}Q^* = \frac{3}{4}Q^*$.

This, of course, is not the end of the story. Since total industry output is now Q_1, the market price of the product must fall to P_1. If firm A attempts to maintain a price of P_0, it will lose part of its market share to firm B. In the Cournot model, firm A will assume that firm B will continue to produce $\frac{1}{4}$Q*. firm A will subsequently adjust its output to maximize its profit based on the remaining $\frac{3}{4}$Q* of the market. This situation is depicted in above figure.

It can be seen in figure below that firm A can maximize its profits by producing half of the remaining three-quarters of the market, or $\frac{3}{8}Q^*$. Combined industry output is now $\frac{1}{4}Q^* + \frac{3}{8}Q^* = \frac{5}{8}Q^*$. Firm B will, of course react by taking firm A's output of $\frac{3}{8}Q^*$ units as given and adjusting output to maximize its profit based on the remaining $\frac{5}{8}Q^*$ of the market. Extending the analysis, this means that firm B will increase its output to $\frac{5}{16}Q^*$. This process of action and reaction, will come to an end when both firms have a market share equal to $\frac{1}{3}Q^*$. When firm A produces $\frac{1}{3}Q^*$, this leaves $\frac{2}{3}Q^*$ remaining for firm B to maximize its profits. Since half of the remaining market is $\frac{1}{3}Q^*$, the process now comes to a halt. The Cournot model can be generalized to include industries comprising of more than two firms.

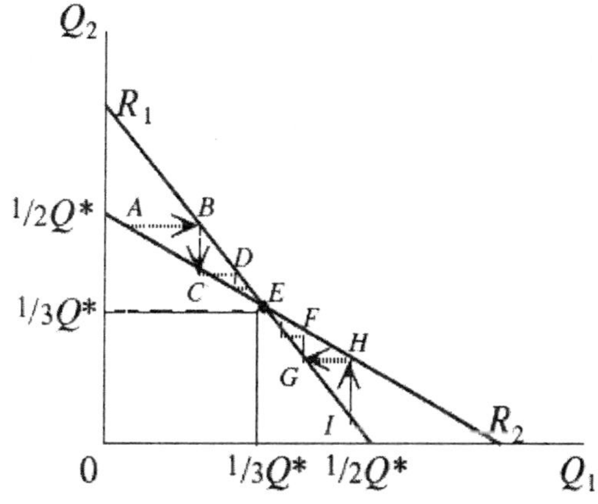

Figure: Reaction functions and the adjustment to a Cournot equilibrium in a duopolistic industry.

$$Q = \frac{nQ^*}{n+1} \tag{8.2}$$

where n is the number of firms in the industry.

From Equation (8.2) it is clearly recognized that as $n \to \infty$, then $Q \to Q^*$. This is the situation of perfect competition described earlier, where MC = 0 and MR = P. It may also be seen that the average market share of each firm in the industry is

$$Q^i = \frac{Q}{n} = \frac{Q^*}{n+1} \tag{8.3}$$

where i represents the ith firm in the industry, Clearly, as the number of firms in the industry increases, the market share of each individual firm will decrease. Recall that for the two-firm case, the average market share of each was $1/(2 + 1)Q^* = \frac{1}{3}Q^*$,

where Q^* is the total output of a perfectly competitive industry.

The adjustment process just described may be illustrated with the use of the reaction functions (to be discussed in greater detail shortly) illustrated in figure above, where R_1 is the reaction function for firm 1 and R_2 is the reaction function for firm 2. Equilibrium at output levels Q_1^* and Q_2^* will be stable provided the reaction curve of firm 1 is steeper than that of firm 2.

Starting at point I in figure above, the output of firm 1 is greater than its equilibrium level of output Q_1^* and the output of firm 2 is lower than its equilibrium level of output Q_2^*. Given firm 1's output, firm 2 will increase its output to point H. Firm 1 will react by reducing its output to point G (iteration 5). Continuing in this manner will eventually lead to the equilibrium output level at point E. Analogous reasoning would produce the same result if the process were to begin at point A with firm 2 producing "too much" and firm 1 producing "too little."

The analysis thus far assumes that the demand functions that confront the two firms are identical and that production occurs at zero marginal cost (MC = 0). Of course, neither of these assumptions will necessarily be valid. To see this, consider the following, more general, description of the Cournot duopoly model. Since the sum of the output of two firms equals the industry output $Q = Q_1 + Q_2$, the market demand function may be written

$$P = f(Q_1 + Q_2) \tag{8.4}$$

where Q_1 and Q_2 represent the outputs of firm 1 and firm 2, respectively. The total revenue of each duopolist may be written as

$$TR_1 = Q_1 f(Q_1 + Q_2) \tag{8.5a}$$

$$TR_2 = Q_2 f(Q_1 + Q_2) \tag{8.5b}$$

The profits of the firm are

$$\pi_1 = Q_1 f(Q_1 + Q_2) - TC_1(Q_1) \tag{8.6}$$

$$\pi_2 = Q_2 f(Q_1 + Q_2) - TC_2(Q_2) \tag{8.7}$$

The basic behavioral assumption underlying the Cournot model is that each duopolist will maximize its profit without regard to the actions of its rival. In other words, the firm assumes that its rival's output is invariant with respect to its own output decision. Thus, each duopolist maximizes profit holding output of its rival constant. Taking the appropriate first partial derivative, setting the results equal to zero we find

$$\frac{\partial \pi_1}{\partial Q_1} = \frac{\partial TR}{\partial Q_1} - \frac{\partial TC_1}{\partial Q_1} = 0 \tag{8.8}$$

or

$$MR_1 = MC_1 \tag{8.9}$$

Similarly for firm 2,

$$\frac{\partial \pi_2}{\partial Q_2} = \frac{\partial TR}{\partial Q_2} - \frac{\partial TC_2}{\partial Q_2} = 0 \tag{8.10}$$

or

$$MR_2 = MC_2 \tag{8.11}$$

The marginal revenue of the duopolists is not necessarily equal. Bearing in mind that $Q = Q_1 + Q_2$, then $\partial Q/\partial Q_1 = \partial Q/\partial Q_2 = 1$. The marginal revenues of the duopolists are, therefore

$$\frac{\partial TR_i}{\partial Q} = P + Q_i\left(\frac{dP}{dQ}\right), i = 1,2 \tag{8.12}$$

Clearly, since $dP/dQ < 0$, the duopolist with the largest output will have the smallest marginal revenue. That is, an increase in the output by either firm will result in a reduction in price, while the marginal revenue of both firms will be affected. The second-order condition for profit maximization is

$$\frac{\partial^2 \pi i}{\partial Q_2^{\ 2}} = \frac{\partial^2 TR_i}{\partial Q_i^{\ 2}} - \frac{\partial^2 TC_i}{\partial Q_2^{\ 2}} < 0, i = 1,2 \tag{8.13}$$

or

$$\frac{\partial^2 TR_i}{\partial Q_i^{\ 2}} < \frac{\partial^2 TC_i}{\partial Q_2^{\ 2}}, i = 1,2 \tag{8.14}$$

This result simply says that the firm's marginal revenue must be increasing less rapidly than marginal cost.

Thus, the Cournot solution asserts that each duopolist (oligopolist) will be in equilibrium if Q_1 and Q_2 maximize each firm's profits and each firm's output remains unchanged. This process may be described more fully by introducing an additional step before solving for the equilibrium output levels. Reaction functions express the output of each firm as a function of its rival's output. Solving the first-order conditions, these reaction functions may be written as

$$Q_1 = R_1(Q_2) \tag{8.15}$$

$$Q_2 = R_2(Q_1) \tag{8.16}$$

In the case of firm 1, the expression states that for any specified value of Q_2 the corresponding value of Q_1 maximizes π_1, and similarly for firm 2. The solution values are illustrated in figure below.

Problem: Suppose that an industry comprising two firms produces a homogeneous product. Consider the following demand and individual firm's cost function: $P = 200 - 2(Q_1 + Q_2)$ $TC_1 = 4Q_1$ $TC_1 = 4Q_2$

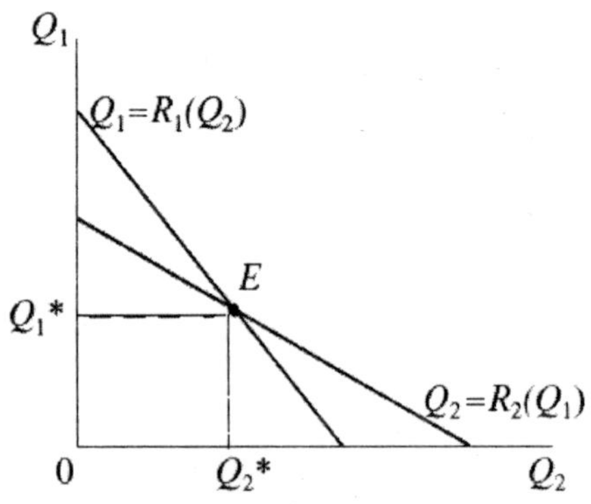

Figure: Cournot equilibrium.

a. Calculate each firm's reaction function.

b. Calculate the equilibrium price, profit-maximizing output levels, and profits for each firm. Assume that each duopolist maximizes its profit and that each firm's output decision is invariant with respect to the output decision of its rival.

Solution:

a. The total revenue function for firm 1 is

$$TR_1 = 200Q_1 - 2Q_1^2 - 2Q_1Q_2$$

therefore, the total profit function for firm 1 is

$$\pi_1 = 200Q_1 - 2Q_1^2 - 2Q_1Q_2 - 4Q_1$$

$$= 196Q_1 - 2Q_1^2 - 2Q_1Q_2$$

For firm 1, taking the first partial derivative with respect to Q_1, setting equal to zero and solving yields

$$\frac{\partial \pi}{\partial Q_1} = 196 - 4Q_1 - 2Q_2 = 0$$

For firm 2,

$$TR_2 = 200Q_2 - 2Q_1Q_2 + 2Q_2^2$$

$$\pi_2 = 200Q_2 - 2Q_1Q_2 - 2Q_2^2 - 4Q_2$$

$$= 196Q_2 - 2Q_1Q_2 - 2Q_2^2$$

Taking the first partial derivative with respect to Q_1, setting equal to zero and solving

$$\frac{\partial \pi_2}{\partial Q_2} = 196 - 2Q_1 - 4Q_2 = 0$$

These first-order conditions yield the reactions functions

$$Q_1 = 49 - 0.5Q_2$$

$$Q_2 = 49 - 0.5Q_1$$

b. These reaction functions may be solved simultaneously to yield the equilibrium output levels

$$Q_1^* = Q_2^* = 32.67$$

Thus,'total industry output is

$$Q_1^* = Q_2^* = 65.34$$

Substituting these results into the profit functions yields

$$\pi_1^* = 196(32.67) - 2(32.67)^2 - 2(32.67)(32.67) = \text{Rs. } 2{,}134$$

$$\pi_2^* = 196(32.67) - 2(32.67)^2 - 2(32.67)(32.67) = \text{Rs. } 2{,}134$$

The equilibrium price can be found by using the demand equation $P^* = 200 - 2(32.67 + 32.67) = \text{Rs. } 69.32$

BERTRAND MODEL

Cournot's constant-output assumption was criticized by the nineteenthcentury French mathematician and economist Joseph Bertrand in 1881. Bertrand argued that each firm sets the price of its product to maximize profits and ignores the price charged by its rival. This assumption is analogous to that adopted by Cournot in that both duopolists expect their rival to keep price, rather than output, constant. The demand curve facing each firm in the Bertrand model is

$$Q_1 = f_1(P_1P_2) \tag{8.17a}$$

$$Q_2 = f_2(P_1P_2) \tag{8.17b}$$

Once again, for simplicity, assume that each firm has constant and equal marginal cost. The total revenue and profit functions for each firm are

$$TR_1 = P_1f_1(P_1P_2) \tag{8.18a}$$

$$TR_2 = P_2f_2(P_1P_2) \tag{8.18b}$$

and

$$\pi_1 = P_1f_1(P_1P_2) - TC_1(P_1P_2) \tag{8.19a}$$

$$\pi_2 = P_2f_2(P_1P_2) - TC_2(P_1P_2) \tag{8.19b}$$

In the Bertrand model, the objective of each firm in the industry is to maximize Equations (8.19) with respect to its selling price, and assuming that the price charged by its rival remains unchanged.

Definition: The Bertrand model is a theory of strategic interaction in which a firm sets the price of its product to maximize profits and ignores the prices charged by its rivals. The Bertrand model is analogous to Cournot model in that the firms expect their rivals to keep prices, rather than output, constant.

Problem: Suppose that an industry comprising two firms producing a homogeneous product. Suppose that the demand functions for two profit maximizing firms in a duopolistic industry are

$$Q_1 = 50 - 0.5P_1 + 0.25P_2$$

$$Q_2 = 50 - 0.5P_2 + 0.25P_1$$

Suppose, further, that the firms' total cost functions are

$TC_1 = 4Q_1$

$TC_2 = 4Q_2$

where P_1 and P_2 represent the prices charged by each firm producing Q_1 and Q_2 units of output.

a. What is the inverse demand equation for this product?

b. What are the equilibrium price, profit-maximizing output levels, and profits for each firm?

Solution:

a. Total industry output is given as

$$Q = Q_1 + Q_2$$

$$= (50 - 0.5P_1 + 0.25P_2) + (50 - 0.5P_2 + 0.25P_1)$$

$$= 100 - 0.25(P_1 + P_2)0.25(P_1 + P_2) = 100 - (Q_1 + Q_2)$$

In equilibrium $P = P_1 = P_2$.

Thus

$$0.25(2P) = 100 - (Q_1 + Q_2)$$

$$0.5P = 100 - (Q_1 + Q_2)$$

$$P = 200 - 2(Q_1 + Q_2)$$

b. The total revenue function for firm 1 is

$$TR_1 = P_1(50 - 0.5P_1 + 0.25P_2)$$

$$= 50P_1 - 0.5P_1^2 + 0.25P_1P_2$$

Similarly, the total revenue function for firm 2 is

$$TR_2 = P_1Q_2 = 50P_2 - 0.5P_2^2 + 0.25P_1P_2$$

The total cost functions for the two firms are

$$TC_1 = 4Q_1 = 4(50 - 0.5P_1 + 0.25P_2) = 200 - 2P_1 + P_2$$

$$TC_2 = 4Q_2 = 200 - 2P_2 + P_1$$

The firms' profit functions are

$$\pi_1 = TR_1 - TC_1 = -200 + 52P_1 - 0.5P_1^2 - P_2 + 0.25P_1P_2$$

$$\pi_2 = TR_2 - TC_2 = -200 + 52P_2 - 0.5P_2^2 - P_1 + 0.25P_1P_2$$

For firm 1, taking the first partial derivative with respect to P_1 and setting the result equal to zero yields

$$\frac{\partial \pi_1}{\partial P_1} = 52 - P_1 + 0.25P_2 = 0$$

From firm 2,

$$\frac{\partial \pi_2}{\partial P_2} = 52 - P_2 + 0.25P_1 = 0$$

These first-order conditions yield the reaction functions

$$P_1 = 52 + 0.25P_2$$

$$P_2 = 52 + 0.25P_1$$

Solving the reaction functions for the equilibrium price yields

$$P_1^* = 52 + 0.25(52 + 0.25P_1) = \text{Rs. } 69.33$$

$$P_2^* = 52 + 0.25(69.33) = \text{Rs. } 69.33$$

The profit-maximizing output levels are

$$P_1{*} = 50 + 0.5(69.33) + 0.25(69.33) = 32.67$$

$$P_2{*} = 50 + 0.5(69.33) + 0.25(69.33) = 32.67$$

Thus, total industry output is $P_1{*} + Q_2{*} = 65.34$

Finally, each firm's profits are

$$\pi_1{*} = -200 + 52(69.33) - 0.5(69.33)^2 - 69.33 + 0.25(69.33)(69.33)$$

= Rs. 2,134.17

$$\pi_2{*} = -200 + 52(69.33) - 0.5(69.33)^2 - 69.33 + 0.25(69.33)(69.33)$$

= Rs. 2,134.17

The reader should verify that for firms producing a homogeneous product, the solution to the Bertrand model will be quite different from the solution to the Cournot model if the firms in the industry do not have identical marginal costs. To see this, suppose, initially, that each firm charges a price greater than MC_2. If $MC_1 > MC_2$, then firm 1 will be able to capture the entire market by charging a price that is only slightly below MC_1.

STACKELBERG MODEL

A variation on the Cournot model, the Stackelberg model posits two firms. Firm 2, which is referred to as the "Stackelberg leader," believes that firm 1 will behave as in the Cournot model by taking the output of firm 2 as constant. Firm 2 will then attempt to exploit the behavior of firm 1, called the "Stackelberg follower," by incorporating the known reaction of the follower into its production decisions. Depending on the total cost functions of the two firms, different solutions may emerge. But, if the two firms have identical total cost equations, the first mover will capture a larger share of the market and earn greater profits.

Definition: The Stackelberg model is a theory of strategic interaction in which one firm, the "Stackelberg leader," believes that its rival, the "Stackelberg follower," will not alter its level of output. The production decisions of the Stackelberg leader will exploit the anticipated behavior of the Stackelberg follower.

Problem: Consider once again the situation described in previous two Problems,where the demand equation for two profit-maximizing firms in a duopolistic industry is $P = 200 - 2(Q_1 + Q_2)$ and the firm's total cost functions are $TC_1 = 4Q_1$ $TC_2 = 4Q_2$ where Q_1 and Q_2 represent the output levels of firm 1 and firm 2, respectively. Assume that firm 2 is a Stackelberg leader and firm 1 is a Stackelberg follower. What are the equilibrium price, profit maximizing output levels, and profits for each firm?

Solution: From the solution to the Cournot duopoly problem, the reaction function of firm 1 is $Q_1 = 49 - 0.5Q_2$

The profit function of firm 2 is $\pi_2 = 196Q_2 - 2Q_2^2 - 2Q_1Q_2$

Substituting firm 1's reaction function into firm 2's profit function yields

$$\pi_2 = 196Q_2 - 2Q_2^2 - 2Q_2(49 - 0.5Q_2) = 98_2 - Q_2^2$$

The first-order condition is $\frac{\partial \pi_2}{\partial Q_2} = 98 - 2Q_2 = 0$ $Q_2{*} = 49$

Substituting into the reaction function, the output of firm 1 is $Q_1{*} = 49 - 0.5(49) = 24.5$

Thus, total industry output is $Q_1{*} + Q_2{*} = 73.5$

The equilibrium price in this market is $P{*} = 200 - 2(49 + 24.5)$

= Rs. 53

The profits of the two firms are

$\pi_1{*} = 98(24.5) - (24.5)^2$ = Rs. 1,800.75

$\pi_2{*} = 98(49) - (49)^2$ = Rs. 2,401

Note that in the Stackelberg solution total industry output is higher (Rs.73.5 > Rs.65.34) and the product price is lower (Rs.53 < Rs.69.3) than in both the Cournot and Bertrand solutions. Moreover, in both the Cournot and Bertrand solutions both firms' profits were Rs.2,134, which is less than the profit of the Stackelberg follower, but greater than the Stackelberg leader. Finally, in the Stackelberg solution firm 1's profit of Rs.1,800.75 is threefourths that of firm 2.

The duopoly models discussed have been criticized for the simplicity of their underlying assumptions. As E. H. Chamberlin (1933) noted: "When a move by one seller evidently forces the other to make a countermove, he is very stupidly refusing to look further than his nose if he proceeds on the assumption that it will not" (p. 46). Chamberlin was quick to realize that mutual interdependence would lead oligopolistic firms to explicitly or tacitly agree to charge monopoly prices and divide the profits. Chamberlin's contribution to the analysis of oligopolies was to recognize that the price and output of one firm will affect, and be affected by, the price and output decisions of other firms in the industry.

On the other hand, we can use game theory, to illustrate the Cournot and Bertrand models as static games, in which in equilibrium the underlying assumptions are fulfilled. The Stackelberg model can be shown to be a dynamic game and, once again, the equilibrium assumptions are satisfied.

Definition: Mutual interdependence in pricing occurs when firms in an oligopolistic industry recognize that their pricing policies depend on the pricing policies of other firms in the industry.

COLLUSION

When duopolists or oligopolists recognize their mutual interdependence, they might agree to coordinate their output decisions to maximize the output of the entire industry. Collusion may take the form of explicit pricefixing agreements, through so-called price leadership, or by means of other practices that lessen competitive pressures. The exact nature of the collusive practices will depend on the particular characteristics of the industry. The implementation of such practices will, however, be constrained by antitrust regulation.

Definition: Collusion represents a formal agreement among firms in an oligopolistic industry to restrict competition to increase industry profits.

Definition: Price fixing is a form of collusion in which firms in an oligopolistic industry conspire to set product prices.

Definition: Price leadership is a form of price collusion in which a firm in an oligopolistic industry initiates a price change that is matched by other firms in the industry.

Perhaps the most well-known manifestation of collusive behavior is the cartel. A cartel is a formal agreement among firms in an oligopolistic industry to allocate market share and/or industry profits. The Organization of Petroleum Exporting Countries (OPEC) is probably the most famous of all cartels. In the mid-1970s, OPEC began to restrict the quantity of oil produced, which resulted in a dramatic increase in oil and gasoline prices.

Many economists have attributed global recession and inflation to these output restrictions.

Definition: A cartel is an explicit agreement among firms in an oligopolistic industry to allocate market share and/or industry profits.

Many people believe that cartels are organized for the purpose of increasing product prices by restricting output, but in fact the opposite might occur. In the mid-1980s an international coffee cartel attempted to lower prices by increasing output! Why? The answer can be found in the price elasticity of demand. If the demand for a product is price inelastic, as was the case of petroleum in the 1970s, producers will be able to increase total revenues by lowering output. On the other hand, if demand is price elastic, as was the case of coffee in the 1980s, producers should be able to earn higher revenues by increasing output and lowering prices. Of course, the actions by coffee producers received very little press coverage. After all, consumers rarely complain about lower prices.

When firms in an industry agree to coordinate their output decisions, the profit-maximizing behavior of the cartel is analytically identical to that of a multiplant monopolist in which the profit function is the difference between the total revenue and total costs functions of each firm. Consider, again, the demand and cost equations given in with industry profit given as Rs.4,802.

Problem: Suppose that the two firms in the industry decide to jointly determine output levels for the purpose of maximizing industry profit. Determine the profit-maximizing levels of output, the equilibrium price, and total industry profit.

Solution: The industry profit function is given as

$$\pi = \pi_1 + \pi_2 = 196Q_1 + 196Q_2 - 2Q_1^2 - 2Q_2^2 - 4Q_1Q_2$$

Taking the first partial derivatives, setting the result equal to zero, and solving yields

$$\frac{\partial \pi}{\partial Q_1} = 196 - 4Q_2 - 4Q_1 = 0$$

$$\frac{\partial \pi}{\partial Q_2} = 195 - 4Q_1 - 4Q_2 = 0$$

The firms' reaction functions are

$$Q_1 = 49 - Q_2$$

$$Q_2 = 49 - Q_1$$

This system of linear equations yields the profit maximizing output levels for Q_1 and Q_2 of $Q_1^* = Q_2^* = 24.5$

The product's price is given as $P^* = 200 - 2(24.5 + 24.5) =$ Rs. 102

GAME THEORY

Today, game theory is perhaps the most important tool in the economist's analytical kit for studying strategic behavior. Strategic behavior is concerned with how individuals and groups make decisions when they recognize that their actions affect, and are affected by, the actions of other individuals or groups. In other words, the decision-making process is mutually interdependent.

Definition: Strategic behavior recognizes that decisions of competing individuals and groups are mutually interdependent.

In each of the models thus far discussed, strategic behavior was central to an understanding of how equilibrium prices and quantities were established in oligopolistic industries. We saw in the discussion of the "kinked" demand curve, for example, that the decision by one firm in an oligopolistic industry to lower its product price to capture increased market share is likely to be countered by lower prices from rivals. On the other hand, unless justified by a mutual increase in the marginal cost of production, a price increase by one firm is likely to go unchallenged by other firms in the industry. Similar considerations of move and countermove were also explicit recognized in the form of reaction functions in our discussions of the Cournot, Bertrand, and Stackelberg models.

Game theory represents an improvement over earlier models discussed in this chapter in that it attempts to analyze the strategic interaction of firms in any competitive environment.

Definition: Game theory is the study of how rivals make decisions in situations involving strategic interaction (i.e., move and countermove) to achieve an optimal outcome.

What is a game? There are a number of elements that are common to all games. To begin with, all games have rules. These rules define the order of play, that is, the sequence of moves by each player. The moves of each player in a game are based on strategies. A strategy is a sort of game plan. It is a decision rule that the player will apply when decisions about the next move need to be made. Knowledge of that player's strategy allows us to predict what course of action that player will take when confronted with choices. The collection of strategies for each player is called a strategy profile. Strategy profiles are often depicted within curly braces {}. Each strategy profile defines the outcome of the game and the payoffs to each player.

Definition: A strategy is a decision rule that indicates what action a player will take when confronted with a decision.

Definition: A strategy profile represents the collection of strategies adopted by a player.

Definition: A payoff represents the gain or loss to each player in a game.

Each of these basic elements of games is illustrated in what is perhaps the best-known of all game theoretic scenarios—the Prisoners' Dilemma. The Prisoners' Dilemma is an example of a two-person, noncooperative, simultaneous-move, one-shot game in which both players have a strictly dominant strategy, that is, one that results in the largest payoff regardless of the strategies adopted by any other player. The Prisoners' Dilemma is an example of a noncooperative game in the sense that the players are unable or unwilling to collude to achieve an outcome that is optimal for both.

In the Prisoners' Dilemma the players are required to move simultaneously. Simultaneous-move games are sometimes referred to as static games. An example of a simultaneous-move game would be the children's game rock–paper–scissors. In this game, both players are required to recite in unison the words "rock, paper, scissors." When they say the word "scissors" both are required to simultaneously show a rock (fist), a paper (open hand), or a scissors (index and middle finger separated). The winner of the game depends on what each player shows. If one player shows rock and the other player shows scissors, then rock wins because rock breaks scissors.

If one player shows rock and the other player shows paper, then paper wins because paper covers rock. If one player shows scissors and the other player shows paper, then scissors wins because scissors cut paper. Strictly speaking, it is not absolutely necessary that both players actually move at the same time. The important thing is that neither player knows what the other player plans to show until both have moved. It is only necessary that neither player be aware of the decision of the other player until after both have moved.

Finally, the Prisoners' Dilemma is an example of a one-shot game. In a one-shot game, both players have one, and only one, move. In fact, most games, such as chess or checkers, involve multiple moves in which the players "take turns" (i.e., move sequentially). Sequential-move games are sometimes referred to as dynamic games. Except for the first move, the move of each player will depend on the moves made by the other player.

Definition: In a simultaneous-move game neither player is aware of the decision of the other player until after a pair of moves has been made.

Definition: A strictly dominant strategy results in the largest payoff to a player regardless of the strategy adopted by any other player.

Definition: The Prisoners' Dilemma is a two-person, simultaneous-move, noncooperative, one-shot game in which each player adopts the strategy that yields the largest payoff, regardless of the strategy adopted by the other player.

		Suspect *B*	
		Do not confess	Confess
Suspect *A*	Do not confess	(6 months in jail, 6 months in jail)	(10 years in jail, 0 years in jail)
	Confess	(0 years in jail, 10 years in jail)	(5 years in jail, 5 years in jail)

Payoffs: (Suspect *A*, Suspect *B*)

Figure: Payoff matrix for the Prisoners' Dilemma.

To illustrate the Prisoners' Dilemma, consider the following situation, which is described in Schotter (1985). Two individuals are taken into custody by the police following the robbery of a store, but after of the booty has been disposed of. Although the police believe the suspects to be guilty, they do not have enough evidence to convict them. In an effort to extract a confession, the suspects are taken to separate rooms and interrogated. If neither individual confesses, the most that either one can be convicted of is loitering at the scene of the crime, which carries a penalty of 6 months in jail.

On the other hand, if one confesses and turns state's evidence against the other, the person who talks will go free by a grant of immunity, while the other will receive 10 years in prison. Finally, if both suspects confess, both will be convicted, but because of a lack of evidence (the stolen items having been disposed of prior to their arrest) the penalty is 5 years on the lesser charge of breaking and entering. The decision problem and outcomes facing each suspect are illustrated in Figure above.

The entries in the cells of the payoff matrix refer to the gain or loss to each player from each combination of strategies. The payoffs are often depicted in parentheses. The first entry in parentheses in each cell refers to the payoff to suspect A, while the second entry refers to the payoff to suspect B. We will adopt the convention that the first entry refers to the payoff to the player indicated on the left of the payoff matrix, while the second entry refers in each cell refers to the payoff to the player indicated at the top. The situation depicted in above figure is sometimes referred to as a normal-form game.

Definition: A normal-form game summarizes the players, possible strategies, and payoffs from alternative strategies in a simultaneous-move game. In the situation depicted in above figure, the worst outcome is reserved for the suspect who does not confess if the other suspect does confess. To see this, consider the lower left-hand cell of the payoff matrix, which represents the decision by suspect A to confess and the decision by suspect B not to confess. The result of the strategy profile {Confess, Do not confess} is that suspect A is set free, while suspect B goes to prison for 10 years. Since the payoff matrix is symmetric, the strategy profile {Do not confess, Confess} results in the opposite outcome.

It should be remembered that the Prisoners' Dilemma is a noncooperative game. Neither suspect has any idea what the other plans to do before making his or her own move. The key element is strategic uncertainty. Since both suspects are being held incommunicado, they are unable to cooperate. Under the circumstances, if both suspects are rational, the decision of each suspect (i.e., the move that will result in the largest payoff), will be to confess. Why?

Consider the problem from suspect A's perspective. If suspect B does not confess, the more advantageous response is to confess, since this will result in no prison time as opposed to 6 months by not confessing. On the other hand, if suspect B confesses, suspect A would be well advised to confess because this would result in 5 years in prison, compared with 10 years by not confessing. In other words, suspect A's best strategy is to confess, regardless of the strategy adopted by suspect B. Since the payoff matrix is symmetric, the same thing is true for suspect B. In this case, both suspects' strictly dominant strategy is to confess. The strictly dominant strategy equilibrium for this game is {Confess, Confess}. In this case, both suspects will receive 5 years in prison.

The foregoing solution is called a Nash equilibrium, in honor of John Forbes Nash Jr. who, along with John Harsanyi and Reinhard Selten, received the 1994 Nobel Prize in economic science for pioneering work in game theory. A noncooperative game has a Nash equilibrium when neither player can improve the payoff by unilaterally changing strategies. Nash created quite a stir in the economics profession in 1950, when he first proposed his now famous solution to noncooperative games, which he called a "fixed-point equilibrium." The reason was that his result seemed to contradict Adam Smith's famous metaphor of the invisible hand, which asserts that the welfare of society as a whole is maximized when each individual pursues his or her own private interests. According to the situation depicted in above figure, it is clearly in the best interest of both suspects to adopt the joint strategy of not confessing. This would result in an optimal solution, at least for the suspects, of only 6 months in prison.

Definition: A Nash equilibrium occurs in a noncooperative game when each player adopts a strategy that is the best response to what is believed to be the strategy adopted by the other players. When a game is in Nash equilibrium, neither player can improve the payoff by unilaterally changing strategies.

The Prisoners' Dilemma provides some very important insights into the strategic behavior of oligopolists. To see this, consider the situation of a duopolistic industry. Suppose that firm A and firm B are confronted with the decision to charge a "high" price or a "low" price for their product. In the case of the "kinked" demand curve model discussed earlier, for example, each firm recognizes that a unilateral change in price is likely to precipitate a response from the rival firm. More specifically, if firm A charges a "high" price, but firm B charges a "low" price, then firm B will gain market share at firm A's expense, and vice versa.

On the other hand, if the two firms were to collude, they could act as a profit-maximizing monopolist and both would benefit. But collusion, at least in the United States, is illegal, so it may be possible to model the strategic behavior of the two firms as a game similar to the Prisoners' Dilemma (i.e., a two-person, noncooperative, simultaneous-move, one-shot game). To see this, suppose that the alternatives facing each firm in the present situation are as summarized in figure below. The numbers in each cell represent the expected profit that can be earned by each firm given any combination of a high price and a low price strategy.

Does either firm have a strictly dominant strategy in this scenario? To answer this question, consider the problem from the perspective of firm B. If firm A charges a "high" price, it will be in firm B's interest to charge a "low" price. Why? If firm B adopts a high-price strategy, it will earn a profit of Rs.1,000,000 compared with a profit of Rs.5,000,000 adopts a low-price strategy.

On the other hand, if firm A charges a "low" price, then firm B will earn a profit of Rs.100,000 if it charges a "high" price and Rs.250,000 if it charges a "low" price. In this case, regardless of the strategy adopted by firm A, it will be in firm B's best interest to charge a "low" price. Thus, firm B's dominant strategy is to charge a "low" price. What about firm A? Since the entries in the payoff matrix are symmetric, the outcome will be identical. If firm B charges a "high" price, it will be in firm A's best interest to adopt a low-price strategy, since it will earn a profit of Rs.5,000,000, compared with a profit of only Rs.1,000,000 by adopting a high-price strategy.

If firm B charges a "low" price, it will again be firm A's best interest to charge a "low" price and earn a profit of Rs.250,000 as opposed to earning a profit of only Rs.100,000 by charging a "high" price. Thus, firm A's dominant strategy is also to charge a "low" price. Thus, in this noncooperative game, where the pricing decision of one firm is independent of the pricing decision of the other firm, it pays for both firms to charge a "low" price, with each firm earning a profit of Rs.250,000. In other words, the strictly dominant strategy equilibrium for this game is {Low price, Low price}.

The reader should note that the solution to the game depicted in figure below is a Nash equilibrium because neither firm can improve its payoff byunilaterally switching to another strategy. On the other hand, if both firms were to cooperate and charge a "high" price, each firm could earn profits of Rs.1,000,000. Note, however, that a (High price, High price) strategy profile is not a Nash equilibrium, since either player could improve its payoff by switching strategies.

That is, firm A could earn profits of Rs.5,000,000 by charging "low" price, provided firm B continues to charge a "high" price. Of course, if firm A were to charge a "low" price, firm B would respond by lowering its price as well.

		Firm B	
		High price	Low price
Firm A	High price	(Rs. 1,000,000 Rs. 1,000,000)	(Rs. 1,000,000 Rs. 5,000,000)
	Low price	(Rs. 5,000,000 Rs. 1,000,000)	(Rs. 250,000 Rs. 250,000)

Payoffs: (Firm A, Firm B)

Figure: Game theory and interdependent pricing behavior.

Historically, such cartels have proven to be highly unstable. Even if both firms were legally permitted to collude, distrust of the other firm's motives and intentions might compel each to charge a lower price anyway. Whether the collusive arrangement is legal or illegal, the incentive for cartel members to cheat is strong. Economic history is replete with examples of cartels that have collapsed because of the promise of gain at the expense of other members of the cartel. For such cartel arrangements to be maintained, it must be possible to enforce the agreement by effectively penalizing cheaters.

CONCLUSION

The characteristics of oligopoly are relatively few sellers, either standardized or differentiated products, price interdependence, and relatively difficult entry into and exit from the industry. A duopoly is an industry comprising two firms producing homogeneous or differentiated products in which entry and exit into and from the industry is difficult.

Two common measures for determining the degree of industrial concentration are the concentration ratio and the Herfindahl–Hirschman Index. Concentration ratios measure the percentage of total industry revenue or market share accounted for by the industry's largest firms. The Herfindahl–Hirschman Index is a measure of the size distribution of firms in an industry but assigns greater weight to larger firms.

Mutual interdependence in pricing decisions, which is characteristic of industries with high concentration ratios, makes it difficult to determine the optimal price for a firm's product. Collusion occurs when firms coordinate their output and pricing decisions to maximize the output of the entire industry. Collusion may take the form of explicit price-fixing agreements, through so-called price leadership, or by means of other practices that lessen competitive pressures. Perhaps the best-known example of collusive behavior is the cartel, which is a formal agreement among producers to allocate market share and/or industry profits.

Four popular models of firm behavior in oligopolistic industries are the Sweezy ("kinked" demand curve) model, the Cournot model, the Bertrand model, and the Stackelberg model. The Sweezy model, which provides insights into the pricing dynamics of oligopolistic firms, assumes that firms will follow a price decrease by other firms in the industry but will not follow a price increase. In the Cournot model, each firm decides how much to produce and assumes that its rival will not alter its level of production in response. The Bertrand model argues that each firm sets the price of its product to maximize profits and ignores the price charged by its rival. Finally, the Stackelberg model assumes that one firm will behave as in the Cournot model by taking the output of its rival as constant, but the rival will incorporate this behavior into its production decisions.

Game theory is perhaps the most important tool in the economist's analytical kit for analyzing strategic behavior. Strategic behavior is concerned with how individuals make decisions when they recognize that their actions affect, and are affected by, the actions of other individuals or groups. The Prisoners' Dilemma is an example of a two-person, noncooperative, simultaneous-move, one-shot game in which both players have a strictly dominant strategy (i.e., one that results in the largest payoff regardless of the strategy adopted by any other players). A Nash equilibrium occurs in a noncooperative game when each player adopts a strategy that is the best response to what is believed to be the strategy adopted by any other player. When a two-person game is in Nash equilibrium, neither player can improve the payoff by unilaterally changing strategies.

Note: Abercrombie & Fitch (A&F) is a specialty retailer selling sportswear apparel, personal care products and accessories. A&F operates in the US, the UK and Canada. The company is headquartered in New Albany, Ohio and employs about 22,000 people. For a case study visit company's site www.abercrombie.com

9

Pricing Practices

We have thus far discussed output and pricing decisions under some very simplistic assumptions. We have assumed, for example, that a firm is a profit maximizer, that it produces and sells a single good or service, that all production takes place in a single location, that the firm operates within a welldefined market structure, and that management has precise knowledge about the firm's production, revenue, and cost functions. In addition, we assumed that the firm sells its output at the same price to all consumers in all markets. These conditions, however, are rarely observed in reality. These in the next two chapters we apply the tools of economic analysis developed earlier to more specific real-world situations, including multiplant and multiproduct operations, differential pricing, and non-profit-maximizing behavior.

PRICE DISCRIMINATION

For firms with market power, price discrimination refers to the practice of tailoring a firm's pricing practices to fit specific situations for the purpose of extracting maximum profit. Price discrimination may involve charging different buyers different prices for the same product or charging the same consumer different prices for different quantities of the same product. Price discrimination may involve pricing practices that limit the consumers' ability to exercise discretion in the amounts or types of goods and services purchased. In whatever guise price discrimination is practiced, it is often viewed by the consumer, when the consumer understands what is going on, as somehow nefarious, or at the very least "unfair."

Definition: Price discrimination occurs when profit-maximizing firms charge different individuals or groups different prices for the same good or service.

The literature generally discusses three degrees of price discrimination. First-degree price discrimination, which involves charging each individual a different price for each unit of a given product, is potentially the most profitable of the three types of price discrimination. First-degree price discrimination is the least often observed because of very difficult informational requirements. Second-degree price discrimination differs from first-degree price discrimination in that the firm attempts to maximize profits by "packaging" its products, rather than selling each good or service one unit at a time. Finally, third-degree price discrimination occurs when firms charge different groups different prices for the same good or service. While not as profitable as first-degree and second-degree price discrimination, third-degree price discrimination is the most commonly observed type of differential pricing. A recurring theme in most, but not all, price discriminatory behavior is the attempt by the firm to extract all or some consumer surplus.

FIRST-DEGREE PRICE DISCRIMINATION

Wc have noted that price discrimination occurs when different groups are charged different prices for the same product subject to certain conditions. Theoretically, price discrimination could take place at any level of group aggregation. Price discrimination at its most disaggregated level occurs when each "group" consists a single individual. First-degree price discrimination occurs when firms charge each individual a different price for each unit purchased. The price charged for each unit purchased is based on the seller's knowledge of each individual's demand curve. Because it is virtually impossible to satisfy this informational requirement, first-degree price discrimination is extremely rare. Nevertheless, an analysis of firstdegree price discrimination is important because it underscores the rationale underlying differential pricing.

Definition: First-degree price discrimination occurs when a seller charges each individual a different price for each unit purchased.

The purpose of first-degree price discrimination is to extract the total amount of consumer surplus from each individual customer. Consumer surplus represents the Rupee value of benefits received from purchasing an amount of a good or service in excess of benefits actually paid for. In Figure below, which illustrates an individual's demand (marginal benefit) curve for a particular product, the market price of the product is Rs.3. At that price, the consumer purchases 10 units of the product. The total expenditure by the consumer, and therefore the total revenues to the firm, is Rs.3 × 10 = Rs.30. It is clear from Figure below, however, that the individual would have been willing to pay much more for the 10 units purchased at Rs.3. In fact, as we will see, only the tenth unit was worth Rs.3 to the consumer. Each preceding unit was worth more than Rs.3.

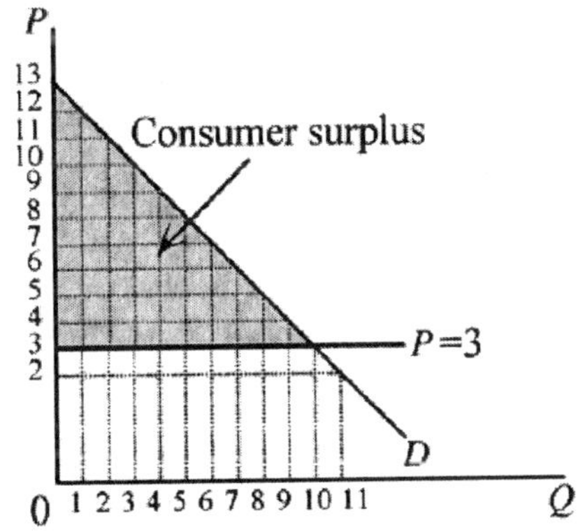

Figure: Consumer surplus.

Suppose that we lived in a world of truth tellers. The consumer whose behavior is represented in figure above enters a shop to purchase some amount of a particular product. The consumer is completely knowledgeable of his or her preferences and the value (to the consumer) of each additional unit. The process begins when the shopkeeper inquires how much the consumer is willing to pay for the first unit of the good. The consumer truthfully states a willingness to pay Rs.12. A deal is struck, the sale is made, and the consumer expends Rs.12, which becomes Rs.12 in revenue to the shopkeeper. The process continues. The shopkeeper then inquires how much the consumer is willing to pay for the second unit. By the law of diminishing marginal utility, the consumer truthfully acknowledges a willingness to pay Rs.11. Once again, a deal is struck, the sale is made, and the consumer expends an additional Rs.11, which becomes an additional Rs.11 in revenue to the shopkeeper.

This process continues until the tenth unit is purchased for Rs.3. The consumer will not purchase an eleventh unit, since the amount paid (Rs.3) will exceed the Rupee value of the marginal benefits received (Rs.2). By proceeding in this manner, the consumer has paid for each item purchased an amount equivalent to the marginal benefit received, or a total expenditure of Rs.75. This amount is Rs.45 greater than would have been paid in a conventional market transaction. In other words, the shopkeeper was able extract Rs.45 in consumer surplus.

Definition: Consumer surplus is the value of benefits received per unit of output consumed minus the product's selling price.

Of course, this mind experiment is unrealistic in the extreme. Moreover, the amount of consumer surplus we calculated is only a rough approximation. With the price variations made arbitrarily small, the actual value of consumer surplus is the value of the shaded area in figure above. Our scenario, however, underscores the benefits to the firm being able to engage in first-degree price discrimination.

Alas, we do not live in a world of truth tellers. Even if we were completely cognizant of our individual utility functions, we would more than likely understate the true value of the next additional unit offered for sale. Moreover, even if the firm knew each consumer's demand equation, the realities of actual market transactions make it extremely unlikely that the firm would be able to extract the full amount of consumer surplus. Transactions are seldom, if ever, conducted in such a piecemeal fashion.

More formally, for discrete changes in sales (Q), consumer surplus may be approximated as

$$CS = \sum_{i=1\rightarrow n} (P_i \times \Delta Q) - P_n Q_n \tag{9.1}$$

where Q_n is the quantity demanded by individual i at the market price, P_n. If we assume that the individual's demand function is linear, that is,

$$P_i = b_0 + b_1 Q_i \tag{9.2}$$

then consumer surplus is approximated as

$$CS = \sum_{i=1\rightarrow n} (b_0 + b_1 Q_i)\Delta Q - P_n Q_n \tag{9.3}$$

Examination of Equation (9.3) suggests that the smaller ΔQ, the better the approximation of the shaded area in figure above. It can be easily demonstrated, and can be seen by inspection, that for a linear demand equation, as $\Delta Q \rightarrow 0$ the value of the shaded area in figure above may be calculated as

$$CS = 0.5(b_0 - P_n)Q_n \tag{9.4}$$

The concept of the integral can be applied in this instance to calculate the value of consumer surplus. Defining the demand curve as P = f(Q), consumer surplus may be defined as $CS = \int f(Q)dQ - P^*Q^*$

where P_n and Q_n are the equilibriums price and quantity, respectively. Substituting Equation (9.2) into the integral equation yields

$$CS = \int_0^n (b_0 + b_1 Q_i) dQ - P_n Q_n$$

$$\left[b_0 Q_i + 0.5 b_1 Q_i^2 \right]_0^n - P_n Q_n$$

$$\left[b_0 Q_n + 0.5 b_1 Q_n^2 \right] - \left[b_0 (0) + 0.5 b_1 (0)^2 \right] - P_n Q_n$$

$$\left[b_0 Q_n + 0.5 b_1 Q_n^2 \right] - P_n Q_n$$

If we assume that the demand equation is linear and that the firm is able to extract consumer surplus, how can we find the profit-maximizing price and output level? If the firm is able to extract consumer surplus, total revenue is

$$TR = PQ + 0.5(b_0 - P)Q \tag{9.5}$$

If we assume that total cost as an increasing function of output, then the total profit function is

$$\pi(Q) = TR(Q) - TC(Q) \tag{9.6}$$

Substituting Equations (9.4) and (9.5) into Equation (9.6) yields

$$\pi = (b_0 - b_1 Q)Q + 0.5\left[b_0 - (b_0 + b_1 Q)Q \right] - TC$$

$$= b_0 Q + 0.5 b_1 Q^2 - TC \tag{9.7}$$

The first- and second-order conditions for profit maximization are

$$\frac{d\pi}{dQ} = b_0 + b_1 Q - MC = 0 \tag{9.8a}$$

$$\frac{d\pi^2}{dQ^7} = \frac{b_1 - dMC}{dQ} < 0 \tag{9.8b}$$

Solving Equation (9.8a) for output yields

$$Q^* = \frac{MC - b_0}{b_1} \tag{9.9}$$

Substituting Equation (9.9) into Equation (9.2) yields

$$P^* = b_0 + b_1\left(\frac{MC - b_0}{b_1}\right) = b_0 + (MC - b_0) = MC \qquad (9.10)$$

Under the circumstances, the firm attempting to extract consumer surplus does not actually charge a price equal to marginal cost. Instead, the firm will calculate consumer surplus by substituting Equation (9.10) into Equation (9.4). It should be noted that Equation (9.10) looks similar to the one the profit-maximizing firm operating in a perfectly competitive industry. Of course, the crucial difference is that P > MC for a profit-maximizing firm facing a downward-sloping demand curve for its product.

Problem: Assume that an individual's demand equation is

$P_i = 20 - 2Q_i$

Suppose that the market price of the product is P_n = Rs.6.

a. Approximate the value of this individual's consumer surplus for $\Delta Q = 1$.

b. What is value of consumer surplus as $\Delta Q \to 0$?

Solution:

a. The equation for approximating the value of consumer surplus for discrete changes in Q when the demand function is linear is

$$CS = \sum_{i=1\to n} (b_0 + b_1 Q_i)\Delta Q - P_n Q_n$$

For P_n = Rs.6 and $\Delta Q = 1$ this equation becomes

$$CS = \sum_{i=1\to n} (20 - 2Q_i) - 42$$

For values of Q_i from 0 to 7 this becomes

$$CS = [20-2(1)]+[20-2(2)]+[20-2(3)]+[20-2(4)]$$
$$+[20-2(5)]+[20-2(6)]+[20-2(7)]-42$$
$$= 18 + 16 + 14 + 12 + 10 + 8 + 6 - 42 = \text{Rs. } 42$$

The approximate value of consuming 7 units of this good is approximately Rs.84 Rupees. If the consumer pays Rs.6 for 7 units of the good, then the individual's total expenditure is Rs.42. The approximate Rupee value of benefits received, but not paid for, is Rs.42.

b. The value of the individual's consumer surplus as $\Delta Q \rightarrow 0$ is given by the expression $CS = 0.5(b_0 - P_n)Q_n$

Substituting into this expression we obtain

$$CS = 0.5(20-6)7 = 0.5(14)7 = \text{Rs. } 49$$

The actual value of consumer surplus is Rs.49, compared with the approximated value of Rs.42 calculated in part a.

SECOND-DEGREE PRICE DISCRIMINATION

Sometimes referred to as volume discounting, second-degree price discrimination differs from first-degree price discrimination in the manner in which the firm attempts to extract consumer surplus. In the case of second degree price discrimination, sellers attempt to maximize profits by selling product in "blocks" or "bundles" rather than one unit at a time. There are two common types of second-degree price discrimination: block pricing and commodity bundling.

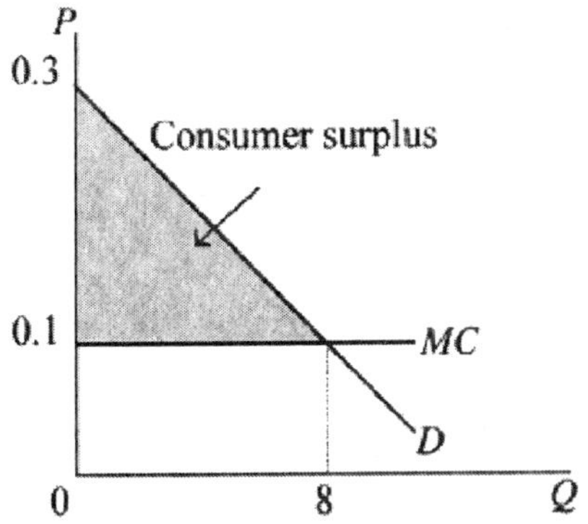

Figure: Block pricing.

Definition: Second-degree price discrimination occurs when firms sell their product in "blocks" or "bundles" rather than one unit at a time.

BLOCK PRICING

Block pricing, or selling a product in fixed quantities, is similar to first degree price discrimination in that the seller is trying to maximize profits by extracting all or part of the buyer's consumer surplus. Eight frankfurter rolls in a package and a six-pack of beer are examples of block pricing.

The rationale behind block pricing is to charge a price for the package that approximates, but does not exceed, the total benefits obtained by the consumer. Suppose, for example, that the estimated demand equation of the average consumer for frankfurter rolls is given as Q = 24 – 80P. Solving this equation for P yields P = 0.3 – 0.0125Q. Suppose, further, that the marginal cost of producing a frankfurter roll is constant at Rs.0.10. This situation is illustrated in above figure.

With block pricing the firm will attempt to get the consumer to pay for the full value received for the eight frankfurter rolls by charging a single price for the package. If frankfurter rolls were sold for Rs.0.10 each, the total expenditure by the typical consumer would be Rs.0.80. The firm will add the value of consumer surplus to the package of eight frankfurter rolls, as follows:

$$TR = PQ + CS = PQ + 0.5(b_0 - P)Q$$

$$= 0.1(8) + 0.5(0.3 - 0.1)8 = \text{Rs. } 1.60$$

The profit earned by the firm is

$$\pi = TR - TC = PQ + 0.5(b_0 - P)Q - (MC \times Q)$$

$$= \$1.60 - \$0.80 = \text{Rs. } 0.80$$

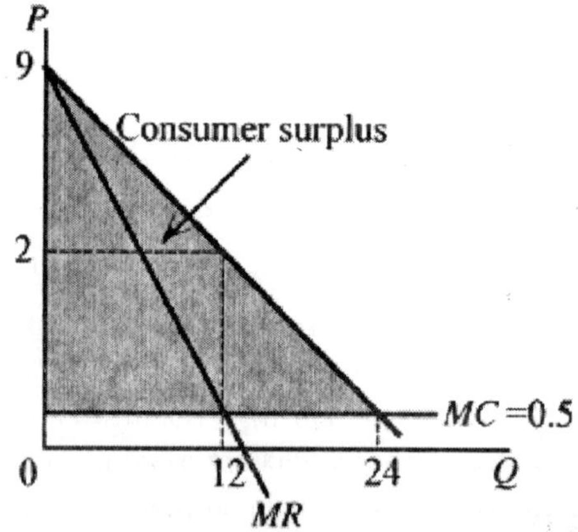

Figure: Amusement park pricing.

If this firm operated in a perfectly competitive industry and frankfurter rolls were sold individually, the selling price would be Rs.0.10 per roll and the firm would break even. In other words, the firm would earn only normal profits, since TR = TC.

One interesting variation of block pricing is amusement park pricing. While it is not possible for the management of an amusement park to know the demand equation for each individual entering the park, and therefore first-degree price discrimination is out of the question, suppose that management had estimated the demand equation of the average park visitor. Figure above illustrates such a demand relationship.

In above figure the marginal cost to the amusement park of providing a ride is assumed to be Rs.0.50. If the amusement park is a profit maximizer, it will set the average price of a ride at Rs.2 per ride (i.e., where MR = MC). At Rs.2 per ride, the average park visitor will ride 12 times for an average total expenditure of Rs.24 per park visitor. The total profit per visitor is $\pi = TR - TC = PQ - (MC - Q) = 2(12) - 0.5(12)$ = Rs. 18

At the profit-maximizing price, however, the average park visitor will enjoy a consumer surplus on the first 11 rides. The challenge confronting the managers of the amusement park is to extract this consumer surplus.

Rather than charging on a per-ride basis, many amusement parks charge a one-time admission fee, which allows park visitors to ride as often as they like. What admission fee should the amusement park charge? The park will calculate consumer surplus as if the price per ride is equal to the marginal cost to the amusement park of providing a single ride. Substituting Equation (9.22) into Equation (9.16), the amount of consumer surplus is $CS = 0.5(9 - 0.5)24$ = Rs. 102

The one-time admission fee charged by the amusement park should equal the marginal cost of providing a ride multiplied by the number of rides, plus the amount of consumer surplus. On average, the amusement park expects each guest to ride approximately 24 times. Thus, the amusement park should charge a one-time admission of Rs.114 [(MC × Q) + CS = Rs.0.5(24) + Rs.102].

The main difference between the block pricing of frankfurter rolls and admission to an amusement park is that while frankfurter rolls are very much a private good, amusement park rides take on the characteristics of a public good. For now, it is enough to say that the ownership rights of private goods are well defined. The owner of the private property rights to a good or service is able to exclude all other individuals from consuming that particular product. Moreover, once the product has been consumed, as in this case frankfurter rolls, there is no more of the good available for anyone else to consume. In other words, private goods have the properties of excludability and depletability.

The situation is quite different with public goods. For one thing, use by one person of a public good such as commercial radio programming or television broadcasts does not decrease its availability to others. Another important characteristic of a public good is unlimited access by individuals who have not paid for the good. This is the characteristic of nonexcludability. While cable television broadcasts possess the characteristic of nondepletability, they are not public goods because nonpayers can be excluded from their use.

In the case of public goods, private markets often fail because consumers are unwilling to reveal their true preferences for the good or service, which makes it difficult, if not impossible, to correctly price the good. This phenomenon is often referred to as the free-rider problem. In the case of pure public goods, the government is often obliged to step in to provide the good or service. The most commonly cited examples of public goods are national defense and police and fire protection. The provision of public goods is financed through tax levies.

Block pricing by amusement parks is similar to block pricing by cable television companies in that the success of this pricing policy depends crucially on management's ability to deny access to nonpayers. This is usually accomplished by controlling access to the park. It is not unusual for large amusement parks, such as the Six Flags, Busch Gardens, or Disney World theme parks, to be isolated from densely populated areas. Access to the park is typically limited to one or a few points, and the perimeter of the park is characterized by high walls, fences, or a natural obstacle, such as a lake, constantly guarded by security personnel.

It is much more difficult for older amusement parks, which are usually located in densely populated metropolitan areas, to engage in a one-time admission fee pricing policy because of the difficulty associated with controlling access to park grounds.

In such cases, an alternative pricing policy to extract consumer surplus is necessary. One such technique is to sell identifying bracelets that enable park visitors to ride as often as they like for a limited period of time, say, two hours. This approach is often advertised as a POP (pay-one-price) plan. Thus, access to rides is not controlled at the park entrance, but at the entrance to individual rides.

Ironically, whatever technique is used to extract consumer surplus by amusement parks, it is good public relations. Park visitors like the convenience of not having to pay per ride. What is more, most park visitors believe that this pricing practice is a by-product of the management's concern for the comfort and convenience of guests, which is probably true. Finally, and most important, many amusement park visitors believe that they are getting their money's worth by being able to ride as many times as they like, which is, of course, true. But do they get more than their money's worth? This may also be true, but it should not be forgotten that the purpose of this type of pricing is to maximize amusement park profits by extracting as much consumer surplus as possible.

Problem: Seven Banners High Adventure has estimated the following demand equation for the average summer visitor to its theme park

$$Q = 27 - 3P$$

where Q represents the number or rides by each guest and P the price per ride in U.S. Rupees. The total cost of providing a ride is characterized by the equation

$$TC = 1 + Q$$

Seven Banners is a profit maximizer considering two different pricing schemes: charging on a per-ride basis or charging a one-time admission fee and allowing park visitors to ride as often as they like.

a. How much should the park charge on a per-ride basis, and what is the total profit to Seven Banners per customer?

b. Suppose that Seven Banners decides to charge a one-time admission fee to extract the consumer surplus of the average park guest. What is the estimated average profit per park guest? How much should Seven Banners charge as a one-time admission fee? What is the amount of consumer surplus of the average park guest?

Solution:

a. Solving the demand equation for P yields

$$P = 9 - \frac{Q}{3}$$

The per-customer total revenue equation is

$$TR = PQ = \left(9 - \frac{Q}{3}\right)Q = 9Q - \frac{Q^2}{3}$$

The per-customer total profit equation is

$$\pi = TR - TC = 9Q - \frac{Q^2}{3} - (1+Q) = -1 + 8Q - \frac{Q^2}{3}$$

The first- and second-order conditions for profit maximization are d π /dQ = 0 and d$^2\pi$ /dQ^2 < 0, respectively. The profit-maximizing output level is

$$\frac{d\pi}{dQ} = 8 - \frac{2Q}{3} = 0$$

$$Q^* = 12$$

To verify that this is a local maximum, we write the second derivative of the profit function

$$\frac{d^2\pi}{dQ^2} = \frac{-2}{3} < 0$$

which satisfies the second-order condition for a local maximum. The profit-maximizing price per ride is, therefore,

$$P^* = 9 - \frac{12}{3} = 5$$

The estimated average profit per Seven Banners guest with per-ride pricing is

$$\pi = -1 + 8(12) - \frac{(12)^2}{3} = \text{Rs. } 47$$

b. If Seven Banners charges a one-time admission fee, it will attempt to extract the total amount of consumer surplus. Since the demand equation is linear, the estimated consumer surplus per average rider is given by the equation

$$CS = 0.5(b_0 - P)Q$$

From Equation (9.7) the profit equation for Seven Banners is

$$\pi = TR - TC = (b_0 + b_1Q)Q + 0.5[b_0 - (b_0 + b_1Q)]Q - TC$$

$$= \left(9 - \frac{Q}{3}\right)Q + 0.5\left[9 - \left(9 - \frac{Q}{3}\right)\right]Q - (1 + Q)$$

$$= 9Q - \frac{Q^2}{3} + \frac{0.5Q^2}{3} - 1 - Q = 8Q - \frac{Q^2}{6} - 1$$

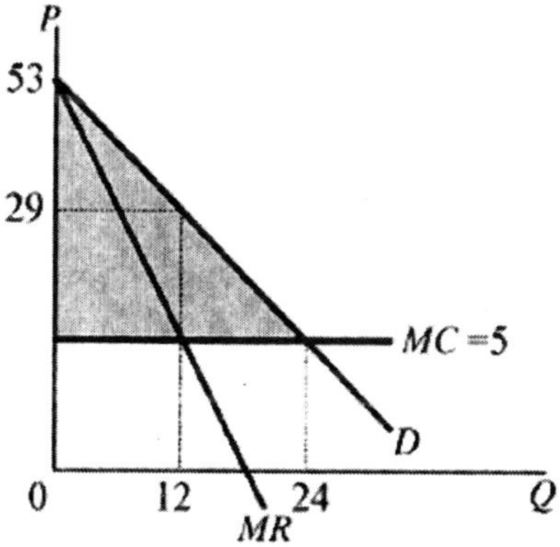

Figure: Two-part pricing.

The first-order condition for profit maximization is

$$\frac{d\pi}{dQ} = 8 - \frac{Q}{3} = 0$$

$$\dot{Q}^* = 24$$

After substituting this value into the demand equation we get

$$P^* = 9 - \frac{24}{3} = 1 = MC$$

Total profit is, therefore,

$$\pi = 8Q - \frac{Q^2}{6} - 1 = 8(24) - \frac{(24)^2}{6} - 1$$

$$= 192 - 96 - 1 = \text{Rs. } 95$$

The one-time admission fee should equal the total cost per guest of providing 24 rides plus the total amount of consumer surplus, that is,

Admission fee $TR = (MC \times Q) + CS = (MC \times Q) + 0.5(b_0 - MC)Q$

$$= 1(24) + 0.5(9-1)24 = 24 + 96 = \text{Rs. } 120$$

Thus the estimated consumer surplus of the average park guest is Rs.96.

Two-Part Pricing

A variation of block pricing is two-part pricing. Two-part pricing is used to enhance a firm's profits by first charging a fixed fee for the right to purchase or use the good or service, then adding a per-unit charge. As in the case of block pricing, two-part pricing is often used by clubs to extract consumer surplus. To see how two-part pricing works, consider above figure, which illustrates the demand for country club membership.

In above figure the per-visit demand to the country club is

$$Q = 26.5 - 0.5P$$

The club's total cost equation is

$$TC = 15 + 5Q$$

If the management of the country club were to charge its members a single price, the profit-maximizing price and output level would be 12 and Rs.29, respectively. The country club's profit would be (Rs.24 × 12) – (Rs.5 × 12) = Rs.288. At this price–quantity combination, each member of the club would receive consumer surplus (value received but not paid for) of 0.5[(53 – 29) × 12] = Rs.144.

If, on the other hand, the country club were to use two-part pricing, it could extract the maximum amount of consumer surplus, which is the shaded area in figure above. In this case, the club would charge an initiation fee of 0.5[(Rs.53 – Rs.5) × Rs.24] = Rs.576 and impose a per-visit charge of Rs.5 to cover the cost of services. It is clear that the initiation fee is pure profit and is a substantial improvement over the profit of Rs.288 earned by charging a single price per visit.

Commodity Bundling

Another form of second-degree price discrimination is commodity bundling. Commodity bundling involves combining two or more different products into a single package, which is sold at a single price. Like block pricing, commodity bundling is an attempt to enhance the firm's profits by extracting at least some consumer surplus.

A vacation package offered by a travel agent that includes airfare, hotel accommodations, meals, entertainment, ground transportation, and so on is an example of commodity bundling. To understand how commodity bundling enhances a company's profits, consider the case of a resort hotel that sells weekly vacation packages. Suppose that the package includes room, board, and entertainment. Let us further suppose that the marginal cost to the resort hotel of providing the package is Rs.1,000.

Management has identified two groups of individuals that would be interested in the vacation package. Although the hotel is not able to identify members of either group, it does know that each group values the components of the package differently. To keep the example simple, assume that there are an equal number of members in each group. To further simplify the example, assume that total membership in each group is a single individual.

If the resort hotel could identify the members of each group, it might engage in first-degree price discrimination and charge members of the first group Rs.3,000 and members of the second group Rs.2,550 for the vacation package. Since the marginal cost of providing the service to each group is Rs.1,000, the hotel's profit would be Rs.3,550 per group. Since the hotel is not able to identify members of each group, what price should the hotel charge for the package?

Suppose the hotel decides to price each component of the package separately. If it charges Rs.2,500 for room and board, it would sell only to the first group, and its total revenue would be Rs.2,500. Members of the second group will not be interested because the price is above what the value they attach to room and board. If, on the other hand, the hotel were to charge Rs.1,800 for room and board, it would sell to both groups for a total revenue of Rs.3,600. Clearly, then, the hotel will charge Rs.1,800.

The same scenario holds true for entertainment. If the hotel charges Rs.750, then only members of the second group will purchase entertainment and the hotel will generate revenues of only Rs.750. On the other hand, if the hotel charges Rs.500, both groups will purchase entertainment and generate revenues of Rs.1,000. Thus, whether the hotel charges per item or charges a package price of Rs.1,800 + Rs.500 = Rs.2,300, the profit from each group will be Rs.1,300. Since we have assumed that there is only one individual in each group, the hotel's total profit is Rs.2,600.

Now, although a package price of Rs.2,300 appears to be reasonable from the point of view of the profit-conscious hotel, the story does not end there. As it turns out, the hotel can do even better if it charges a package price of Rs.1,800 + Rs.750 = Rs.2,550. The reason is simple. Management knows that the value of the package to the first group is Rs.2,500 + Rs.500 = Rs.3,000. It also knows that the value to the second group is Rs.1,800 + Rs.750 = Rs.2,550. By bundling room, board, and entertainment and selling the package for Rs.2,550, the hotel will sell both components of the package to members of both groups. At a package price of Rs.2,550, the hotel earns a profit of Rs.1,550, instead of Rs.1,300, from each group. Again, since we have assumed that there is only one person in each group, the hotel's total profit is now Rs.3,100.

Table: Commodity bundling and new car options I.

Group	Power steering	CD stereo system
1	Rs.1,700	Rs.300
2	Rs.1,600	Rs.320
3	Rs.1,500	Rs.340

In the foregoing example, by bundling room, board, and entertainment and charging a single package price, the hotel has enhanced its profits by Rs.250 per group member. The hotel has extracted the entire amount of consumer surplus from members of the second group and some consumer surplus from members of the first group.

Problem: A car dealership offers power steering and a compact disc stereo system as options in all new models. Suppose that the dealership sells to members of three different groups of new car buyers and that there are five individuals in each group. Table above illustrates how the members of each group value power steering and a compact disc stereo sound system.

Suppose that the per-unit cost of providing power steering and a CD stereo system is Rs.1,200 and Rs.250, respectively.

a. If the dealership sold each option separately, how much profit would it earn from each group member?

b. If the dealership cannot easily identify the members of each group, how should it price a package consisting of power steering and a CD stereo system? What will be the dealership's profit on each package sold?

Solution:

a. If the dealership sells each item separately, it would change Rs.1,500 for power steering, for a profit of Rs.300 per sale.

Given that there are five members in each group, the dealership has generated total profits of Rs.4,500. By contrast, if the dealership sells power steering for Rs.1,600, it will earn a profit of Rs.400 per sale. But since only members of the second and third groups will purchase power steering, the dealership's total profit will only be Rs.4,000.

Similarly, the dealership will sell compact disc stereo systems for Rs.300, for a profit of Rs.50 per sale. Again, since there are five members in each group, the dealership's total profit will be Rs.750. By contrast, if the dealership sells the option for Rs.320 it will earn a profit of Rs.70 per sale. Since, however, only members of the first and second group will opt for the CD stereo system at this price, the dealership's total profit will be Rs.700.

b. If the dealership sells power steering and a CD stereo system at a package price of Rs.1,800, as suggested in the answer to part a, the total

Table: Commodity bundling and new car options II.

Group	Power steering	CD stereo system
1	Rs.2,000	Rs.300
2	Rs.1,800	Rs.350
3	Rs.1,500	Rs.400

Profit will be Rs.4,700. However, if the dealership sells the package for Rs.1,840, it will appeal to members of all three groups. In this way, the dealership will extract total consumer surplus from members of the third group, and at least some consumer surplus from the remaining two groups. The dealership's total profit will be Rs.5,850.

THIRD-DEGREE PRICE DISCRIMINATION

In some cases, it is possible for the firm to charge different groups different prices for its goods or services. It is a common practice, for example, for theaters, restaurants, and amusement parks to offer senior citizen, student, and youth discounts. This kind of pricing strategy, which is perceived as altruistic or community spirited, has considerable public relations appeal. In reality, however, this third-degree price discrimination in fact results in increased company profits.

Definition: Third-degree price discrimination occurs when firms segment the market for a particular good or service into easily identifiable groups, then charge each group a different price.

For third-degree price discrimination to be effective, a number of conditions must be satisfied. First, the firm must be able to estimate each group's demand function. As we will see, the degree of price variation will depend of differences in each group's price elasticity of demand. In general, groups with higher price elasticities of demand will be charged a lower price.

A second condition that must be satisfied for a firm to engage in third degree price discrimination is that members of each group must be easily identifiable by some distinguishable characteristic, such as age; or perhaps groups can be identified in terms of the time of the day in which the good or service, such as movie tickets, is purchased.

Finally, for third-degree price discrimination to be successful, it must not be possible for groups purchasing the good or service at a lower price to be able to resell that good or service to groups changed the higher price. If resales are possible, the firm would not be able to sell anything to the group paying the higher price because they would simply buy the good or service from the group eligible for the lower price.

The rationale behind third-degree price discrimination is straightforward. Different individuals or groups of individuals with different demand functions will have different marginal revenue functions. Since the marginal cost of producing the good is the same, regardless of which group purchases the good, the profit-maximizing condition must be $MC = MR_1 = MR_2 = ... = MR_n$, where n is the number of identifiable and separable groups. To see why this must be the case, suppose that $MR_1 > MC$. Clearly, in this case, it would pay for the firm to produce one more unit of the good or service and sell it to group 1, since the addition to total revenues would exceed the addition to total cost from producing the good. As more of the good or service is sold to group 1, marginal revenue will fall until $MR_1 = MC$ is established.

The mathematics of this third-degree price discrimination is fairly straightforward. Assume that a firm sells its product in two easily identifiable markets. The total output of the firm is, therefore,

$$Q = Q_1 + Q_2 \tag{9.11}$$

By the law of demand, the quantity sold in each market will vary inversely with the selling price. If the demand function of each group is known, the total revenue earned by the firm selling its product in each market will be

$$TR(Q) = TR_1(Q_1) + TR_2(Q_2) \tag{9.12}$$

where $TR_1 = P_1Q_1$ and $TR_2 = P_2Q_2$. The total cost of producing the good or service is a function of total output, or,

$$TC(Q) = TC(Q_1 + Q_2) \tag{9.13}$$

Note that the marginal cost of producing the good is the same for both markets. By the chain rule,

$$\frac{\partial TC(Q)}{\partial Q_1} = \left(\frac{dTC}{dQ}\right)\left(\frac{\partial Q}{\partial Q_1}\right) = \frac{\partial TC}{dQ} \tag{9.14}$$

since $\partial Q / \partial Q_1 = 1$. Likewise for Q_2,

$$\frac{\partial TC(Q)}{\partial Q_2} = \left(\frac{dTC}{dQ}\right)\left(\frac{\partial Q}{\partial Q_2}\right) = \frac{\partial TC}{dQ} \tag{9.15}$$

since $\partial Q / \partial Q_2 = 1$. Equations (9.14) and (9.15) simply affirm that the marginal cost of producing the good or service remains the same, regardless of the market in which it is sold.

Upon combining Equations (9.11) to (9.15), the firm's profit function may be written

$$\pi(Q_1, Q_2) = TR_1(Q_1) + TR_2(Q_2) - TC(Q_1 + Q_2) \tag{9.16}$$

Equation (9.16) indicates that profit is a function of both Q_1 and Q_2. The objective of the firm is to maximize profit with respect to both Q_1 and Q_2. Taking the first partial derivatives of the profit function with respect to Q_1 and Q_2, and setting the results equal to zero, we obtain

$$\frac{\partial \pi}{\partial Q_1} = \frac{\partial TR_1}{\partial Q_1} - \left(\frac{dTC}{dQ}\right)\left(\frac{\partial Q}{\partial Q_1}\right) = 0 \tag{9.17a}$$

$$\frac{\partial \pi}{\partial Q_2} = \frac{\partial TR_2}{\partial Q_2} - \left(\frac{dTC}{dQ}\right)\left(\frac{\partial Q}{\partial Q_2}\right) = 0 \tag{9.17b}$$

Solving Equations (9.17) simultaneously with respect to Q_1 and Q_2 yields the profit-maximizing unit sales in the two markets. Assuming that the second-order conditions are satisfied, the first-order conditions for profit maximization may be written as

$$MC = MR_1 = MR_2 \tag{9.18}$$

Finally, since $TR_1 = P_1Q_1$ and $TR_2 = P_2Q_2$, then

$$MR_1 = P_1\left(\frac{dQ_1}{dQ_1}\right)+\left(\frac{dP_1}{dQ_1}\right)$$

$$= P_1\left[1+\left(\frac{dP_1}{dQ_1}\right)\left(\frac{Q_1}{P_1}\right)\right] = P_1\left(1+\frac{1}{\varepsilon_1}\right) \tag{9.19}$$

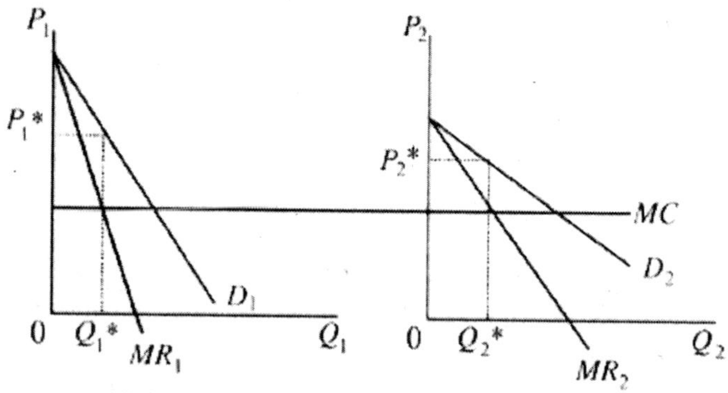

Figure: Third-degree price discrimination.

$$MR_2 = P_2\left(1+\frac{1}{\varepsilon_2}\right) \tag{9.20}$$

where ε_1 and ε_2 are the price elasticities of demand in the two markets. By the profit-maximizing condition in Equations (9.17), it is easy to see that the firm will charge the same price in the two markets only if $\varepsilon_1 = \varepsilon_2$. When $\varepsilon_1 \neq \varepsilon_2$, the prices in the two markets will not be the same. In fact, when $\varepsilon_1 > \varepsilon_2$, the price charged in the first market will be greater than the price charged in the second market. figureabove illustrates this solution for linear demand curves in the two markets and constant marginal cost.

Problem: Red Company sells its product in two separable and identifiable markets. The company's total cost equation is $TC = 6+10Q$

The demand equations for its product in the two markets are

$$Q_1 = 10 - (0.2)P_1$$

$$Q_2 = 10 - (0.2)P_2$$

where $Q = Q_1 + Q_2$.

a. Assuming that the second-order conditions are satisfied, calculate the profit-maximizing price and output level in each market.

b. Verify that the demand for Red Company's product is less elastic in the market with the higher price.

c. Give the firm's total profit at the profit-maximizing prices and output levels.

Solution:

a. This is an example of price discrimination. Solving the demand equations in both markets for price yields

$$P_1 = 50 - 5Q_1$$

$$P_2 = 30 - 2Q_2$$

The corresponding total revenue equations are

$$TR_1 = 50Q_1 - 5Q_1^2$$

$$TR_2 = 30Q_2 - 2Q_2^2$$

Red Company's total profit equation is

$$\pi = TR_1 + TR_2 - TC = 50Q_1 - 5Q_1^2 + 30Q_2 - 2Q_2^2 - 6 - 10(Q_1 + Q_2)$$

Maximizing this expression with respect to Q_1 and Q_2 yields

$$\frac{\partial \pi}{\partial Q_1} = 50 - 10Q_1 - 10 = 40 - 10Q_1 = 0$$

$$Q_1^* = 4$$

$$\frac{\partial \pi}{\partial Q_2} = 30 - 4Q_2 - 10 = 20 - 4Q_2 = 0$$

$$Q_2^* = 5$$

$$P_1^* = 50 - 5(4) = 50 - 20 = 30$$

$$P_2^* = 30 - 2(5) = 30 - 10 = 20$$

b. The relationships between the selling price and the price elasticity of demand in the two markets are

$$MR_1 = P_1\left(1 + \frac{1}{\varepsilon_1}\right)$$

$$MR_2 = P_2\left(1 + \frac{1}{\varepsilon_2}\right)$$

where

$$\varepsilon_1 = \left(\frac{dQ_1}{dP_1}\right)\left(\frac{P_1}{Q_1}\right)$$

$$\varepsilon_2 = \left(\frac{dQ_2}{dP_2}\right)\left(\frac{P_2}{Q_2}\right)$$

From the demand equations, $dQ_1/dP_1 = -0.2$ and $dQ_2/dP_2 = -0.5$. Substituting these results into preceding above relationships, we obtain

$$\varepsilon_1 = (-0.2)\left(\frac{30}{4}\right) = \frac{-6}{4} = -1.5$$

$$\varepsilon_2 = (-0.5)\left(\frac{20}{5}\right) = \frac{-10}{5} = -2$$

This verifies that the higher price is charged in the market where the price elasticity of demand is less elastic.

c. The firm's total profit at the profit-maximizing prices and output levels are

$$\pi^* = 50(4) - 5(4)^2 + 30(5) - 2(5)^2 - 6 - 10(4+5)$$

$$= 200 - 80 + 150 - 50 - 6 - 90 = 124$$

Problem: Brahmaputra Mountain is a world-famous ski resort in India. Brahmaputra Resorts operates the resort's ski-lift and grooming operations. When weather conditions are favourable, Brahmaputra's total operating cost, which depends on the number of skiers who use the facilities each year, is given as

$$TC = 10S + 6$$

where S is the total number of skiers (in hundreds of thousands). The management of Brahmaputra Resorts has determined that the demand for ski-lift tickets can be segmented into adult (S_A) and children 12 years old and under (S_C). The demand curve for each group is given as

$$S_A = 10 - 0.2\,P_A$$

$$S_C = 15 - 0.5\,P_C$$

where P_A and P_C are the prices charged for adults and children, respectively.

a. Assuming that Brahmaputra Resorts is a profit maximizer, how many skiers will visit Copperline Mountain?

b. What prices should the company charge for adult and child's ski-lift tickets?

c. Assuming that the second-order conditions for profit maximization are satisfied, what is Brahmaputra's total profit?

Solution:

a. Total profit is given by the expression

$$\pi = TR - TC = (TR_A + TR_C) - TC$$

$$= P_A S_A + P_C S_C - TC$$

$$= (50 - 5S_A)S_A + (30 - 2S_C)S_C - [10(S_A + S_C) + 6]$$

$$= -6 + 40S_A + 20S_C - 5S_A^2 - 2S_C^2$$

Taking the first partial derivatives with respect to S_A and S_C, setting the results equal to zero, and solving, we write

$$\frac{\partial \pi}{\partial S_A} = 40 - 10S_A = 0$$

$$S_A = 4$$

$$\frac{\partial \pi}{\partial S_C} = 20 - 4S_C = 0$$

$$S_C = 5$$

The total number of skiers that will visit Brahmaputra Mountain is $S = S_A = S_C = 4 + 5 = 9(\times 10^5)$ skiers

b. Substituting these results into the demand functions yields adult and child's, ski-lift ticket prices.

$$4 = 10 - 0.2P_A$$

$$P_A = \$30$$

$$5 = 15 - 0.5P_C$$

P_C = Rs. 20

c. Substituting the results from part a into the total profit equation yields

$$\pi = -6 + 40(4) + 20(5) - 5(4)^2 - 2(5)^2$$

$$= -6 + 160 + 100 - 80 - 50 = \$124(\times 10^3)$$

Problem: Suppose that a firm sells its product in two separable markets. The demand equations are $Q_1 = 100 - P_1$ $Q_2 = 50 - 0.25P_2$

The firm's total cost equation is $TC = 150 + 5Q + 0.5Q^2$

a. If the firm engages in third-degree price discrimination, how much should it sell, and what price should it charge, in each market?

b. What is the firm's total profit?

Solution:

a. Assuming that the firm is a profit maximizer, set MR = MC in each market to determine the output sold and the price charged. Solving the demand equation for P in each market yields $P_1 = 100 - Q_1$ $P_2 = 200 - 4Q_2$

The respective total and marginal revenue equations are

$$TR_1 = 100Q_1 - Q_1^2$$

$$TR_2 = 200Q_2 - Q_2^2$$

$$MR_1 = 100 - 2Q_1$$

$$MR_2 = 200 - 8Q_2$$

The firm's marginal cost equation is

$$MC = \frac{dTC}{dQ} = 5 + Q$$

Setting MR = MC for each market yields

$$100 - 2Q_1 = 5 + Q_1$$

$$200 - 8Q_2 = 5 + Q_2$$

$$Q_1{}^* = 31.67$$

$$Q_2{}^* = 15$$

$$Q_1{}^* = 100 - 31.67 = \$68.33$$

$$Q_2{}^* = 200 - 4(15) = \$140.00$$

b. The firm's total profit is

$$\pi^* = P_1{}^*Q_1{}^* + P_2{}^*Q_2{}^* - \left[150 + 5(P_1{}^* + Q_2{}^*) + 0.5(P_1{}^* + Q_2{}^*)^2\right]$$

$= 68.33(31.67) + 140(15) - (150 + 233.35 + 1{,}089.04) =$ Rs. 2,791.62

Problem:. Suppose that the firm in previous Problem charges a uniform price in the two markets in which it sells its product.

a. Find the uniform price charged, and the quantity sold, in the two markets.

b. What is the firm's total profit?

c. Compare your answers to those obtained in previous Problem.

Solution:

a. To determine the uniform price charged in each market, first add the two demand equations:

$Q = Q_1 + Q_2 = 100 - P_1 + 50 - 0.25P_2 = 150 - 1.25P$

Next, solve this equation for P: $P = 120 - 0.8Q$

The total and marginal revenue equations are

$TR = PQ = 120Q - 0.8Q^2 \; MR = 120 - 1.6Q$

The profit-maximizing level of output is

$MR = MC$

$120 - 1.6Q = 5 + Q$

$Q^* = 44.23$

That is, the profit-maximizing output of the firm is 44.23 units. The uniform price is determined by substituting this result into the combined demand equation:

$P^* = 120 - 0.8(44.23) = 120 - 35.38 =$ Rs. 84.62

The amount of output sold in each market is

$P_1^* = 100 - 84.62 = 15.38$

$Q_2^* = 50 - 0.25(84.62) = 50 - 21.16 = 28.85$

Note that the combined output of the two markets is equal to the total output Q* already derived.

b. The firm's total profit is

$\pi^* = P^*Q^* - (150 + 5Q^* + 0.5Q^{*2})$

$= 84.62(44.23) - \left[150 + 5(44.23) + 0.5(44.23)^2\right]$

$= 3,742.74 - (150 + 221.15 + 978.15) =$ Rs. 2,393.44

c. The uniform price charged (Rs.84.62) is between the prices charged in the two markets (Rs.68.33 and Rs.140.00) when the firm engaged in third-degree price discrimination. When the firm engaged in uniform pricing, the amount of output sold is lower in the first market (15.38 units compared with 31.67 units) and higher in the second market (28.85 units compared with 15 units). Finally, the firm's total profit with uniform pricing (Rs.2,393.44) is lower than when the firm engaged in third-degree price discrimination.

When third-degree price discrimination is practiced in foreign trade it is sometimes referred to as dumping. This rather derogatory term is often used by domestic producers claiming unfair foreign competition. Recall that when resale between two markets is not possible, the monopolist will sell its product at a lower price in the market in which demand is more price elastic. In international trade theory, the difference between the home price and the foreign price is called the dumping margin.

NONMARGINAL PRICING

Most of the discussion of pricing practices thus far has assumed that management is attempting to optimize some corporate objective. For the most part, we have assumed that management attempts to maximize the firm's profits, but other optimizing behavior has been discussed, such as revenue maximization. In each case, we assumed that the firm was able to calculate its total cost and total revenue equations, and to systematically use that information to achieve the firm's objectives. If the firm's objective is to maximize profit, for example, then management will produce at an output level and charge a price at which marginal revenue equals marginal cost. This is the classic example of marginal pricing.

In reality, however, firms do not know their total revenue and total cost equations, nor are they ever likely to. In fact, because firms do not have this information, and in spite management's protestations to the contrary, most firms are (unwittingly) not profit maximizers. Moreover, even if this information were available, there are other corporate objectives, such as satisficing behavior, that do not readily lend themselves to marginal pricing strategies. Consequently, most firms engage in nonmarginal pricing. The most popular form of nonmarginal pricing is cost-plus pricing.

Definition: Firms determine the profit-maximizing price and output level by equating marginal revenue with marginal cost. When the firm's total revenue and total cost equations are unknown, however, management will often practice nonmarginal pricing. The most popular form of nonmarginal pricing is cost-plus pricing, also known as markup or full-cost pricing.

COST-PLUS PRICING

As we have seen, profit maximization occurs at the price–quantity combination at which where marginal cost equals marginal revenue. In reality, however, many firms are unable or unwilling to devote the resources necessary to accurately estimate the total revenue and total cost equations, or do not know enough about demand and cost conditions to determine the profit-maximizing price and output levels.

Instead, many firms adopt rule-of-thumb methods for pricing their goods and services. Perhaps the most commonly used pricing practice is that of cost-plus pricing, also known as mark up or full-cost pricing. The rationale behind cost-plus pricing is straightforward: approximate the average cost of producing a unit of the good or service and then "mark up" the estimated cost per unit to arrive at a selling price.

Definition: Cost-plus pricing is the most popular form of nonmarginal pricing. It is the practice of adding a predetermined "markup" to a firm's estimated per-unit cost of production at the time of setting the selling price.

The firm begins by estimating the average variable cost (AVC) of producing a good or service. To this, the company adds a per-unit allocation for fixed cost. The result is sometimes referred to as the fully allocated per-unit cost of production. With the per-unit allocation for fixed cost denoted AFC and the fully allocated, average total cost ATC, the price a firm will charge for its product with the percentage mark up is

$$P = ATC(1 + m) \tag{9.21}$$

where m is the percentage markup over the fully allocated per-unit cost of production. Solving Equation (9.21) for m reveals that the mark up may also be expressed as the difference between the selling price and the perunit cost of production.

$$m = \frac{P - ATC}{ATC} \tag{9.22}$$

The numerator of Equation (9.22) can also be written as P – AVC – AFC. The expression P – AVC is sometimes referred to as the contribution margin per unit. The marked-up selling price, therefore, may be referred to as the profit contribution per unit plus some allocation to defray overhead costs.

Problem: Suppose that the Nimrod Corporation has estimated the average variable cost of producing a spool of its best-selling brand of industrial wire, Mithril, at Rs.20. The firm's total fixed cost is Rs.20,000.

a. If Nimrod produces 500 spools of Mithril and its standard pricing practice is to add a 25% markup to its estimated per-spool cost of production, what price should Nimrod charge for its product?

b. Verify that the selling price calculated in part a represents a 25% markup over the estimated per-spool cost of production.

Solution:

a. At a production level of 500 spools, Nimrod's per-unit fixed cost allocation is

$$AFC = \frac{20,000}{500} = 40$$

The cost-plus pricing equation is given as $P = ATC(1+m)$

where m is the percentage markup and ATC is the sum of the average variable cost of production (AVC) and the per-unit fixed cost allocation (AFC). Substituting, we write

$$P = (20+40)(1+0.25) = 60(1.25) = \text{Rs. } 75$$

Nimrod should charge Rs.75 per spool of Mithril. In other words, Nimrod should charge Rs.15 over its estimated per-unit cost of production.

b. The percentage markup is given by the equation

$$m = \frac{(P - ATC)}{ATC}$$

Substituting the relevant data into this equation yields

$$m = \frac{75-60}{60} = \frac{15}{60} = 0.25$$

Of course, the advantage of cost-plus pricing is its simplicity. Cost-plus pricing requires less than complete information, and it is easy to use. Care must be exercised, however, when one is using this approach. The usefulness of cost-plus pricing will be significantly reduced unless the appropriate cost concepts are employed. As in the case of break-even analysis, care must be taken to include all relevant costs of production. Cost-plus pricing, which is based only on accounting (explicit) costs, will move the firm further away from an optimal (profit-maximizing) price and output level. Of course, the more appropriate approach would be to calculate total economic costs, which include both explicit and implicit costs of production.

There are two major criticisms of cost-plus pricing. The first criticism involves the assumption of fixed marginal cost, which at fixed input prices is in defiance of the law of diminishing marginal product. It is this assumption that allows us to further assume that marginal cost is approximately equal to the fully allocated per-unit cost of production. If it can be argued, however, that marginal cost is approximately constant over the firm's range of production, this criticism loses much of its sting.

A perhaps more serious criticism of cost-plus pricing is that it is insensitive to demand conditions. It should be noted that, in practice, the size of a firm's markup tends to reflect the price elasticity of demand for of goods of various types. Where the demand for a product is relatively less price elastic, because of, say, the paucity of close substitutes, the markup tends to be higher than when demand is relatively more price elastic. As will be presently demonstrated, to the extent that this observation is correct, the criticism of insensitivity loses some of its bite.

Recall from our discussion of the relationship between the price elasticity of demand and total revenue, the relationship between marginal revenue, price, and the price elasticity of demand may be expressed as

$$MR = P\left(1 + \frac{1}{\varepsilon_p}\right) \tag{4.15}$$

The first-order condition for profit maximization is MR = MC. Replacing MR with MC in Equation (4.15) yields

$$MC = P\left(1 + \frac{1}{\varepsilon_p}\right) \tag{9.23}$$

Solving Equation (9.23) for P yields

$$P = \frac{MC}{1 + 1/\varepsilon_p} \tag{9.24}$$

If we assume that MC is approximately equal to the firm's fully allocated per-unit cost (ATC), Equation (9.24) becomes,

$$P = \frac{ATC}{1 + 1/\varepsilon_p} \tag{9.25}$$

Equating the right-hand side of this result to the right-hand side of

Equation (9.21), we obtain

$$\frac{ATC}{1+1/\varepsilon_p} = ATC(1+m)$$

where m is the percentage markup. Solving this expression for the markup yields

$$m = \frac{-1}{\varepsilon_p + 1} \tag{9.26}$$

Equation (9.26) suggests that when demand is price elastic, then the selling price should have a positive markup. Moreover, the greater the price elasticity of demand, the lower will be the markup. Suppose, for example, that $\varepsilon_p = -2.0$. Substituting this value into Equation (9.26), we find that the markup is m = –1/(–2 + 1) = –1/–1 = 1, or 100%. On the other hand, if $\varepsilon_p = -5.0$, then m = –1/(–5 +1) = –1/–4 = 0.25, or a 25% markup.

What happens, however, if the demand for the good or service is price inelastic? Suppose, for example, that $\varepsilon_p = -0.8$. Substituting this into Equation (9.26) results in a markup of m = –1/(–0.8 +1) = –1/0.2 = –5. This result suggests that the firm should mark down the price of its product by 500%! Equation (9.26) suggests that if the demand for a product is price inelastic, the firm should sell its output at below the fully allocated per-unit cost of production, a practice that is clearly not observed in the real world. Fortunately, this apparent paradox is easily resolved.

It will be recalled, and is easily seen from Equation (4.15), that when the demand for a good or service is price inelastic, it marginal revenue must be negative. For the profit-maximizing firm, this suggests that marginal cost is negative, since the first-order condition for profit maximization is MR = MC, which is clearly impossible for positive input prices and positive marginal product of factors of production.

Problem: What is the estimated percentage markup over the fully allocated per-unit cost of production for the following price elasticities of demand?

a. $\varepsilon_p = -11$

b. $\varepsilon_p = -4$

c. $\varepsilon_p = -2.5$

d. $\varepsilon_p = -2.0$

e. $\varepsilon_p = -1.5$

Solution:

a. $m = \dfrac{-1}{\varepsilon_p + 1} = \dfrac{-1}{-11+1} = 0.10$ or a 10% mark up

b. $m = \dfrac{-1}{\varepsilon_p + 1} = \dfrac{-1}{-4+1} = 0.333$ or a 33.3% mark up

c. $m = \dfrac{-1}{\varepsilon_p + 1} = \dfrac{-1}{-2.5+1} = 0.667$ or a 66.7% mark up

d. $m = \dfrac{-1}{\varepsilon_p + 1} = \dfrac{-1}{-2.0+1} = 1.0$ or a 100% mark up

e. $m = \dfrac{-1}{\varepsilon_p + 1} = \dfrac{-1}{-1.5+1} = 2.0$ or a 200% mark up

Problem: What is the percentage markup on the output of a firm operating in a perfectly competitive industry?

Solution: A firm operating in a perfectly competitive industry faces an infinitely elastic demand for its product. Substituting $\varepsilon_p = -\infty$ into Equation (9.26) yields

$$m = \frac{-1}{\varepsilon_p + 1} = \frac{-1}{-\infty + 1} = 0$$

A firm operating in a perfectly competitive industry cannot mark up the selling price of its product. This is as it should be, since such a firm has no market power; that is, the firm is a price taker. The firm must sell its product at the market-determined price.

Problem: Suppose that a firm's marginal cost of production is constant at Rs.25. Suppose further that the price elasticity of demand (ε_p) for the firm's product is +5.0.

a. Using cost-plus pricing, what price should the firm charge for its product?

b. Suppose that ε_p = –0.5. What price should the firm charge for its product?

Solution:

a. The firm's profit-maximizing condition is $MR = MC$

$$MR = P\left(1 + \frac{1}{\varepsilon_p}\right)$$

Substituting this result into the profit-maximizing condition yields

$$MC = P\left(1 + \frac{1}{\varepsilon_p}\right)$$

Since MC is constant, then MC = ATC. After substituting, and rearranging, we obtain

$$P^* = ATC\frac{\varepsilon_p}{\varepsilon_p + 1} = 25\left(\frac{-5}{-5+1}\right) = 25\left(\frac{-5}{-4}\right) = \text{Rs. } 31.25$$

b. If ε_p = –0.5, then

$$P^* = 25\left(\frac{-0.5}{-0.5+1}\right) = 25\left(\frac{-0.5}{0.5}\right) = \text{Rs. } -25.00$$

This result, however, is infeasible, since a firm would never charge a negative price for its product. Recall that a profit-maximizing firm will never produce along the inelastic portion of the demand curve.

MULTIPRODUCT PRICING

We have thus far considered primarily firms that produce and sell only one good or service at a single price. The only exception to this general statement was our discussion of commodity bundling, in which a firm sells a package of goods at a single price. We will now address the issue of pricing strategies of a single firm selling more than one product under alternative scenarios. These scenarios include the optimal pricing of two or more products with interdependent demands, optimal pricing of two or more products with independent demands that are jointly produced in variable proportions, and optimal pricing of two or more products with independent demands that are jointly produced in fixed proportions.

Definition: Multiproduct pricing involves optimal pricing strategies of firms producing and selling more than one good or service.

Optimal Pricing of Two or More Products with Interdependent Demands and Independent Production

Often a firm will produce two or more goods that are either complements or substitutes for each other. Dell Computer, for example, sells a number of different models of personal computers. These models are, to a degree, substitutes for each other. Personal computers also come with a variety of accessories (mouses, printers, modems, scanners, etc.). These options not only come in different models, and are, therefore, substitutes for each other, but they are also complements to the personal computers.

Because of the interrelationships inherent in the production of some goods and services, it stands to reason that an increase in the price of, say, a Dell personal computer model will lead to a reduction in the quantity demanded of that model and an increase in the demand for substitute models. Moreover, an increase in the price of the Dell personal computer model will lead to a reduction in the demand for complementary accessories. For this reason, a profit-maximizing firm must ascertain the optimal prices and output levels of each product manufactured jointly, rather than pricing each product independently.

The problem may be formally stated as follows. Consider the demand for two products produced by the same firm. If these two products are related, the demand functions may be expressed as

$$Q_1 = f_1(P_1, Q_2) \tag{9.27a}$$

$$Q_2 = f_2(P_2, Q_1) \tag{9.27b}$$

By the law of demand, $\partial Q_1/\partial P_1$ and $\partial Q_2/\partial P_2$ are negative. The signs of $\partial Q_1/\partial Q_2$ and $\partial Q_2/\partial Q_1$ depend on the relationship between Q_1 and Q_2. If the values of these first partial derivatives are positive, then Q_1 and Q_2 are complements. If the values of these first partials are negative, then Q_1 and Q_2 are substitutes.

Upon solving Equation (9.27a) for P_1 and Equation (9.27b) for P_2, and substituting these results into the total revenue equations, we write

$$TR_1(Q_1, Q_2) = P_1Q_1 = h_1(Q_1, Q_2)Q_1 \tag{9.28a}$$

$$TR_2(Q_1, Q_2) = P_2Q_2 = h_2(Q_1, Q_2)Q_2 \tag{9.28b}$$

Since the two goods are independently produced, the total cost functions are

$$TC_1 = TC_1(Q_1) \tag{9.29a}$$

$$TC_2 = TC_2(Q_2) \tag{9.29b}$$

The total profit equation for this firm is, therefore,

$$\pi = TR_1(Q_1, Q_2) + TR_2(Q_1, Q_2) - TC_1(Q_1) - TC_2(Q_2)$$

$$= P_1Q_1 + P_2Q_2 + TC_1(Q_1) - TC_2(Q_2)$$

$$h_1(Q_1, Q_2)Q_1 - h_2(Q_1, Q_2)Q_2 - TC_1(Q_1) - TC_2(Q_2) \tag{9.30}$$

The first-order conditions for profit maximization are

$$\frac{\partial \pi}{\partial Q_1} = \frac{\partial TR_1}{\partial Q_1} + \frac{\partial TR_2}{\partial Q_1} - \frac{\partial TC_1}{\partial Q_1} = 0 \tag{9.31a}$$

$$\frac{\partial \pi}{\partial Q_2} = \frac{\partial TR_2}{\partial Q_2} + \frac{\partial TR_1}{\partial Q_2} - \frac{\partial TC_2}{\partial Q_2} = 0 \tag{9.31b}$$

which may be expressed as

$$MC_1 = \frac{\partial TR_1}{\partial Q_1} + \frac{\partial TR_2}{\partial Q_1} \tag{9.32a}$$

$$MC_2 = \frac{\partial TR_2}{\partial Q_2} + \frac{\partial TR_1}{\partial Q_2} \tag{9.32b}$$

We will assume that the second-order conditions for profit maximization are satisfied.

Equations (9.32) indicate that a firm producing two products with interrelated demands will maximize its profits by producing where marginal cost is equal to the change in total revenue derived from the sale of the product itself, plus the change in total revenue derived from the sale of the related product. If the second term on the right-hand side of Equation (9.31) is positive, then Q_1 and Q_2 are complements. If this term is negative, then Q_1 and Q_2 are substitutes.

Problem: Gizmo Brothers, Inc., manufactures two types of hi-tech yo-yo: the Exterminator and the Eliminator. Denoting Exterminator output as Q_1 and Eliminator output as Q_2, the company has estimated the following demand equations for its yo-yos:

$$Q_1 = 10 - 0.2P_1 - 0.4Q_2$$

$$Q_2 = 20 - 0.5P_2 - 2Q_1$$

The total cost equations for producing Exterminators and Eliminators are

$$TC_1 = 4 + 2Q_1^2$$

$$TC_2 = 8 + 6Q_2^2$$

a. If Gizmo Brothers is a profit-maximizing firm, how much should it charge for Exterminators and Eliminators? What is the profitmaximizing level of output for Exterminators and Eliminators?

b. What is Gizmo Brothers's profit?

Solution:

a. Solving the demand equations for P1 and P2, respectively, yields

$$P_1 = 50 - 5Q_1 - 2Q_2$$

$$P_2 = 40 - 2Q_2 - 4Q_1$$

The profit equation is

$$\pi = TR_1(Q_1, Q_2) + TR_2(Q_1, Q_2) - TC_1(Q_1) - TC_2(Q_2)$$

$$= P_1Q_1 + P_2Q_2 - TC_1(Q_1) - TC_2(Q_2)$$

Substitution yields

$$\pi = (50 - 5Q_1 - 2Q_2)Q_1 + (40 - 2Q_2 - 4Q_1)Q_2 - (4 + 2Q_1^2) - (8 + 6Q_2^2)$$

$$= 50Q_1 + 40Q_2 - 6Q_1Q_2 - 7Q_1^2 - 8Q_2^2 - 12$$

The first-order conditions for profit maximization are

$$\frac{\partial \pi}{\partial Q_1} = 50 - 14Q_1 - 6Q_2 = 0$$

$$\frac{\partial \pi}{\partial Q_2} = 40 - 6Q_1 - 16Q_2 = 0$$

The second-order conditions for profit maximization are

$$\frac{\partial^2 \pi}{\partial Q_1^2} < 0 \quad \frac{\partial^2 \pi}{\partial Q_2^2} < 0$$

$$\left(\frac{\partial^2 \pi}{\partial Q_1^2}\right)\left(\frac{\partial^2 \pi}{\partial Q_1^2}\right) - \left(\frac{\partial^2 \pi}{\partial Q_1 \partial Q_2}\right) > 0$$

The appropriate second partial derivatives are

$$\frac{\partial^2 \pi}{\partial Q_1^2} = -14 < 0$$

$$\frac{\partial^2 \pi}{\partial Q_2^2} = -16 < 0$$

$$\frac{\partial^2 \pi}{\partial Q_1 \partial Q_2} = -6$$

$$(-14)(-16) - (6)^2 = 244 - 36 = 208 > 0$$

Thus, the second-order conditions for profit maximization are satisfied. Solving the first-order conditions for Q_1 and Q_2 we obtain

$$14Q_1 + 6Q_2 = 50$$

$$6Q_1 + 16Q_2 = 40$$

which may be solved simultaneously to yield $Q_1{*} = 2.979$ $Q_2{*} = 1.383$

Upon substituting these results into the price equations, we have

$$P_1{*} = 50 - 5(2.979) - 2(1.383) = \text{Rs. } 32.34$$

$$P_2{*} = 40 - 2(1.383) - 4(2.979) = \text{Rs. } 25.32$$

b. Gizmo Brothers's profit is

$$\pi = 50(2.979) + 40(1.383) - 6(2.979)(1.383) - 7(2.979)^2 - 8(1.383)^2 - 12$$

$$= \text{Rs. } 90.17$$

Optimal Pricing of Two or More Products with Independent Demands Jointly Produced in Variable Proportions

Let us now suppose that a firm sells two goods with independent demands that are jointly produced in variable proportions. An example of this might be a consumer electronics company that produces automobile taillight bulbs and flashlight bulbs on the same assembly line. In this case, the demand functions are given by the expressions

$$Q_1 = f_1(P_1) \tag{9.33a}$$

$$Q_2 = f_2(P_2) \tag{9.33b}$$

where $\partial Q_1/\partial P_1$ and $\partial Q_2/\partial P_2$ are negative. The total cost function is given by the expression

$$TC = TC(Q_1, Q_2) \tag{9.34}$$

The firm's total profit function is

$$\pi = TR_1(Q_1) + TR_2(Q_2) - TC(Q_1, Q_2) \tag{9.35}$$

Solving the demand equations for P_1 and P_2 and substituting the results into Equation (9.35) yields

$$\pi = P_1Q_1 + P_2Q_2 - TC(Q_1, Q_2)$$

$$= h_1(Q_1)Q_1 + h_2(Q_2)Q_2 - TC(Q_1, Q_2) \tag{9.36}$$

The first-order conditions for profit maximization are

$$\frac{\partial \pi}{\partial Q_1} = \frac{\partial TR_1}{\partial Q_1} - \frac{\partial TC_1}{\partial Q_1} = 0 \tag{9.37a}$$

$$\frac{\partial \pi}{\partial Q_2} = \frac{\partial TR_2}{\partial Q_2} - \frac{\partial TC_2}{\partial Q_2} = 0 \tag{9.37b}$$

which may be written as

$$MR_1 = MC_1 \tag{9.38a}$$

$$MR_2 = MC_2 \tag{9.38b}$$

We will assume that the second-order conditions for profit maximization are satisfied.

Equations (9.38) indicate that a profit-maximizing firm jointly producing two goods with independent demands that are jointly produced in variable proportions will equate the marginal revenue generated from the sale of each good to the marginal cost of producing each product.

Problem: Suppose Gizmo Brothers also produces Tommy Gunn action figures for boys ages 7 to 12, and Bonzey, a toy bone for pet dogs. Except for the molding phase, both products are made on the same assembly line. Denoting Tommy Gunn as Q_1 and Bonzey as Q_2, the company has estimated the following demand equations: $Q_1 = 10 - 0.5P_1$

$$Q_2 = 20 - 0.2P_2$$

The total cost equation for producing the two products is

$$TC = Q_1^2 + 2Q_1Q_2 + 3Q_2^2 + 10$$

a. As before, Gizmo Brothers is a profit-maximizing firm. Give the profitmaximizing levels of output for Tommy Gunn and for Bonzey. How much should the firm charge for Tommy Gunn and Bonzey?

b. What is Gizmo Brothers's profit?

Solution:

a. Solving the demand equations for P_1 and P_2, respectively, yields

$$P_1 = 20 - 2Q_1$$

$$P_2 = 100 - 5Q_2$$

Gizmo Brothers's profit equation is

$$\pi = TR_1(Q_1) + TR_2(Q_2) - TC_1(Q_1, Q_2) = P_1Q_1 + P_2Q_2 - TC_1(Q_1, Q_2)$$

Substituting the demand equations into the profit equation yield

$$\pi = (20 - 2Q_1)Q_1 + (100 - 5Q_2)Q_2 - (Q_1^2 + 2Q_1Q_2 + 3Q_2^2 + 10)$$

$$= -10 + 20Q_1 + 100Q_2 - 3Q_1^2 - 8Q_2^2 - 2Q_1Q_2$$

The first-order conditions for profit maximization are

$$\frac{\partial \pi}{\partial Q_1} = 20 - 6Q_1 - 2Q_2 = 0$$

$$\frac{\partial \pi}{\partial Q_2} = 100 - 16Q_2 - 2Q_1 = 0$$

The second-order conditions for profit maximization are

$$\frac{\partial^2 \pi}{\partial Q_1^2} < 0 \quad \frac{\partial^2 \pi}{\partial Q_2^2} < 0$$

$$\left(\frac{\partial^2 \pi}{\partial Q_1^2}\right)\left(\frac{\partial^2 \pi}{\partial Q_1^2}\right) - \left(\frac{\partial^2 \pi}{\partial Q_1 \partial Q_2}\right)^2 > 0$$

The appropriate second-partial derivatives are

$$\frac{\partial^2 \pi}{\partial Q_1^2} = -6 < 0$$

$$\frac{\partial^2 \pi}{\partial Q_2^2} = -16 < 0$$

$$\frac{\partial^2 \pi}{\partial Q_1 \partial Q_2} = -2$$

$$(-6)(-16) - (-2)^2 = 96 - 4 = 92 > 0$$

Thus, the second-order conditions for profit maximization are satisfied. Solving the first-order conditions for Q_1 and Q_2 yields

$$6Q_1 + 2Q_2 = 20$$

$$2Q_1 + 16Q_2 = 100$$

which may be solved simultaneously to yield

$$Q_1^* = 1.304$$

$$Q_2^* = 6.087$$

Substituting these results into the price equations yields

$$P_1^* = 20 - 2(1.304) = \text{Rs. } 17.39$$

$$P_2^* = 100 - 2(6.087) = \text{Rs. } 69.66$$

b. Gizmo Brothers's profit is

$$\pi = 20(1.304) + 100(6.087) - 2(1.304)(6.087) - 3(1.304)^2 - 8(6.087)^2 - 10$$

$$= \text{Rs. } 88.17$$

OPTIMAL PRICING OF TWO OR MORE PRODUCTS WITH INDEPENDENT DEMANDS JOINTLY PRODUCED IN FIXED PROPORTIONS

Now, let us assume that a firm jointly produces two goods in fixed proportions but with independent demands. In many cases, the second product is a by-product of the first, such as beef and hides. With joint production in fixed proportions, it is conceptually impossible to consider two separate products, since the production of one good automatically determines the quantity produced of the other.

Suppose that the demand functions for two goods produced jointly are given as Equations (9.33). The total cost equation is given as Equation (9.13).

$$TC(Q) = TC(Q_1 + Q_2) \tag{9.13}$$

The analysis differs, however, in that Q_1 and Q_2 are in direct proportion to each other, that is,

$$Q_2 = kQ_1 \tag{9.39}$$

where the constant $k > 0$. Solving Equation (9.33) for P_1 and P_2 yields

$$P_1 = h_1(Q_1) \tag{9.40a}$$

$$P_2 = h_2(Q_2) \tag{9.40b}$$

Substituting Equation (9.39) into Equations (9.13) and (9.40b) yields

$$P_1 = h_1(Q_1)$$

$$P_2 = h_2(Q_1) \tag{9.41}$$

$$TC(Q) = TC(Q_1) \tag{9.42}$$

Substituting Equations (9.39), (9.40a), (9.41), and (9.42) into Equation (9.36) yields the firm's profit equation:

$$\pi = P_1Q_1 + P_2(kQ_1) - TC(Q_1)$$

$$= h_1(Q_1)Q_1 + h_2(Q_1)(kQ_1) - TC(Q_1) \tag{9.43}$$

Stated another way, the firm's total profit function is

$$\pi(Q_1) = TR_1(Q_1) + TR_2(Q_1) - TC(Q_1) \tag{9.44}$$

Equation (9.44) indicates that total profit is a function of the single decision variable, Q_1. Equation (9.44) may also be written

$$\pi(Q_2) = TR_1(Q_2) + TR_2(Q_2) - TC(Q_2) \tag{9.45}$$

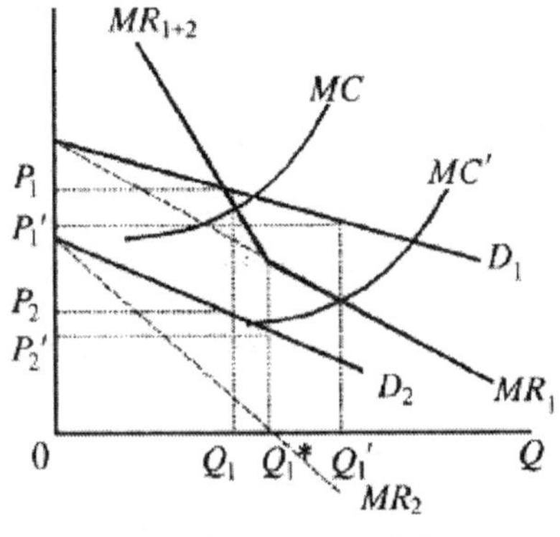

Figure: Optimal pricing of two goods jointly produced in fixed proportions with independent demands.

From Equation (9.44), the first-order condition for profit maximization is

$$\frac{d\pi}{dQ_1} = \frac{dTR_1}{dQ_1} + \frac{dTR_2}{dQ_1} - \frac{dTC_1}{dQ_1} = 0$$

Equation (9.46) may be rewritten

$$\frac{dTR_1}{dQ_1} + \frac{dTR_2}{dQ_1} = \frac{dTC_1}{dQ_1}$$

$$MR_1(Q_1) + MR_2(Q_1) = MC(Q_1)$$

Equation (9.47) says that a profit-maximizing firm that jointly produces two goods in fixed proportions with independent demands will equate the sum of the marginal revenues of both products expressed in terms of one of the products with the marginal cost of jointly producing both products expressed in terms of the same product. This situation is depicted diagrammatically in above figure.

In above figure the marginal cost curve is labeled MC. According to Equation (9.47) the firm should produce Q_1 units where marginal cost is equal to the sum of MR_1 and MR_2. The amount of Q_2 produced is proportional to Q_1. At that output level the firm charges P_1 for Q_1 and P_2 for Q_2. It should be noted that beyond output level Q_1* in above figure, MR_2 becomes negative and MR_{1+2} becomes simply MR_1.

Suppose that marginal cost increases to MC'. In this case, the firm should produce Q_1',, but still only sell Q_1* units. Any output in excess of Q_1* should be disposed of, since the firm's marginal revenue beyond Q_1* is negative. The amount of Q_2 produced will be in fixed proportion to Q_1'. The price of Q_1 * is P_2', and the price of Q_2 is P_1'.

Problem: Suppose that a firm produces two units of Q_2 for each unit of Q_1. Suppose further that the demand equations for these two goods are $Q_1 = 10 - 0.5P_1$ $Q_2 = 20 - 0.2P_2$

The total cost of production is $TC = 10 + 5Q^2$

a. What are the profit-maximizing output levels and prices for Q_1 and Q_2?

b. At the profit-maximizing output levels, what is the firm's total profit?

Solution:

a. Solving the demand equations for P1 and P2 yields

$P_1 = 20 - 2Q_1$

$P_2 = 100 - 5Q_2$

The firm's total profit equation is $\pi = P_1Q_1 + P_2Q_2 - TC(Q_1 + Q_2)$

$= (20 - 2Q_1)Q_1 + (100 - 5Q_2)Q_2 - (10 + 5Q^2)$

$= 20Q_1 - 2Q_1^2 + 100Q_2 - 5Q_2^2 - 10 - 5(Q_1 + Q_2)^2$

Since $Q_2 = 2Q_1$, this may be rewritten as

$$\pi = 20Q_1 - 2Q_1^2 + 100(2Q_1) - 5(2Q_1)^2 - 10 - 5(Q_1 + 2Q_1)^2$$

$$= -10 - 220Q_1 - 67Q_1^2$$

The first-order condition for profit maximization is

$$\frac{d\pi}{dQ_1} = 220 - 134Q_1 = 0$$

The second-order condition for profit maximization is $\frac{d^2\pi}{dQ_1^2} < 0$

Since $d_{2\pi}/dQ_1^2 = -137$ the second-order condition is satisfied. Solving the first-order condition for Q_1 yields $Q_1^* = 1.64$

The profit-maximizing level of Q_2 is $Q_2^* = 2Q_1^* = 3.28$

Substituting these results into the price equations yield $P_1^* = 20 - 2(1.64) =$ Rs. 16.72 $P_2^* = 100 - 5(3.28) =$ Rs. 83.60

b. The firm's total profit is

$$\pi = 220(1.64) - 67(1.64)^2 - 10$$

$$= 360.80 - 180.20 - 10 = \text{Rs. } 170.60$$

Problem: Suppose that a firm jointly produces two goods. Good B is a by-product of the production of good A. The demand equations for the two goods are $Q_A = 200 - 10P_A$ $Q_B = 120 - 5P_B$

The firm's total cost equation is $TC = 500 + 15Q + 0.05Q^2$

a. What is the profit-maximizing price for each product?

b. What is the firm's total profit?

Solution:

a. Solving the demand equation for price yields $P_A = 20 - 0.1Q_A$

$$P_B = 24 - 0.2Q_B$$

The respective total and marginal revenue equations are

$TR_A = 20Q_A - 0.1Q_A^2$

$MR_A = 20 - 0.2Q_A$

$TR_B = 24Q_B - 0.2Q_B^2$

$MR_B = 24 - 0.4Q_B$

The firm's marginal revenue equation is

$MR = MR_A + MR_B$

$= 20 - 0.2Q_A + 24 - 0.4Q_B = 44 - 0.6Q$

The firm's marginal cost equation is

$$MC = \frac{dTC}{dQ} = 15 + 0.1Q$$

The profit-maximizing rate of output is

$MR = MC$

$44 - 0.6Q = 15 + 0.1Q$

$Q^* = 41.43$

The profit-maximizing prices for the two goods are

$P_A^* = 20 - 0.1(41.43) = 20 - 4.14 =$ Rs. 15.86

$P_B^* = 20 - 0.2(41.43) = 24 - 8.29 =$ Rs. 15.71

b. The firm's total profit is

$\pi^* = P_A{}^*Q^* + P_B{}^*Q^* - (500 + 15Q^* + 0.05Q^{*2})$

$= 15.86(41.43) + 15.71(41.43) - [500 - 15(41.43) + 0.05(41.43)^2]$

= Rs. 1,343.57

PEAK-LOAD PRICING

In many markets the demand for a service is higher at certain times than at others. The demand for electric power, for example, is higher during the day than at night, and during summer and winter than during spring and fall. The demand for theater tickets is greater at night and on the weekends or for midweek matinees. Toll bridges have greater traffic during rush hours than at other times of the day. The demand for airline travel is greater during holiday seasons than at other times. During such "peak" periods it becomes difficult, if not impossible, to satisfy the demands of all customers. Thus the profit-maximizing firm will charge a higher price for the product during "peak" periods and a lower price during "off-peak" periods. This kind of pricing scheme is known as peak-load pricing.

Definition: Peak-load pricing is the practice of charging a higher price for a service when demand is high and capacity is fully utilized and a lower price when demand is low and capacity is underutilized.

Figure below illustrates an example of peak-load pricing for a profitmaximizing firm. Here the marginal cost of providing a service is assumed to be constant until capacity is reached at a peak output level of O_p. At the peak output level the marginal cost curve becomes vertical. This reflects the fact that to satisfy additional demand at O_p, the firm must increase its capacity, by building a new bridge, installing a new hydroelectric generator, or other high-cost measure.

The short-run production function is typically defined in terms of a time interval over which certain factors of production are "fixed." Strictly speaking, this assertion is incorrect. In principle, virtually any factor may be varied if the derived benefits are great enough. It is certainly the case, however, that some factors of production are more easily varied that others. It is clearly easier and less expensive to hire an additional worker at a moment's notice than to build a new bridge.

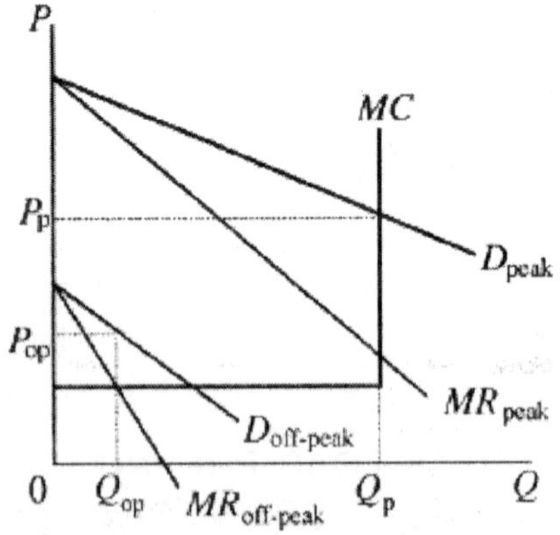

Figure: Peak-load pricing.

Thus, it is reasonable to assume that the short-run marginal cost of expanding bridge traffic or increasing hydroelectric capacity is infinite. For that reason, the marginal cost curve at Q_p is assumed to be vertical.

To maximize profits subject to capacity limitations, the firm will charge different prices at different times. Off-peak prices are determined by equating marginal revenue to marginal operating costs. Peak prices, on the other hand, are determined by equating marginal revenue to the marginal cost of increasing capacity. In above figure, for example, MR = MC for off-peak users at output level Q_{op}. At that output level the firm will charge off-peak users a price of P_{op}. On the other hand, the profit-maximizing level of output for peak users is at the firm's capacity, which in above figure occurs at output level Q_p. At that output level the marginal cost curve of producing the service becomes vertical. The profit-maximizing price at that output level is P_p.

Peak-load pricing suggests that users of, say, congested bridges during rush hours, ought to be charged a higher toll than users during non–rush hour periods when there is excess capacity. Since peak-period demand strains capacity, the cost of additional capital investment ought to be borne by peak-period users. This tends to run contrary to the common practice on trains and toll bridges of offering multiple-use discounts to commuters traveling during rush hour, such as lower per-ride prices for, say, monthly tickets on commuter railways.

Problem: The Gotham Bridge and Tunnel Authority (GBTA) has estimated the following demand equations for peak and off-peak automobile users of the Frog's Neck Bridge:

$$\text{Peak: } T_p = 10 - 0.02Q_p$$

$$\text{Off-peack: } T_{op} = 5 - 0.05Q_{op}$$

where T is the toll charged for a one-minute trip (Q) across the bridge. The marginal cost of operating the bridge has been estimated at Rs.2 per automobile bridge crossing. The peak capacity of the Frog's Neck Bridge has been estimated a 50 automobiles per minute. What toll should the GBTA charge peak and off-peak users of the bridge?

Solution: This is a problem of peak-load pricing. If the GBTA is a profit maximizer, then off-peak drivers should be charged a price consistent with the first-order condition for profit maximization, MC = MR. The total revenue equation for off-peak users of the bridge is given as

$$TR_{op} = T_{op}Q_{op} = (5 - 0.05Q_{op})Q_{op} = 5Q - 0.05Q_{op}^{2}$$

The marginal revenue equation is

$$MR_{op} = \frac{dTR}{dQ_{op}} 5 - 0.1Q_{op}$$

Equating marginal revenue to marginal cost yields

$$MR_{op} = MC_{op}$$

$$5 - 0.1Q_{op} = 2$$

$$Q_{op} = 30$$

Substituting this result into the off-peak demand equation yields the toll charged to off-peak automobile users of the bridge:

$$T_{op} = 5 - 0.05Q_{op} = 5 - 0.05(30) = \text{Rs. } 3.50$$

At a bridge capacity of 50 automobiles per minute, the marginal cost curve is vertical. Substituting bridge capacity into the peak demand equation yields the toll that should be charged to peak automobile users of the bridge:

$$T_{p} = 10 - 0.02(50) = \text{Rs. } 9$$

Peak users of the bridge should be charged Rs.9 per crossing.

TRANSFER PRICING

In recent years, the growth of large, conglomerate corporations producing a multitude of products has been accompanied by the parallel development of semiautonomous profit centers or subsidiaries. The creation of these "companies within a company" was an attempt to control rising production costs that accompanied the burgeoning managerial and adminis trative superstructure necessary to coordinate the activities of multiple corporate divisions.

Often the output of a division or subsidiary of a parent company is used as a productive input in the manufacture of the output of another division. A subsidiary of a large, multinational firm, for example, might assemble automobiles, while another subsidiary manufactures automobile bodies. Still another subsidiary might produce air and oil filters, while yet another produces electronic ignition systems, all of which are used in the production of automobiles.

Transfer pricing concerns itself with the correct pricing of intermediate products that are produced and sold between divisions of a parent company. For example, what price should one division of a company that produces, say, ignition systems, charge another division that assembles automobiles. The optimal pricing of intermediary goods is important because the organizational objective of each division is to maximize profit. What is more, the price charged for the output of one division that is used as an input in the production of another division affects not only each division's profits but also profits of the parent company as a whole.

Definition: Transfer pricing involves the optimal pricing of the output of one subsidiary of a parent company that is sold as an intermediate good to another subsidiary of the same parent company.

The literature dealing with transfer pricing typically focuses on three possible scenarios. In the first scenario, there is no external market for the output of the division or subsidiary producing the intermediate good. In other words, the division producing the final product is the sole customer for the output of the division producing the intermediate good. In the second scenario there exists a perfectly competitive external market for the intermediate good. In the third scenario the division or subsidiary operates in an industry that may be characterized as imperfectly competitive.

TRANSFER PRICING WITH NO EXTERNAL MARKET

Assume that a parent company comprises two subsidiary companies. One subsidiary sells its output, Q_1, exclusively to the other subsidiary that is used in the production of Q_2, for final sale in an external market. Assume further that there exists no other demand for Q_1; that is, there is no external market for the intermediate good. Finally assume that one unit of Q_1 is used to produce one unit of Q_2.

Since the parent company comprises only two subsidiaries, the marginal cost of producing Q_2 for final sale must include the marginal cost of producing Q_1. The rationale for this is straightforward. Although the company has been divided into separate profit centers, in the final analysis the company is in the business of producing and selling Q_2 for final sale. The marginal cost of producing Q_2 must, of course, include the marginal cost of producing Q_1. If we assume that the parent company is a profit maximizer, it will produce at the output level where $MR_2 = MC_2$. This situation is illustrated in figure below.

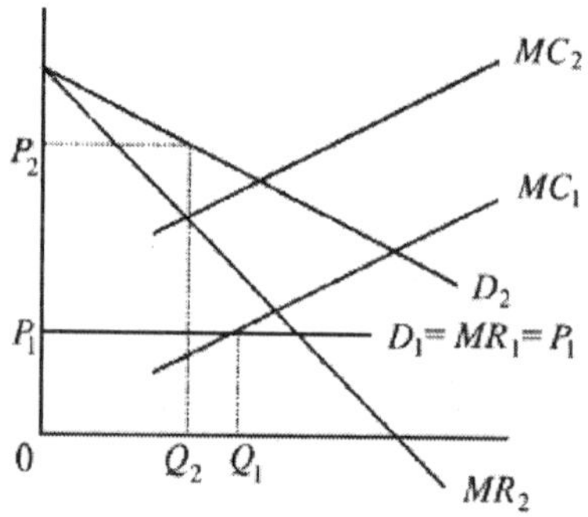

Figure: Transfer pricing with no external market for the intermediate good.

Since Q_1 and Q_2 are used on a one-to-one basis, the output level that maximizes profit of Q_2 will be the same output level as Q_1. The selling price of Q_2 is P_2. Since the output level of Q_1 has been determined by the output level of Q_2, the profit-maximizing price for Q_1 must be P_1 (i.e., where $MC_1 = MR_1$). Thus, the correct transfer price for the intermediate good Q_1 must be P_1. It should be noted that any increase in the marginal cost of producing Q_1 will result in an increase in the marginal cost of producing Q_2, which will further result in an increase in the selling price of Q_2 and an increase in the transfer price (i.e., the price of the intermediate good that is sold between divisions).

On the other hand, suppose that the marginal cost curve of producing Q_1 remains unchanged, but the marginal cost curve of producing Q_2 shifts upward, perhaps because of an increase in factor or intermediate goods prices purchased in the external market. The result will be an increase in P_2, a decline in the output of Q_2 and Q_1, and, assuming an upward sloping marginal cost curve for Q_1, a fall in the transfer price. When the marginal cost of producing Q_1 is constant, the transfer price remains unaffected by the additional increase in the marginal cost of producing Q_2.

Problem: Parallax Corporation produces refractive telescopes for amateur astronomers. The demand equation for Parallax telescopes was estimated by the operations research department as $Q_T = 2{,}000 - 20P_T$

Parallax's total cost equation was estimated as $TC_T = 100 - 2Q_T^2$

Although the company procures most of its components from outside vendors, each Parallax telescope requires three highly polished lenses that are manufactured on site. Because these components are manufactured to exact specifications, there is no outside market for Parallax lenses. The total cost equation for producing Parallax lenses is $TC_L = 200 - 0.025Q_L^2$

Because of the rapid growth of the company in the 1980s, Parallax management decided to divide the company into two separate profit centers to control costs—the telescope division and the lens division.

a. What is the profit-maximizing price and quantity for Parallax telescopes?

b. What is Parallax's total profit?

c. What transfer price should the lens division charge the telescope division?

Solution:

a. Solving the demand equation for PT yields $P_T = 100 - 0.05Q_T$

The corresponding total revenue equation for Parallax telescopes is

$$TR_T = P_T Q_T = (100 - 0.05Q_T)Q_T = 100Q_T - 0.05Q_T^2$$

The total profit equation for Parallax telescopes is

$$\pi_T = TR_T - TC_T = (100Q_T - 0.05Q_T^2) - (100 + 2Q_T^2)$$

$$= -100 + 100Q_T - 2.05Q_T^2$$

The first-order condition for profit maximization is d π /dQT = 0. Taking the first derivative of the profit equation yields

$$\frac{d\pi}{dQ} = 100 - 4.1Q_T = 0$$

solving, we that $Q_T{}^* = 24.39$

The second-order condition for profit maximization is d π /dQT < 0. After taking the second derivative of the profit equation, we obtain

$$\frac{d^2\pi}{dQ^2} = -4.1 < 0$$

which guarantees that this output level represents a local maximum. The profit-maximizing price, therefore, is $P_T{*} = 100 - 0.05(24.39) =$ Rs. 98.78

b. Parallax's profit at the profit-maximizing price and quantity is

$$\pi = -100 + 100(24.39) - 2.05(24.39)^2 = \text{Rs. } 1{,}119.51$$

c. Since there is no external market for Parallax lenses, the transfer price is equal to the marginal cost of producing the lenses at the profitmaximizing output level. Parallax's marginal cost equation for producing lenses is

$$MC_L = \frac{dTC_1}{dQ_L} = 0.05Q_L$$

Since Parallax needs three lenses for every telescope produced, the total number of lenses required by the telescope division is 73.17 lenses (3 × 23.39 telescopes). The marginal cost of producing these lenses, therefore, is

$$MC_I = 0.05(70.17) = \text{Rs. } 3.51$$

The transfer price of the lenses, therefore, is Rs.3.51 per lens.

TRANSFER PRICING WITH A PERFECTLY COMPETITIVE EXTERNAL MARKET

We will now consider the situation in which there exists an external market for the intermediate good. That is, the division or subsidiary producing the final product has the option of purchasing the intermediate good either from a subsidiary of its own parent company or from an outside vendor. If the intermediate good is purchased from within, what will its transfer price be? The answer to this question will depend on whether the external market for the intermediate good is or is not perfectly competitive. We will begin by assuming that there exists a perfectly competitive external market for the intermediate good produced by the subsidiary.

Since both divisions are assumed to be profit maximizers, it stands to reason that the division producing the final good will pay no more for the intermediate good than it would pay in the perfectly competitive external market. Similarly, the division producing the intermediate good will sell its output for nothing less than the perfectly competitive external market price. Thus, the transfer price for the intermediate good is the perfectly competitive price in the external market. This situation is depicted in figurebelow, where the price for the intermediate good is the same price depicted in figure above.

It should be noted that because the price of the intermediate good in figure below is assumed to be the same price depicted in figure above, the marginal cost of producing the final good remains unchanged. Thus, the profitmaximizing price and the quantity for the final good remain unchanged at P_2 and Q_2.

Unlike the situation depicted in figure above, the amount of output produced by the intermediate good division no longer needs to equal the output of the final good division. Moreover, the transfer price for the intermediate good is the perfectly competitive price in the external market. In the preceding case, with no external market for the intermediate good, the transfer price was determined by the level of output that maximized profits for the final goods division.

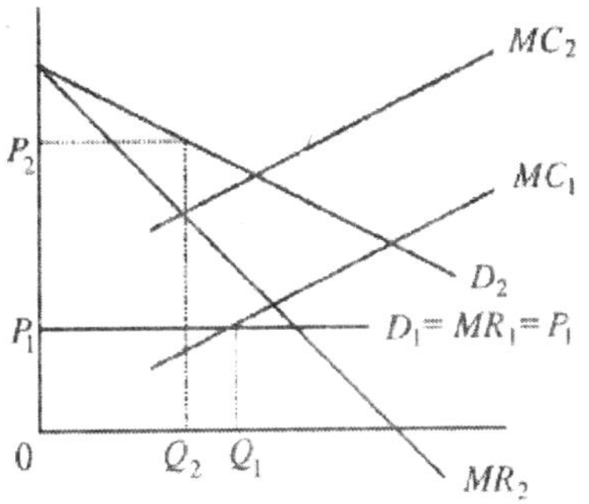

Figure: Transfer pricing with a perfectly competitive external market for intermediate good.

In the situation depicted in figure above, the marginal cost of producing the intermediate good is lower than that depicted in figure above. The profit maximizing, intermediate good division will produce at an output level at which $MC_1 - MR_1$. This occurs at an output level that is greater than Q_2. The division producing the intermediate good will sell Q_2 to the division producing the final good and will sell the surplus output of Q_1 -Q_2 in the external market at the perfectly competitive price, P_1.

Problem: Suppose that in the Parallax telescope example of previous problem, the lenses produced by the subsidiary are of a standard variety produced by a perfectly competitive firm. Suppose further that the marketdetermined price of these lenses is Rs.4.

a. Find the profit-maximizing price and quantity for Parallax telescopes. What is Parallax's total profit?

b. What transfer price should the lens division charge the telescope division?

c.. How many lenses will the lens division produce? Will the number of lenses produced be sufficient to satisfy the requirements of the telescope division? If not, what should the telescope division do? If the lens division produces more lenses than the telescope division requires, what should the overproducing division do?

Solution:

a. Since there is no change in the demand for Parallax telescopes, there is no change in the firm's total revenue function. However, since lenses are now Rs.0.49 more expensive than before, Parallax must spend Rs.1.47 more to produce each telescope. Parallax's total cost equation for telescopes is now $TC_T = 100 - 2Q_T^2 + 1.47Q_T$

Parallax's total profit equation is

$$\pi = TR - TC_T = \left(100Q_T - 0.05Q_T^2\right) - \left(100 + 2Q_T^2 + 1.4Q_T\right)$$

$$= -100 + 100Q_T - 2.05Q_T^2 - 1.47Q_T = -100 + 98.53Q_T - 2.05Q_T^2$$

The first-order condition for profit maximization is dπ/dQT = 0. Taking the first derivative of the profit equation yields

$$\frac{d\pi}{dQ} = 98.53 - 4.1Q_T = 0$$

Solving, we have

$$Q_T{}^* = 24.03$$

The second-order condition for profit maximization is dπ/dQT < 0. Taking the second derivative of the profit equation yields

$$\frac{d^2\pi}{dQ^2} = -4.1 < 0$$

which guarantees that this output level represents a local maximum. The profit-maximizing price, therefore, is $P_T{}^* = 100 - 0.05(24.03) =$ Rs. 98.80

Parallax's total profit at the profit-maximizing price and quantity is

$$\pi = -100 - 98.53(24.03) - 2.05(24.03)^2 = \text{Rs. } 1{,}083.93$$

b. The transfer price for lenses is the price set in the perfectly competitive market (i.e., P_L = Rs.4).

c. The lens division will maximize profit by setting the marginal cost of producing lenses equal to the marginal revenue of selling lenses, that is, $MC_L = MR_L$

Since lens production takes place in a perfectly competitive industry, the marginal revenue from selling lenses is Rs.4 per lens. The marginal cost equation of lens production is

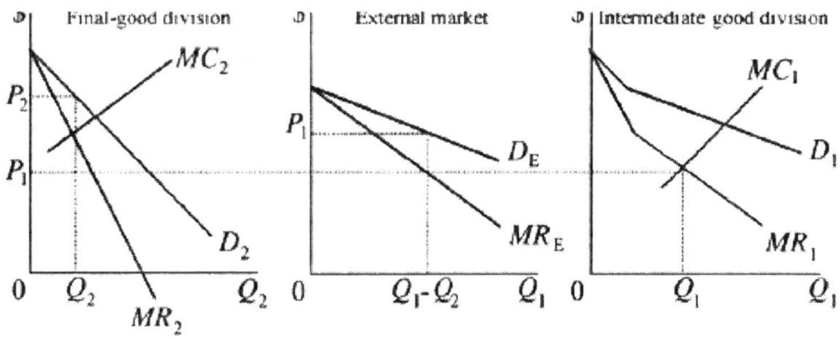

Figure: Transfer pricing with an imperfectly competitive external market for the intermediate good.

$$MC_L = \frac{dTC_L}{dQ_L} = 0.05Q_L$$

Substitution yields $4 = 0.05Q_L \quad Q_L^* = 80$

The lens division should produce 80 lenses. Since the telescope division needs 72.09 lenses (3 ¥ 24.03 telescopes), the lens division should sell the remaining 7.91 lenses in the external market.

TRANSFER PRICING WITH AN IMPERFECTLY COMPETITIVE EXTERNAL MARKET

Finally, let us consider an imperfectly competitive external market for the intermediate good. In this case, the price charged by the intermediate good division to the final good division will differ from the price of the intermediate good in the imperfectly competitive external market. The prices charged internally and externally by the intermediate good division become a matter of third-degree price discrimination.

In above figure, the intermediate good division faces a downward-sloping demand curve for its output. The total demand for Q_I includes the demand for the intermediate good by the final-good division and the demand by the external market. This demand curve is labeled D_I. Once again, the marginal cost of producing the final good Q_2 includes the marginal cost of producing Q_I. The profit-maximizing level of output for the intermediate good division is Q_I. The corresponding $MR_I = MC_I$ will determine the selling price of the intermediate good to the final good division. This will be the transfer price of the intermediate good.

The amount of Q_I that will be sold to the final good division will be determined by the profit-maximizing level of output Q_2, since $Q_I = Q_2$. This leaves $Q_I - Q_2$ units of Q_I available for sale in the external market. The intermediate good division will maximize its profits by charging a price in the external market such that $MC_I = MR_E$. In above figure, the intermediate good division engages in third-degree price discrimination by charging more in the external market than it charges the final good division.

OTHER PRICING PRACTICES

This chapter has so far focused on the pricing behavior of profit-maximizing firms operating under somewhat unique circumstances. In each case, the firm's pricing practices were predicated on subtle economic concepts. It was also assumed that management had complete information about the realities of the market in which the firm operated. In practice however, a firm's pricing practices are much looser in the sense that they are based less on detailed mathematical analysis than on perception, custom, and intuition. The remainder of this chapter is devoted to a review of five of these alternative pricing practices-price leadership, price skimming, penetration pricing, prestige pricing, and psychological pricing.

PRICE LEADERSHIP

Price leadership is a phenomenon that is likely to be observed in oligopolistic industries. Oligopolistic industries are characterized by the interdependence of managerial decisions between and among the firms in the industry. Firms in oligopolistic industries are keenly aware that the pricing and output decisions of any individual firm will provoke a reaction by competing firms. A consequence of this interdependence is relatively infrequent price changes.

Definition: Price leadership occurs when a dominant company in an industry establishes the selling price of a product for the rest of the firms in the industry. Two forms of price leadership are barometric price leadership and dominant price leadership.

Barometric Price Leadership

We saw in our discussion of the kinked demand curve that in oligopolistic industries, marginal cost may fluctuate within a fairly narrow range without evoking a price change. The reason for this is the discontinuity in the firm's marginal revenue curve. As a result, prices are relatively stable at the "kink" in the demand curve. What happens, however, when cost conditions for the typical firm in the industry increase significantly because of some exogenous shock?

Definition: Barometric price leadership occurs when a price change by one firm in an oligopolistic industry, usually in response to perceived changes in macroeconomic or market conditions, is quickly followed by price changes by other firms in the industry.

In an oligopolistic industry characterized by firms of roughly the same size, price changes may sometimes be explained by barometric price leadership. In this case, a typical firm in the industry initiates, say, a price increase based on management's belief that changes in macroeconomic or market conditions will have a uniform impact on all other firms in the industry. If other firms believe that the firm's interpretations of economic events are correct, they will quickly follow suit. If they disagree, the firm initiating the price increase will be forced to reevaluate its decision and may modify or repeal the price increase. If the price increase is modified, the evaluation process begins again. Ultimately, member firms in the industry will form a consensus and a new, stable, price will be established.

An example of this type of price leadership can be seen in the commercial banking industry. Based on its reading of macroeconomic conditions, a leading money-center commercial bank, such as Citibank, may announce its decision to raise or lower the prime rate (the interest rate on loans to its best customers). If the rest of the industry agrees with Citibank's interpretation of macroeconomic conditions, other money-center commercial banks will quickly follow suit. If not, they will not raise their prime rates and Citibank will quietly lower its prime rate to a level consistent with the sentiments of the industry.

Dominant Price Leadership

Some industries are characterized by a single, dominant firm and many smaller competitors. The dominant firm may be the industry leader because of its leadership in product innovation, or because of economies of scale. If the firm is large enough or efficient enough, it may be able to force smaller competitors out of business by undercutting their prices, or it may simply buy them out.

Definition: Dominant price leadership occurs when one firm in the industry is able to establish the industry price as a result of its profit-maximizing behavior. Once a price has been established by the dominant firm, the remaining firms in the industry become price takers and face a perfectly elastic demand curve for their output.

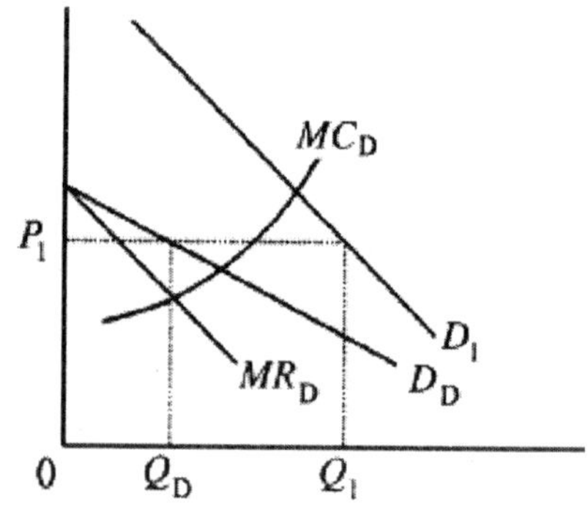

Figure: Dominant price leadership.

Industries dominated by a single large firm are characterized by price stability. The reason for this is that the dominant firm establishes the selling price of the product, and the smaller firms quickly adjust their price and output decisions accordingly. This situation is illustrated in above figure, which indicates that the dominant firm in the industry will behave like a monopolist by producing at output level Q_D, where its marginal cost is equal to its marginal revenue, $MC_D = MR_D$.

The profit-maximizing price P_I will then serve as the industry standard. The amount of output provided by the rest of the industry will be $Q_I - Q_D$.

What is interesting about this analysis is that once the industry price has been established by the dominant firm, the remaining firms take on the appearance of a perfectly competitive industry in which the demand curve for their product is perfectly elastic.

The other words, other firms in the industry are price takers. If entry and exit into and from the industry are relatively easy, the existence of above-normal profits will attract new firms into the industry, while below-normal profits will provide an incentive for firms to leave.

It is speculative whether the influx or outflow of firms into the industry weakens or strengthens the market power of the dominant firm. In large part, this will depend on the circumstances explaining the firm's rise to industry dominance, and whether those factors are sufficient to maintain the firm's preeminent position.

PRICE SKIMMING

If a firm is first to market with a new product, it may engage in a form of first-degree price discrimination called price skimming. As with firstdegree price discrimination, price skimming is an attempt to extract consumer surplus. During the interval between the firm's introduction of a new product and the competition's development of their own versions of the new product, the innovating firm is a virtual monopoly. If the innovating firm wants to extract consumer surplus, however, it must act fast.

Definition: Price skimming is an attempt by a firm that introduces a new product to extract consumer surplus through differential pricing before competitors develop their own versions of the new product.

The firm begins by initially charging a very high price for its product. Consumers willing and able to pay this price will buy first. Before competitors have a chance to sell their versions of the new product, the innovating firm will lower its price just a bit to attract the next, lower tier of consumers. This process is continued until the price charged equals the marginal cost of production.

Pricing in this manner will enable the innovating firm to extract consumer surplus to enhance profits. Of course, for this pricing scheme to be successful the firm must have knowledge of the demand curve of the product. Management is unlikely to have such knowledge, however, because of the novel nature of the product. The firm could, of course, conduct consumer surveys, market experiments, and so on, to develop information regarding the demand for the product, but care would have to be taken not to "tip off" the competition.

PENETRATION PRICING

Penetration pricing occurs when a firm entering a new market charges a price that is below the prevailing market price to gain a foothold in the industry. A form of penetration pricing is dumping. Dumping is defined by the U.S. Department of Commerce as selling a product at less than fair market value. The most egregious form of this kind of pricing behavior is predatory dumping, the attempt by a foreign producer to gain control of the market in another country by selling a product there at less than fair market value with the goal of driving out domestic producers.

Definition: Penetration pricing is the practice of charging a price that is lower than the prevailing market price to gain a foothold in the industry.

PRESTIGE PRICING

Prestige pricing is essentially an attempt by firms to increase sales of certain products by capitalizing on snob appeal. Many consumers derive a degree of personal identity from the ostentatious display of certain brandname items. For them, an enhanced personal image from the conspicuous consumption of upscale products is as valuable, and sometimes more so, than the usefulness or quality of the product itself. The mere fact that a product sells for a higher price often conveys the impression of higher quality, which may or may not be supported by reality.

Prestige pricing is an attempt by some firms to exploit this perception by charging higher prices because of the increased prestige that they believe ownership of their products confers. An often cited example is the luxury automobile market, where higher priced automobiles are perceived to be superior to lower priced automobiles of similar quality.

Definition: Prestige pricing is the practice of charging a higher price for a product to exploit the belief by some consumers that a higher price means better quality, which in turn confers on the owner greater prestige.

PSYCHOLOGICAL PRICING

Finally, psychological pricing is a marketing ploy designed to create the illusion in the mind of the consumer that a product is being sold at a significantly lower price when, in fact, the price differential is inconsequential. Retailer sale of a product for Rs.4.99 instead of Rs.5.00 is psychological pricing. Retailers who engage in psychological pricing are attempting to exploit consumers' initial impressions or their lack of familiarity with the product. The effects of psychological pricing tend to be transitory, however, as initial impressions wear off or the consumer becomes more knowledgeable about the product.

Definition: Psychological pricing is a marketing ploy designed to create the illusion in the mind of the consumer that a product is being sold at a significantly lower price when, in fact, the price differential is inconsequential.

CONCLUSION

Earlier chapters discussed output and pricing decisions under some very simplistic assumptions. We assumed, for example, that profit-maximizing firms produce a single good or service, that production takes place in a single location, that these firms sell their products in a well-defined market, that managements have perfect information about production, revenue, and cost functions, and that the firms sell their output at a uniform price to all customers. In reality, these assumptions are rarely valid. For that reason, we considered alternative pricing practices, which in some cases are derivatives of the more general cases already encountered.

In price discrimination, a firm sells identical products in two or more markets at different prices. Economists have identified three degrees of price discrimination. First-degree price discrimination occurs when a firm charges each buyer a different price based on what he or she is willing to pay. In practice, first-degree price discrimination is virtually impossible.

In second-degree price discrimination, often referred to as volume discounting, different prices are charged for different blocks of units, or different products are bundled and sold at a package price. An example of second-degree price discrimination is block pricing, in which there are different prices for different blocks of goods and services. Second-degree price discrimination requires that a firm be able to closely monitor the level of services consumed by individual buyers.

In third-degree price discrimination, which is by far the most frequently practiced type of price discrimination, firms segment the market for a particular good or service into easily identifiable groups and then charge each group a different price. Such market segregation may be based on such factors as geography, age, product use, or income. For third-degree price discrimination to be successful, firms must be able to prevent resale of the good or service across segregated markets.

Cost-plus pricing, also known as markup or full-cost pricing, is an example of nonmarginal pricing. Firms that engage in nonmarginal pricing are unable or unwilling to devote the resources required to accurately estimate the total revenue and total cost equations, or do not know enough about demand and cost conditions to determine the profit-maximizing price and output levels. In cost-plus pricing, a firm sets the selling price of its product as a markup above its fully allocated per-unit cost of production. One criticism of cost-plus pricing is that it is insensitive to demand conditions. In practice, however, the size of a firm's markup tends to be inversely related to the price elasticity of demand for a good or service.

Multi product pricing involves optimal pricing strategies of firms producing and selling more than one good or service. Firms that independently produce two products with interrelated demands will maximize profits by producing at a level at which marginal cost is equal to the change in total revenue derived from the sale of the product itself, plus the change in total revenue derived from the sale of the related product. A profit-maximizing firm selling two goods with independent demands that are jointly produced in variable proportions will equate the marginal revenue generated from the sale of each good to the marginal cost of producing each product.

Finally, a profit-maximizing firm that jointly produces two goods in fixed proportions with independent demands will equate the sum of the marginal revenues of both products expressed in terms of one of the products with the marginal cost of jointly producing both products expressed in terms of the same product.

Peak-load pricing occurs when a profit-maximizing firm charges a one price for a service when capacity is fully utilized and a lower price when capacity is underutilized. Off-peak prices are determined by equating marginal revenue to marginal operating costs. Peak prices, on the other hand, are determined by equating marginal revenue to the marginal cost of increasing capacity.

Price leadership appears when an oligopolist establishes a price that is quickly adopted by other firms in the industry. There are two types of price leadership: barometric price leadership and dominant price leadership.

Barometric price leadership exists when a price change by one firm in an oligopolistic industry, usually in response to perceived changes in macro economic or market conditions, is quickly followed by price changes by other firms in the industry.

Dominant price leadership exists when the largest firm in the industry establishes the industry price as a result of its profit-maximizing behavior.

Once the industry price has been established, the remaining firms become price takers in the sense that they face a perfectly elastic demand curve for their output.

Other important pricing practices include transfer pricing, price skimming, penetration pricing, prestige pricing, and psychological pricing.

Transfer pricing is a method of correctly pricing a product as it is transferred from one stage of production to another.

Price skimming is the practice of taking advantage of weak or nonexistent competition to change a higher price for a new product than is justified by economic analysis. While competitors are trying to catch up, the firm may have monopoly pricing power.

Penetration pricing is found when a firm entering a new market charges less than its competitors to gain a foothold in the industry.

Prestige pricing is the setting of a high price for a product in the belief that demand will be higher because of the prestige that ownership bestows on the buyer.

Finally, psychological pricing is a marketing ploy designed to create the illusion in the mind of the consumer that a product is being sold at a significantly lower price when, in fact, the price differential is inconsequential. A retailer that sells a product for Rs.4.99 instead of Rs.5.00 is engaging in psychological pricing. The effect of psychological pricing tends to be transitory.

Note: AnnTaylor Stores Corporation (AnnTaylor Stores) is a leading US-based specialty retailer of women's apparel, shoes and accessories. The company offers its merchandise under a number of brand names including Ann Taylor, LOFT, Ann Taylor Factory and LOFT Outlet. The company also sells products through the Internet. The company primarily operates in the US. It is headquartered in New York City, New York and employs about 18,400 people. For a very good case study regarding this topic, reader can visit company's website www.anntaylor.com

Bibliography

A. A. Alchian, "Reliability of Progress Curves in Airframe Production," *Econometrica*, 1963.

A. Taylor, "Detroit Buffs Up," *Fortune,* February, 2004.

A.G. Dawson, "Administrators Settle into New Digs," *Delaware Coast Press,* July, 2003.

A.P. Hare, "Types of Roles in Small Groups: A Bit of History and a Current Perspective," *Small Group Research*, 1994.

B. Bremner and C. Dawson, "Can Anything Stop Toyota?" *Business-Week.* November, 2003.

B.J. Pine, *Mass Customization: The New Frontier in Business Competition*, Boston: Harvard Business School Press, 1993.

B.W. Tuckman and M.A.C. Jensen, "Stages of Small-Group Development Revisited," *Group and Organization Studies,* 1977.

Banai and L.M. Sama, "Ethical Dilemma in MNCs' International Staffing Policies," *Journal of Business Ethics,* June 2000.

Belson, "In U.S., Cell Phone Users Are Often All Talk," *The New YorkTimes,* December, 2004.

Birkinshaw, A. Morrison, and J. Hulland, "Structural and Competitive Determinants of a Global Integration Strategy," *Strategic Management Journal,* 1995.

C. W.L. Hill, *International Business,* 6th ed., New York: McGraw-Hill, 2007.

C.A. Beatty and B.A. Barker, *Building Smart Teams: Roadmap to High Performance*, Thousand Oaks, CA: Sage Publications, 2004.

C.K. Prahalad and Y.L. Doz, *The Multinational Mission: Balancing Local Demands and Global Vision*, New York: Free Press, 1987.

C.K. Swank, "The Lean Service Machine," *Harvard Business Review,* October, 2003.

C.K.W. De Dreu et al., "A Theory-Based Measure of Conflict Management Strategies in the Workplace," *Journal of Organizational Behavior*, 2001.

C.M. Solomon, "Success Abroad Depends upon More Than Job Skills," *Personnel Journal,* April 1994.

C.M. Solomon, "Unhappy Trails," *Workforce,* August 2000.

Competitive Advantage," *Strategic Management Journal,* 1995.

D. Barboza, "An Unknown Giant Flexes Its Muscles," *The New York Times,* December, 2004.

D. Bertsimas and S. de Boer, "Dynamic Pricing and Inventory Control for Multiple Products," *Journal of Revenue and Pricing Management,* January, 2005.

D. Pritchard, "Are Federal Tax Laws and State Subsidies for Boeing 7E7 Selling America Short?" *Aviation Week,* April, 2004.

D. Robb, "Global Workgroups," *Computerworld,* August, 2005.

D. Robey, H.M. Khoo, and C. Powers, "Situated Learning in Cross-Functional Virtual Teams," *Technical Communication,* February, 2000.

D. Welch and K. Kerwin, "Detroit Tries It the Japanese Way," *Business Week,* January, 2004.

D.C. Feldman, "The Development and Enforcement of Group Norms," *Academy of Management Review,* 1984.

D.L. Miller, "The Stages of Group Development: A Retrospective Study of Dynamic Team Processes," *Canadian Journal of Administra-tive Sciences*, 2003.

Data reported in J. Palmer, "Can Anyone Stop Toyota," *Barrons,* September, 2004.

E. Hart, "Manager of the Year: John Mang," *Iron & Steelmaker,* June, 2003.

E. Horwitt, "Knowledge, Knowledge, Who's Got the Knowledge," *Computerworld,* April, 1996.

E. Ulich and W.G. Weber, "Dimensions, Criteria, and Evaluation of Work Group Autonomy," in *Handbook of Work Group Psychology,* ed. M.A. West, Chichester, UK: John Wiley and Sons, 1996.

E.T. Hall and M.R. Hall, *Understanding Cultural Differences,* Yar-mouth, ME: Intercultural Press, 1990.

G. Callioni et al., "Inventory Driven Costs," *Harvard Business Review,* March, 2005.

G. Johns, "Absenteeism Estimates by Employees and Managers: Divergent Perspectives and Self-Serving Perceptions," *Journal of Applied Psychology*, 1994.

G. Oddou and M. Mendenhall, "Expatriate Performance Appraisal: Problems and Solutions," in *International Human Resource Manage-ment,* ed. G. Mendenhall and M. Oddou, Boston: PWS-Kent, 1991.

G. Rice, "Doing Business in Saudi Arabia," *Thunderbird International Business Review,* January-February 2004.

G.Buckler, "Staking One for the Team," *Computing Canada,* October, 2004.

H. Luft, J. Bunker, and A. Enthoven, "Should Operations Be Regionalized?" *New England Journal of Medicine*, 1979.

I.D. Steiner, *Group Process and Productivity*, New York: Academic Press, 1972.

J. Bowles, "Is American Management Really Committed to Quality?" *Management Review,* April 1992.

J. Gordon, "Do Your Virtual Teams Deliver Only Virtual Performance?" *Training,* June, 2005.

J. Schlosser, "Cashing In on the New World of Me," *Fortune,* December, 2004

J. Yang and K.W Mossholder, "Decoupling Task and Relationship Conflict: The Role of Intergroup Emotional Processing," *Journal of Organizational Behavior,* 2004.

J.Ci. Fernald and V. Greenfield, "The Fall and Rise of the Global Economy," *Chicago Fed Letters.* April 2001.

J.H. Gilmore and BJ. Pine II, "The Four Faces of Mass Customization," *Harvard Business Review,* January-February, 1997.

J.J. Dose and R.J. Klimoski, "The Diversity of Diversity: Work Values Effects on Formative Team Processes," *Human Resource Management Review,* Spring 1999.

J.Z. Namenwirth and R.B. Weber, *Dynamics of Culture*, Boston: Alien & Unwin, 1987.

K. Jelin, "A Multimethod Examination of the Benefits and Detriments of Intra-group Conflict," *Administrative Science Quarterly*, 1995.

K.T. Dirks and D.L. Ferrin, "The Role of Trust in Organizations," *Organization Science*, July-August, 2004.

L. Adams, "Medrad Works and Wins as a Team," *Quality Magazine,* October, 2004.

L. Coch and J. French, J.P..R, "Overcoming Resistance to Change," *Human Relations*, 1948.

M. Friedman and R. Fried-man, *Free to Choose*, London: Penguin Books, 1980.

M. Hammer, "Deep Change: How Operational Innovation Can Transform Your Company," *Harvard Business Review,* April 2004.

M. Hammer, "Process Management and the Future of Six Sigma," *MIT Sloan Management Review,* Winter 2002.

Metthee, "Playing a Large Part," *Seattle Post-Intelligencer,* April, 1994.

N. Greenwood, *Implementing Flexible Manu-facturing Systems*, New York: Halstead Press, 1986.

N.L. Kerr and S.R. Tindale, "Group Performance and Decision Making," *Annual Review of Psychology,* 2004.

O. Port and G. Smith, "Quality," *Business-Week,* November, 1992.

O.E. Williamson, "Calculativeness, Trust, and Economic Organization," *Journal of Law and Economics*, 1993.

P. Haw, "Learning from Lean Principles," *Business Day,* July, 2003.

P. Nemetz and L. Fry, "Flexible Manufacturing Organizations: Im-plications for Strategy Formulation," *Academy of Management Review*, 1988.

P. Sullivan, J. and D.L. Feltz, "The Relationship between Intrateam Conflict and Cohesion within Hockey Teams," *Small Group Research,* June, 2001.

R. Cross, "Looking before You Leap: Assessing the Jump to Teams in Knowledge-Based Work," *Business Horizons,* September, 2000.

R. Hallowell, D. Bowen, and C.-I. Knoop, "Four Seasons Goes to Paris," *Academy of Management Executive*, November 2002.

R. Mead, *International Management: Cross Cultural Dimensions*, Oxford: Blackwell Business, 1994.

R. Rosmarin, "Your Custom Car Is Ready at Toyota," *Business 2.0,* October, 2004.

R.C. Liden et al., "Social Loafing: A Field Investigation," *Journal of Management*, 2004.

R.M. Belbin, *Team Roles at Work*, Oxford, UK: Butterworth-Heine-mann, 1993.

S. Beatty, "Bass Talk: Plotting Plaid's Future," *The Wall Street Journal,* September, 2004.

S. Chambers and R. Johnston, "Experience Curves in Services," *International Journal of Operations and Production Management*, 2000.

S. Fisher, R. Sahay, and C.A. Vegh, "Stabilization and the Growth in Transition Economies: The Early Experience," *Journal of Economic Perspectives*, Spring 1996

S. Kotha, "Mass Customization: Implementing the Emerging Paradigm for Competitive Advantage," *Strategic Management Journal*, 1995.

S. Leung, "Armchairs, TVs, and Espresso: Is It McDonald's?" *The Wall* A *Street Journal,* August, 2002..

S. Prashad, "Building Trust Tricky for 'Virtual' Teams," *Toronto Star,* October, 2003.

S.E. Nedleman, "Recruiters Repeal Their Top Interview Questions," *Financial News Online,* February, 2005.

S.F. Jablonsky and N.P. Barsky, *The Manager's Guide to Financial Statement Analysis*, New York: Wiley, 2001.

S.H.N. Leung, J.W.K. Chan, and WB. Lee, "The Dynamic Team Role Behavior: The Approaches of Investigation," *Team Performance Management,* 2003.

S.J. Karau and K.D. Williams, "Social Loafing: A Meta-Analytic Review and Theoretical Integration," *Journal of Personality and Social Psychology*, 1993.

S.J. Kobrin, "Geocentric Mindset and Multinational Strategy," *Journal of International Business Studies*, 1994..

S.P. Seith, "The Impact of Flexible Automation on Business Strategy and Organizational Structure," *Academy of Management Review*, 1992.

S.S. Webber and L.M. Donahue, "Impact of Highly and Less Job-Related Diversity on Work Group Cohesion and Performance: A Meta-Analysis," *Journal of Management*, 2001.

T. Copeland, T. Koller, and J. Murrin, *Valuation: Measuring and Managing the Value of Companies*, New York: Wiley, 1996.

T. Levitt, "The Globalization of Markets," *Harvard Business Review*. May-June 1983.

The NTSB and NASA studies are summarized in J.R. Hackman, "New Rules for Team Building," *Optimize,* July, 2002.

United Nations, *World Investment Report 2005*, New York & Geneva: United Nations, 2005.

United Nations, *World Investment Report 2005.*

United Nations, *World Investment Report 2005.*

V.S. Borland, "Global Technology in the Twenty-First Century," *Textile World,* January 2003.

W.B. Scott, "Blue Angels," *Aviation Week & Space Technology,* March,. 2005.

W.G. Dyer, *Team Building: Current Issues and New Alternatives,* 3rd ed., Reading, MA: Addison-Wesley, 1995.

W.M. Bulkeley, "IBM to Export Highly Paid Jobs to India," *The Wall Street Journal.* December, 2003.

World Trade Organization, *2004 Annual Report*, Geneva: WTO, 2005.

Index

D

E

Q

R

S